Effective Managerial Leadership

James J. Cribbin

A DIVISION OF AMERICAN MANAGEMENT ASSOCIATIONS

Library of Congress catalog card number: 71-166554
ISBN: 0-8144-5277-9
ISBN: 0-8144-7504-3 pbk

First AMACOM paperback edition 1978.

Fifth Printing

Preface

"I am a leader. These people just won't follow me." In two sentences, this harried executive summed up the difficulties inherent in managerial leadership. Line managers have several alternatives. They can listen to the siren songs of facile prescriptions; unfortunately, such enticements rarely produce the promised salvation without effort. They can give ear to the retrospective reflections of proven leaders; although it is wise to heed the wisdom contained in autobiographical reminiscences, it may be lethal to assume that what has worked well for one manager will be equally effective for another. They can delve into more carefully conducted research; yet few operating managers enjoy the luxury of time for this admirable venture. They can rely on their personal experience; but generalizing from a single case indicates a peculiar form of pride, which goeth before a fall.

This book has been written only in response to the repeated requests of line managers for realistic guidelines that they can translate into appropriate behavior in their workaday situations. The chapters that follow are aimed at the manager who must achieve objectives despite the distractions and irritations of an all-too-pressured existence in the corporate "zoo." Hence, it seeks to avoid two pitfalls: the dogmatically stated nonsense of which Chester A. Barnard complained years ago, the "Do this and thou shalt be saved" approach; and the semantic morass of research jargon. The chapters try to ask the right questions, present some of the more important research findings in a readily understandable manner, and offer realistic suggestions that will give the manager not puffery or pep talks but solid material simply expressed. If the chapters encourage the average busy executive to think through the leadership pattern effective for him personally within the unalterable matrix of his particular company, department, and work environment, they will have served their modest purposes in a measure pressed down and flowing over.

Without the gracious cooperation of authors and publishers for the reproduction of copyrighted materials, without the stimulation of many other unnamed authorities, and without the educational influence that many executives and managers have had on the writer, especially his associates in the Presidents Association, no book would have been possible. The beneficial impact of all three groups is appreciatively recognized. Special thanks are due Mrs. Margaret Kelly, who with great good humor not only put up with the writer's eccentricities but also painstakingly typed the manuscript. Finally, a word of gratitude is due the editors and the peculiar alchemy they employ to change a manuscript into something that it might otherwise never have become.

James J. Cribbin
Professor of Management
St. John's University
Principal
The Greenhouse Group

Contents

sophically Determined Variable; Concepts of Man; Concepts in Action; Leadership Is a Technologically Determined Variable; Leadership Is an Organizationally Determined Variable; Analyzing and Navigating the Organizational Force Field; Leadership Is a Skill-Mix-Determined Variable

Effective
Managerial
Leadership

managerial leadership: fulcrum for profitability

Ask a group of executives what the initials *ROI* stand for, and they will respond in Pavlovian chorus, *"Return on investment."* To the manager-leader, however, these initials have a subtler meaning. He is well aware that return on investment is the name of the game. But he is sensitive to the fact that a principal means to this end is *return on individuals.* Unless he succeeds in securing a rich return in quality and quantity of output from the people who work with (rather than merely for) him, he will find it difficult to obtain his intended return on investment. A simple formula, adapted from some ideas of Victor H. Vroom,[1] illustrates this truth: $P = C \times M$.

The job of the manager is to be constantly concerned with P as spelled out in terms of performance, proficiency, productivity, and profit. This in turn is the product of two factors: the competence of the work group, C, multiplied by its motivation, M.

In a sense, half of the manager-leader's task is to seek persistently to raise the competence level of his people. An old Chinese saying maintains that if the son does not turn out a better man than his father, both have failed. How many executives in modern business could face up honestly to this criterion? One suspects that few could give a ready answer to this direct question: During the past six months, how much have your key subordinates grown in knowledge about and skill in their work?

References appear at the end of the book.

The second factor has to do with the manager's ability to motivate his people to become self-starting achievers. To paraphrase the Bible, "Though I have all competence, so that I could remove mountains, and have no motivation, I am nothing." Motivation multiplies the efficacy of individual effort. Motivation builds cohesive work groups committed to an objective. Motivation maximizes the impact of group competence. It is a blunt fact of life that many executives have a deficit of ability to motivate subordinates. Others do an outstanding job; still others are noted more for demotivating than for motivating.

Napoleon, a practitioner with a splendid record up to a point, once remarked that morale accounts for three-quarters of a victory in battle, the relative balance of manpower accounting for the remaining quarter. And Rockefeller—the early profit maker, not the later political pundit—was willing to pay more for the ability to handle people than for any other executive talent. Contrast these contentions with the two most common phenomena in American industry today—what Thorstein Veblen long ago called employees' systematic withdrawal of competence from the objectives of top management and middle management *malaise,* an ailment of men once filled with zest who plateau out and are content to go through the motions. Little wonder that both Pope John XXIII and Nikita Khrushchev were reported to have replied to the question, "How many people work for you?" with the terse answer, "About half." Perhaps this is inevitable in a bureaucracy. It need never be the case in a dynamic organization where the prime movers are leaders rather than caretakers.

Management: The Role and the Functions

At times, the concepts of management, administration, and leadership are confused or even considered identical. It might be well, therefore, to make certain distinctions among them even at the risk of seeming a bit pedantic.

A Formal View of the Manager's Job

Management is the scientific art of attaining intended organizational objectives by working effectively with and through the human and material resources of the firm. Thus, management as a process is a sine qua non in any organization, be it a corporation, church, prison, or hospital.

The job of the manager is first to determine what is to be done and second to see that it gets done, whether he goes about these tasks in a democratic, autocratic, or other fashion. His responsibility is to insure that needed corporate inputs are provided to achieve overall goals while coordinating these inputs with those of other departments in order to facilitate the work of the whole organization. Over and beyond this, the manager's role is that of a change agent, introducing innovations that will enhance the performance and promote the improvement of his work group, changes that would not occur in his absence. If they would take place without him, then he is merely an overseer with a high-sounding title and is probably overpaid.

A standardized litany of the manager's ritual responsibilities can easily be formulated.

1. He *plans,* for if the thinkers do not think ahead, the doers will have nothing to do that is worth their time and energy. He tries to anticipate the future so as to control it if possible, to capitalize on the opportunities that the future always offers the thoughtful and denies the unthinking, or at the very least to avoid becoming its victim.

2. He *organizes* the manpower, money, machines, methods, and materials of the firm into well-integrated units so that objectives may be attained with a maximum of efficiency and a minimum of wasted effort.

3. He *staffs* not merely to get today's job done but, more importantly, to insure that the human resources of the company will develop so as to enable it to enjoy increasing prosperity.

4. He *directs* by allocating authority, by determining necessary functions, by assigning personnel to specific tasks, by allowing key people the autonomy to perform and achieve, by setting criteria for acceptable output, and by exacting accountability for results according to those criteria.

5. He *coordinates* the work of individuals and groups so that they operate as a unified whole.

6. He *gains cooperation* from and among his people by arranging conditions so that they can achieve organizational ends while satisfying some of their job-related needs, by giving an ex-

ample, and by creating a climate of cooperation and mutual assistance.

7. He *controls* the efforts of his subordinates by maintaining a feedback system that provides him with valid data early enough in the game to take corrective action and that allows him to reward or punish performance on the basis of justice rather than politics or charity.

8. He *reviews and evaluates* the work of his people informally and formally not merely to satisfy the requirements of the firm but also to help them become more productive and more valuable to the organization.

9. He *leads* his people so as to stimulate them to do willingly what must be done and do well what might otherwise be done in a barely acceptable manner.

10. He *budgets* the four major assets he has going for him—his time, his thought, his talent, and his behavior—to make certain that he and the firm secure the best possible return on investment, with the corporation getting at least a fair and adequate return on its dollar.

An Informal View of the Manager's Job

Whereas no one would find much to criticize in these ten commandments of the manager's job, they suffer from oversimplification. They are too neat and tidy. As every manager knows and every business school graduate is destined to discover to his dismay, they never seem to work out as formulated. They concentrate on what the manager should do rather than on what he actually does, often perforce, in that zoo we call a company or department. They give a Platonic description of the ideal firm under ideal conditions in which the executive is master of his fate and captain of his soul.

The evident truth is that the manager spends as much time and energy reacting as acting, and perhaps more. He is involved and embedded in an amazing variety of relationships, few of which he can directly or solely control. A more realistic description of the day-to-day job of the manager, as Leonard Sayles [2] and others have pointed out, might read as follows:

1. He *works to implement* his personal career plan, using the firm as a vehicle for so doing while seeking to meet its requirements.

2. He *endeavors to be sensitive* to the expressed or, more often, implied expectations of his immediate superiors. He seeks to tune in on new pressures, new developments, and new requirements that may subtly or sharply alter how he goes about his work.

3. He *negotiates* continuously with his peers in other departments on whom he depends and who depend on him and his work group to get the total job done effectively.

4. He *cultivates* good relations with staff and service groups whose attitudes and actions can make his job easier or harder, for he realizes that at times support groups have the ear of the throne.

5. He *responds* to the requests, demands, and requirements of significant individuals and groups in his occupational life space so as to retain their goodwill or at least not alienate them. He must be flexible in adjusting to an astounding variety of personalities, cliques, and in groups, parochial loyalties, expertise, and eccentricities.

6. He *oversees* the flow of work into, within, and out of his department to insure that it proceeds with a minimum of interruption or static that may draw unwanted attention from superiors.

7. He *is alert* to the work output, needs, desires, and morale of his subordinates, interacting with them, yet maintaining his managerial position.

8. He *represents* his people and their views in his dealings with his superiors and other departments.

9. He *tries to remain his own man* while accommodating himself to the legitimate demands of the organization. He must establish a valid order of priorities balancing out what is rightly due his firm, his family, and himself.

10. He *attempts to cope* adequately with his own tensions so as to receive a fair share of psychic as well as economic income from his work.

Management, the Learnable but Unteachable Art

A bright young business school graduate with a sound background in systems analysis, operations research, and statistics was hired by one of the "big eight" accounting firms and assigned to long-range planning. He was given more in the way of autonomy than guidance and went his merry way studying and cogitating about the future in general and the company in particular. After a few months, he was scheduled for an appearance before the executive committee to make a presentation of work completed. Armed with his sources, findings, data, visual aids, and other appropriate paraphernalia, he went through his intellectual exercise. He made one lethal mistake. He assumed that the members of the committee were as conversant as he with the intricacies of operations research and statistics. Unhappily for him, they were not. By the end of his presentation, his blood was spattered around the room, and shortly after, he was let go.

This M.B.A. learned to his regret that management is a learnable but not directly teachable art. The manager has the task of *translating* his knowledge into behavior that a given group or department will find meaningful and acceptable. He must accommodate himself to the tides and eddies, the rocks and shoals of the life stream that flows in every company. In this sense, the formal and informal views of the executive's job are complementary. Management is like medicine and law. All three have a scientific base that is absolutely necessary but hardly sole sufficient. An artistic dimension arises from the need to adapt one's expertise to the given realities in a department or firm. Medicine, law, and management are all practical arts; competence comes not from abstract knowledge alone but from the blend of learning and prudent application.

Managers and Administrators

In any organization, there are three generically different types of personnel. First, there are the technicians, those who possess expertise of a doing nature. Thus, both a plumber and a surgeon are technicians. With markedly different degrees of sophistication, both have the know-how to do a first-rate job, each in his own order of activity. Their emphasis is on the task to be performed; their skills are geared to this task; they are not expected to delve into questions of policy; they are more concerned with the how than with the why of the work they do.

At a different level are the managers, whose responsibility it is to interpret and implement the plans, policies, and objectives of the organization as they apply to those subunits for which they are accountable. Having a subsystem viewpoint, they must utilize their intellectual and practical talents to translate organizational goals from paper into appropriate action.

If managers have a subsystem perspective, as Daniel Katz and Robert Kahn [3] have noted, executives should have a total-system viewpoint. Enjoying the advantages of a bird's-eye view, although often unaware of the limitations of this single line of vision, administrators are responsible for charting the course of the whole company—formulating long-range plans, evolving adequate policies and controls, and making those essential decisions on which the fortunes of the entire enterprise will ultimately depend. It is they who determine the direction the firm will take, the business it will be in, the objectives it will strive for, the principles and philosophy that will guide it, the climate and tone and tempo that will characterize it.

The rank and file in any department or firm are essentially doers. Supervisors, even when a good deal of their time is occupied with doing, are paid to get things done with and through employees. Managers, if they really perform as managers, are supposed to have left behind a considerable amount of their doing ability as they perfect their competence in leading and energizing others to perform as expected. Theirs is a new know-how quite distinct from that of the worker. Executives are rightly expected to be more concerned with questions of "To what end?" than with day-to-day operations. In fact, the administrator who is not reasonably incompetent in the expertise he began his career with probably has a real need to redefine his function in the organization.

It would be a mistake, however, to assume that the supervisor, manager, and administrator are paid to perform totally different functions. They may well live in radically different social and economic worlds, but they are responsible for fulfilling similar roles. As Lawrence A. Appley, chairman of the board of the American Management Association, has pointed out over several decades, the differences that exist are more quantitative than qualitative. They are basically differences in number of people managed, amount of money involved, magnitude of decisions made, and level of problems resolved. The supervisor may be responsible for 10 people, the manager for 100, and the administrator for 5,000. One may plan for next week, the second for next year, and the third for the next five years. In fact, a company would be naive indeed, as James L. Hayes, president of AMA, has observed, were it to put 50 people in the charge of a supervisor or manager who could not carry out managerial functions effectively with 10. Yet this occurs over and over in more than a few organizations.

Managers and Leaders

Emphasis has been placed on the role and responsibilities of the manager lest the reader get the idea that if he simply becomes an effective leader, all else will be added unto him. Such is hardly the case. There is much more to being a manager than becoming a leader. Leadership is but one element of the overall managerial job. This is something that many behavioral scientists have failed to recognize. Is it any wonder that at times line people, knowing unconsciously that they were dealing with staff people who have never felt the burning white light of ultimate accountability, have responded to their suggestions with an attitude of "You must be kidding. What do you think I'm running, an annex of the Salvation Army?" Yet leadership is obviously a desirable, even necessary ingredient of executive success.

One can manage a concentration camp without necessarily being the leader of the inmates. Leadership is not so much a function of status or authority as it is of the quality of the relationship, the interaction that takes place between the leader and his followers. It is not a question of having *power over* subordinates; it is a matter of having *influence with* them. Accordingly, certain distinctions must be made.

First, management and administration are geared to the achievement of organizational objectives. Leadership may be exercised to thwart the attainment of these very objectives. Specifically, the leader may use his abilities to further not the welfare of the firm but his own interests. Again, management always has a strong input of the logical, the rational, the financial, the impersonal, the analytical, the quantitative. Leadership, in contrast, always involves the chemistry that exists between the alpha fish and those he leads. The manager has ample organizational resources to make subordinates engage in required behavior. He is primarily responsible to higher management. The leader, on the contrary, relies chiefly on his personal resources to get people to do as he wishes. He may well be primarily responsible to his "constituency," those who follow him. Finally, supervision, management, and administration are intrinsically connected with levels within a given company. Leadership, however, may be exercised by anyone at any level, depending on the situation and circumstances that define the kind of leadership required. In a sense, then, the title to manage others is a gift of the higher echelons, but the title to lead others is a gift of the followers.

The Nature of Managerial Leadership

Defining leadership in any clear, concise, and comprehensive manner is like dealing with a Hydra with dandruff. As Daniel Katz and Robert L. Kahn have pointed out, leadership is a slippery and a catchall concept. At times, reference is made to *positions of leadership;* in this sense, a company president is more a leader than is a supervisor. At other times, leadership is attributed to a *kind of behavior;* thus, a department head may be a mere figurehead whereas his assistant may well be the power behind the "drone." Again, leadership may refer to certain *qualities or characteristics* a person has; for better or worse, people still speak in terms of so-called leaders and nonleaders, of born leaders and developed leaders.

Some Sense About Managerial Leadership

Leadership can be described as a process of influence on a group in a particular situation, at a given point in time, and in a specific set of circumstances that stimulates people to strive willingly to attain organizational objectives, giving them the experience of helping attain the common objectives and satisfaction with the type of leadership provided. Certain key ideas in this description require explanation.

Process of influence. If managers must manage, then leaders must lead. They must relate to and interact with their subordinates. Leadership is not a now-and-then thing, exercised when emergencies arise. It is a continuous effort on the part of the manager. It seeks not reflex responses to organizational demands but rather that plus factor which makes the difference between mediocrity and excellence. The manager is the leader of his people when—note the verb—they *allow* him to influence their thinking, their attitudes, and their behavior. Influence implies that the manager is accepted by his subordinates, is looked to for guidance and direction, is perceived by them as capable of helping them satisfy their needs and aims. At the heart of the influence process is the impact that one human being has on another or a group.

In a particular situation, at a given point in time, and in a specific set of circumstances. The quest for an abstraction called *leadership* has been as fruitless and frustrating as that for the universal solvent. Leadership, like medicine, is never general, always particular. Despite the tendency of executives to act on the basis of habit and past successes rather than insight into present realities, it seems rather evident that a type of leadership behavior well suited to one situation may be entirely inappropriate in another. This is a deadly truth that Khrushchev and a host of other erstwhile leaders have learned to their regret.

Semon Knudsen, of General Motors, was personally selected by Henry Ford II to be the president of the Ford empire. It may never be known exactly what happened to bring about his downfall. But a palace revolution occurred, resulting in his dismissal from a position that had as much authority, power, and prestige associated with it as any other at the operating level in American industry. Whether or not Lee Iacocca engineered Knudsen's demise is a moot point. Two things are certainly clear. The former's leadership style was inappropriate in that it did not attain the results intended, and the latter appeared to be the real leader. Given his set of circumstances, perhaps no one could have done better than Knudsen. Even so, the replacement of a president implies that his efforts to lead are congruent with neither the corporate realities nor the needs and purposes of his subordinates.

Stimulates people to strive willingly to attain organizational objectives. As the late Vince Lombardi once remarked, "Coaches who can outline plays on a blackboard are a dime a dozen. The ones who succeed are those who can get inside their players and motivate them." Managers who can get things done by resorting to pressure, power, and punishment are also a dime a dozen. There is a tendency in most organizations to be oversecretive, to oversupervise, and to overcontrol. Getting inside people so as to energize them will tax the resources of even the best manager-leader. It begins with his defining just what his objective is, namely, to weld a group of self-starters into a cohesive group committed to organizational goals. When it is within the competence and responsibility of his subordinates, he allows them to set up their own objectives and procedures, provided these conform with those of the firm and its policies. The simple fact is that some managers have neither enough understanding of nor enough interest in their people to adopt this trusting approach. They work on the assumption that, given half a chance, employees will goof off.

In all organizations, many plans and goals come down the chain of command. Even though the manager may have had no say in establishing them, his duty is obvious. He must do his utmost to get his people to accept organizational aims and, if possible, to help them identify with them as a means for attaining their own goals. He always has the right to *dissent;* he may even have the obligation to make his dissent known to higher authority. But he has no right to *resist* the legitimate demands of superiors; this would be simple disloyalty. Far too frequently, the plans and aims of top management do not get a genuine chance to succeed because lower-level managers cut the ground out from under them with an attitude that says to their employees, "You know it won't work and I know it won't work. But some darn fool at headquarters thinks it will work." Under such conditions, obviously, every effort is made to prove that top management was wrong in the first place.

At times, higher management does not give lower-level men much chance to cooperate with it. It often fails to indicate the advantages that can accrue to subordinate managers and the rank and file by producing the results that the higher echelons request or require.

One of the reasons that, as the evidence shows, most management development programs are less than overwhelming successes is this failure to inspire people to work willingly toward organizational objectives. The participants are rarely asked what they feel a need to learn or how they learn most efficiently. By a form of unilateral bludgeoning, the program's sponsors alone determine the content, methodology, and instructional techniques on the assumption that they know better than the participants not only what should be learned but also how it should be learned. The meager amount that seems to be carried from the sessions and revealed in changed on-the-job behavior makes one wonder at times whether the time, activities, and money might not have been spent in other directions with greater wisdom.

The experience of helping attain the common objectives. Managers often make the mistake of projecting their attitudes toward certain jobs onto the people who do them. Because the managers would find the work boring and inconsequential, they tend to think of the people doing it as unimportant and dimwitted. To some people, some jobs are so dull that they should be outlawed by an act of Congress. On the other hand, there are no glamorous jobs. All involve routine, repetition, and built-in irritants. In a sense, there are no uninteresting positions; there are only uninterested workers occupying them. The wife who revels in being a mother and the one who finds this role unchallenging and bothersome must contend with the same dirty diapers, the same annoying behavior, the same childhood illnesses. What makes the difference are the perceptions and attitudes that the two mothers have.

A large manufacturer of earth-moving equipment once held a demonstration of its machines to which the public was invited. One employee was observed bending down to a small section of a monster, one wheel of which cost about $10,000. Taking his small son's hand and pointing to a part of the earth mover, he was overheard to say, "Son, if your daddy didn't make this unit just right, this earth mover wouldn't go anywhere."

If employees are to have some identification with the undertaking and some responsibility for its success, the manager-leader must do at least two things. He must help the subordinate understand just how his job contributes to an operational end result, and he must thank the employee for his contribution, however mundane or unglamorous it may be. The switchboard operator's job may seem tedious and dumdum to a manager. But it can be very rewarding and important to her if she realizes that she is the firm's avant-garde public relations expert, since the first image of the firm that an outsider gets is the way she greets him and treats him.

Satisfaction with the type of leadership provided. As Rensis Likert has pointed out, it is possible occasionally and for a short time to increase productivity through pressure and punishment. Unhappily, over the long term, employees can demonstrate remarkable ingenuity in taking out resentments against the organization in petty ways that never show up directly in accounting or production figures. Where the amateur manager is out to win battles, the manager-leader is intent on winning wars. He is interested not only in making people *perform*—after all, prisoners perform in a jail—but also, and more importantly, in helping them to *achieve,* to satisfy their work-relevant needs and aspirations while meeting the requirements of the company. Thus, although he does his best to influence subordinates, he allows them ample latitude for influencing him when they are competent to do so. When they are knowledgeable enough to be of assistance, he consults with his key people; he seeks their suggestions and advice; he provides honest opportunities for them to participate in the formulation of decisions that will affect them, their status, or their work. Where the piddler runs a one-man show, the professional knows that leadership is a shared function, to be exercised in any one instance by the person who is most competent to lead. Thus, where the former clutches to his breast all the prerogatives of leadership, the latter shares with his people—he shares credit, he shares blame, he shares ideas, he shares opinions and experiences.

Some Nonsense About Managerial Leadership

Despite the lack of empirical evidence to support them, certain myths concerning on-the-job leadership seem to have more lives than the liveliest cat. Among current ones are the following.[4]

Leadership connotes being "nice" to people or making them happy. Being considerate of others is a characteristic of well-bred human beings and has nothing per se to do with leadership. Making people happy is a fatuous endeavor since the pursuit of happiness is an individual quest; every man is a Don Quixote as far as happiness is concerned.

Leadership must be democratic. Democracy is a political philosophy and a way of life. No business organization can be a democracy in a real sense any more than a family can. The manager-leader who insists on being democratic all the time ends up with a peculiar form of pseudo-democracy—a naive attempt to attain wisdom by pooling well-intentioned ignorance. To state that the leader must be supportive and share the leadership function when appropriate is a far cry from claiming that everyone has a right to an opinion about any subject, regardless of his ignorance of it. At times, the manager-leader may be open to the ideas of his subordinates. At other times, for good and sufficient reasons, he may make forceful and conclusive decisions alone. The true leader takes his cues not from an idealized picture of his role but from the realities of the situation. In fact, a persistent effort to be democratic may actually be a not too subtle evasion of his responsibilities as a manager.

Leadership can be turned into a clever form of manipulation. Obviously, leadership may be utilized to deceive subordinates. Of themselves, the skills and techniques have a neutral ethical quality. In the long run, however, manipulation is self-defeating. It is not leadership but conmanship. Since there are few country boys left in this vale of tears, sooner or later people will catch on that they are being used and abused. Then the clever con man will reap a whirlwind of resentment and subversion. Kant said a long time ago that one should never use another human being as a mere means to his personal ends or allow himself to be so used. In an era when the educational level and sophistication of subordinates are ever rising, any attempt to manipulate them would endanger the manager's self-interest, to say nothing of his moral integrity.

Leaders are born, not made. No one is born with a divine right to ride herd on others; none are born to be the peons. Leadership is an achievement, not a birthright or happy accident of heredity. Everyone has some leadership potential that can be more fully actualized than it has been in the past. There is a certain amount of truth in the saying that one becomes not what he thinks he is nor even what others think he is but rather what he thinks *others* think he is. If subordinates have never been given opportunities to exercise leadership functions, if they have had no chance to spread their leadership wings, then predictably they will be followers.

It would be foolish to deny that heredity, environment, past opportunities, formal education, personality, and a host of other factors play important roles in the development of the manager-leader. But even so-called born leaders must be developed. As Shakespeare has it, everyone is born a baby, not a leader. A famous writer was once asked how he became so adroit at his craft. He replied, "I really do not know. But I do know that I wanted to become a good writer awfully badly." Exceptional leaders may owe more than most to an unusually bountiful award of gifts and talents by the good Lord or Mother Nature, but the skills of the typical manager-leader come through perspiration rather than inspiration. After all, Lincoln lost his first seven or eight elections, and Nixon lost out on not only the presidency but also a governorship only to pick himself up off the floor and walk away with the grand prize.

Leaders have a charisma that followers lack. Certain rare people, such as Gandhi, Martin Luther King, Churchill, and Hitler, undoubtedly have a special charisma. But for the majority of business leaders, this is simply not the case. No leader has been found to possess unique characteristics that other people lack. In fact, the research does not reveal any consistent personality pattern that distinguishes leaders from followers. It seems more a matter of having intensified common human traits, of having honed one's skills, than of being the recipient of any special boon from a benevolent deity.

The Major Dimensions of Managerial Leadership

If leadership on the job can be viewed as the ability to influence the thinking, attitudes, and activities of others so that they willingly direct their behavior toward organizational objectives, then four sets of variables are important. These are the personality of the manager, the personality of the group, the situation in which leadership is exercised, and organizational factors.

The personality of the manager-leader. It is not possible for any manager to be all things to all men. Each executive has a unique patterning of abilities, skills, attitudes, habits, past experiences, perceptions, values, interests, and what have you. Each has his own peculiar sensitivities, preferences, aversions, blind spots, and likes and dislikes. Thus, the makeup of one manager gives him a comfortable feeling when things are predictable and highly structured, whereas that of another puts him at ease when things are informal and freewheeling. Where one executive likes to interact with the troops and even rub shoulders with them, a second prefers to maintain a certain social and psychological distance. Leaders come in all sizes, temperaments, and personalities. Some are the man-of-distinction type; others are plain Joes. Some are gregarious and outgoing, others introverted and reserved. Some reveal their emotions readily whereas others are quietly self-controlled. This one may be hyperactive and that one may move at a measured pace. There is no mold from which all are poured.

The personality of the group. A group consists of two or more people who have an explicit psychological relationship to each other. A collection of individuals may be a crowd or a mob but not a group. By definition, a group is characterized by a greater or lesser degree of attraction among its members, internal cohesion, interdependence, ability of the members to affect and influence one another, exclusiveness, and shared values, objectives, and interests. Since this is so, the manager-leader is well advised to take the time to gain insight into the dynamics of his work unit. A resentful or hostile group will require a different style of leadership from one that will work with a well-intentioned and friendly group. Leadership behavior that may be successful with a self-confident and self-reliant group may prove a dismal failure with a dependent or apathetic one.

The situation. Probably no two situations call for the exact same type of leadership behavior. Yet there is a human proclivity to seek to impose what has worked in the past on present situations, which may very well be radically different. The manager-leader must accommodate his leadership actions to the mandates of the situation, not expect that the situation will meet his premises. This seems so obvious that it is astonishing how often executives overlook it. Unless he is on guard, a man who has been an outstanding success in private enterprise may endeavor to follow his habitual ways when he moves into government service, forgetting that the latter situation is by definition political. The same thing tends to occur when a manager whose experience has been limited to a very large corporation joins a medium-size or small company.

As an experiment, a large university hired several successful executives as professors, waiving the requirement that they possess the union card of a doctorate. One executive, who had been president of a very large firm and vice-chairman of the board, developed into a superior teacher. When asked what his greatest difficulty or shock had been in making the transition to professorial life, he replied: "When one of the students told me to my face that he disagreed with me and felt my position was not only entirely wrong but lacking any basis in evidence, I was so taken aback that I came within an inch of firing him on the spot. Then I remembered that he was paying a small part of my salary." In the business situation, this executive's subordinates may have felt a need to be somewhat circumspect in expressing their disagreement with him, a feeling that the student in no way shared.

Organizational factors. Before the manager-leader ever appears on the scene, organizational realities and givens have taken root to which he must become attuned. Every firm or department has its own unique history, traditions, folkways, mores, taboos, and unwritten rules of conduct; each has its peculiar power structure and its own ways of cooperating, coordinating, and getting the job done. Friendships and frictions, affiliations and alienations abound. The climate in one department may be cordial and in another competitively jealous. Where one company may move at a sedate and even leisurely pace, the tempo in another may be not only hurried but harried. It is not necessary that the manager-leader either agree with or approve of such organizational features. It is essential that he be sensitive to them if he is not to become a "dead" manager long before he ever is recognized as a dynamic leader.

fifty-seven varieties
of leader

An annoying aspect of managerial leadership is that the phenomenon is readily observed in any organization; yet how one becomes a leader defies precise explanation. Some people have a knack for assuming a leadership role and being accepted and followed by a group, whereas others would have difficulty leading a horde of hungry orphans to a hot-dog stand. There is no science of leadership; there are no prescriptions that will guarantee success in influencing others, no formulas that can be followed. To make matters worse, at times even the most unlikely people seem to achieve a leadership status. Leadership is more an art than management itself. Thus, the dilemma remains: leaders abound; explanations of how they attained their position elude convincing analysis.

In the face of such frustration, it is not surprising that authorities have been tempted to construct managerial taxonomies. Certainly they have not lacked imagination in conjuring up descriptive terminology for various sorts of leaders. Terms like "democratic," "impoverished," "task-oriented," "manipulative," "psychologically distant," "custodial," "free-rein," "exploitative," "autocratic," "missionary," and "nondirective" fill the literature. Each writer not only seems quite content with his own nomenclature but tends to ignore those of his peers. To help the executive thread his way through the maze, this chapter considers some of the more rhetorical descriptions of leaders. The next chapter examines some of the research-oriented discussions of the subject.

Formal Versus Nonformal Leadership

Any company can be considered an arena in which the organizers meet the organized. To insure that its objectives are attained, the firm appoints formal leaders, who are given the right to direct and control the activities of subordinates. They are vested with the authority to carry out their functions and duties. By and large, they execute their responsibilities through the mechanisms of the organization structure. They are readily recognized from their titles, their status, and the way they are treated by subordinates, at least in public. Not too surprisingly, the organized often muster their resources to safeguard what they consider to be their legitimate rights, needs, and wants. Quite apart from, or indeed in spite of, the wishes of higher authority, the work group often *silently selects* and *silently elects* other leaders. To them it looks for guidance; from them it accepts direction.

One day a consultant doing some work for a firm asked a certain vice-president's secretary if he was available. "Why do you want to see him?" was the rather surprising reply. "Among other reasons," replied the consultant, "because he is a vice-president." She smiled and answered, "Oh, no. He's the president's brother-in-law. If you really want to know how things are done around here and what's going on, talk with Mr. X. He's the one everybody turns to for help."

This incident illustrates the fact that the manager does not become a leader because he occupies a given niche in the organization totem pole. Until he wins his spurs with the group, he may remain a merely nominal leader, a figurehead or position holder. Although it is popular to speak of the so-called informal group, there is little that is informal about it. A better term is *nonformal*, since such a group is not recognized by higher management. Nor, of course, does it fit into the formal organizational structure in any rational or planned way.

This divergence of values and views between the organizers and the organized can at times place the manager in a rather uncomfortable situation. He is supported by the firm, which charges him with welding a team out of mismatched parts, people whom he has inherited, selected, or had imposed on him. The nonformal leader, on the other hand, has the support of the work group. The manager or supervisor has the twin task of satisfying the rightful demands of the organization while helping his people satisfy their needs and aspirations. The nonformal leader seeks only to help his followers achieve their personal and group goals. As a result, the manager or supervisor in a very real sense can end up as the man in the middle of two opposing forces. What can he do in such a situation?

He must simply accept the fact that his *legal* right to manage others does not qualify him to lead them. He must earn a *psychological* and *sociological* right to do so. Influence is merited and gained, not coerced and demanded.

He can prevent his own insecurities from compelling him to look upon the nonformal leaders as the enemy. Companies at times make this mistake in their promotion policies. Instead of seeking out, winning over, and advancing the competent natural leaders, they pick men who are more docile and less troublesome. The drawback of such an approach is demonstrated by a study showing that union people who were made supervisors tended to develop both promanagement and contraunion attitudes, whereas those who were elected shop stewards became more prounion but not more antimanagement. If the supervisor or manager has negative or jealous feelings toward the nonformal leaders, it will be difficult or impossible for him to relate to them in any constructive manner.

Barnard pointed out long ago that the existence of nonformal work groups was a natural and inevitable phenomenon and generally a healthy one, since they helped the formal organization adjust to changing corporate realities. In a word, nonformal groups often make the organization work in spite of its built-in rigidities. If the manager can accept this as a fact of organizational life, then he can evolve tactics for cooperating or at least coping with a group's chosen head.

Nonformal leaders derive their positions from various strengths: they are the natural leaders; they often represent and verbalize the real feelings and reactions of the work group; they can color the group's thinking and attitudes; they can help or hinder management's plans or procedures; they are at times key factors in the communications network since people depend on them for a straight story; they can more often than not provide rewards and punishments that may be more compelling than those offered by the department or firm.

Since few if any managers or supervisors can become the non-formal leaders of their work groups, the would-be manager-leader should study his nonformal counterpart to ascertain the role he plays as far as the work force is concerned. After all, the nonformal leader is a result, not a cause. The more the officially designated leader can help his people attain their goals through the organization, the less they will need to turn to the nonfor-mal leader.

The manager should do his best to build a relationship with the nonformal leader based on mutual respect and considera-tion, avoiding the two extremes of giving the company away in petty private deals and of fighting him tooth and nail. It is piti-ful to see some supervisors and managers bending their efforts to increasing the psychological and sociological distance be-tween their employees and themselves instead of seeking to in-teract with them and help them identify more fully with the company or department.

Authoritarian, Democratic, and Laissez-Faire Leaders

A man is both the beneficiary and the victim of his culture. The social milieu in which he lives and has his being exerts a powerful influence on his values, perceptions, and attitudes. It is not surprising, therefore, that about the time of World War II, the public began to pigeonhole leaders as democratic, auto-cratic, or laissez-faire. The successes of fascism terrified the world; the upsurge of antihumanistic political philosophies stunned it. Centuries of painful effort to protect and extend human rights were in danger of being wiped out by a Cro-Mag-non concept of man and freedom. In such conditions, it was in-evitable perhaps that the authoritarian leader was considered a child of darkness, the democratic leader a child of light. The former was doomed to being perceived as self-insistent, dicta-torial, harsh, punitive, threatening, power-conscious, restrictive, and all too eager to seek out scapegoats; the latter was seen as egalitarian, facilitative, group-centered, permissive, participative, responsive to the needs of his followers, and geared to consent and consensus.

There is considerable evidence that a so-called democratic leadership style has many advantages over an authoritarian one and *under certain conditions* can yield rich results; this is not the problem. The real difficulty is that dividing all leaders into three parts, like Caesar's Gaul, is a bit too pat. Democracy per se has nothing to do with leadership in business and industry. It is a political philosophy or a commitment to a way of life that is supercharged with emotional allegiances. Autocracy has the converse hypersensitive aura. The tenor of the times was such, however, that democracy was purported to be inevitable in the modern firm. This may be a laudable, even desirable goal. But the simple fact is that for the foreseeable future it is more a holy grail than a practical strategy that will enable the general run of executives to improve their leadership behavior on the day-to-day job.

Robert McMurry and Eugene Jennings, authorities who would yield to none in their loyalty to the philosophy of democracy, affirmed that in certain situations there might well be a proper place for the directive type of manager-leader.[1] For the most part, however, theirs were small voices that were drowned in the emotional winds. In retrospect, the whole labeling process was somewhat self-defeating. In a democracy, it is clear, the good guy with the white hat will be a democratic leader, and the script will call for the authoritarian manager to end his days wearing a black hat. Unhappily, in an autocratic philosophy or climate, the reverse will be true. Neither approach lends itself to a clearer understanding of the subject. It is perhaps prudent to lay to rest views of the leadership process in business that have their roots in highly emotional political convictions.

Leaders in Bureaucracies

In an engaging book, Anthony Downs describes bureaucratic leaders in eye-catching terms.[2] He divides them into climbers, conservers, zealots, advocates, and statesmen.

Climbers, as the name implies, are self-propelled in their quest for ever-increasing power and prestige. They are sensitively opportunistic in seeking out avenues for personal progress and self-aggrandizement. Weaker managers feel their aggressive strategies. Departments whose resources for resistance are low are likely targets for take-over. When a frontal assault is blocked, climbers are likely to consolidate their present positions or to move obliquely to increase their sphere of influence.

Conservers are antithetical to climbers. Where the latter are ever on the move, the former yearn to stand pat and maintain the status quo. Climbers welcome and foster change, provided it affords them opportunities to advance. Conservers resist and resent change, since it has an unsettling effect on well-structured and well-known relationships. Where the former seek power, the latter seek security and convenience. Climbers wish to break out and break through, conservers to dig in and hold fast to what they have.

Conservers tend to cluster at the middle management level, perhaps because they realize that they have gone as far as they are likely to go. They also tend to be found in organizations that rely extensively on formal regulations, protocol, and doing things by the book. It is interesting that the older the age of the key officials of an organization, the greater the number of conservers in it—probably, as Peter Drucker says, clinging to the crimson curse of red tape and bundling up yesterday in neat packages.

Zealots "have visions" and manifest an evangelistic zeal for the improvement of the organization—as they see it. Hence, they are single-minded, energetic, altruistic, aggressive, determined, and hard-driving. Unlike climbers, zealots have the interests and progress of the company at heart. Unlike conservers, they are impatient to improve and innovate. Their outspokenness is likely to irritate higher-echelon people who do not have the same visions. Opposition means little to zealots, who are more noted for their ability to bruise sensibilities than for their human relations skills. They are excellent instruments for stirring up an apathetic organization or getting a new one off the launching pad as speedily and vigorously as possible. They make far better task force leaders than overall administrators for the reason that they place their "sacred objectives" first and foremost, often to the neglect of other, more important goals.

Advocates are concerned for the improvement of the organization, especially the section of it they represent. They are tigers in fighting for their people and programs. Unlike zealots, who are basically loners, advocates are responsive to the ideas and influence of their superiors, peers, and subordinates. Unlike climbers, who are ever self-centered, advocates will at times promote programs that do not benefit them personally but have long-term favorable implications for the organization. Where zealots tend to take on all adversaries, advocates will engage in conflict only if supported by their colleagues. Externally, they defend their group or department in a partisan manner; internally, they are fair and impartial.

Statesmen, according to Downs, are generally found at the bottom and top of a given organization. They have an aversion to internecine warfare and petty politics, and they try to stand above parochial interests. They seek to reconcile factional clashes by pointing to the overall objectives or mission of the firm. They are found at the lower levels of the managerial hierarchy because few organizations promote statesmen; at the top, statesmanship is a requisite, since the incumbent must be above provincial affiliations.

A Psychoanalytical View of Managerial Leadership

Erich Fromm has described diverse types of individuals, and Ernest Dale has adapted these classifications to different kinds of managers and executives.[3]

The receptive manager. The motto of the receptive leader is, "It is better to receive than to give." He does things not out of conviction but to win the approbation of others. He relies on others rather than himself to secure the good things of life. Weak and dependent, he finds it difficult to say no. This gets him into the hot water of conflicting loyalties and promises. For him, love implies being loved, not freely offering affection to others who deserve it. Left to his own resources, the receptive manager feels alone and helpless. Not surprisingly, he is usually submissive, friendly, adaptable, responsive, agreeable, and easy to live with. On the other hand, he is likely to be opinionless, unable to stand up and be counted, and perhaps overly eager to please and be accepted. Hence, he is normally a good worker and a fine producer, but innovation and the creative idea are beyond his talents.

The exploitative manager. The exploitative manager is a different breed of cat entirely. His motto is, "It is better to rape than to receive." He typically sets out to use, abuse, and manipulate others to satisfy his own ends. Everything and everyone are targets for raiding. Even when he is capable of coming up with good ideas or innovations, he seems to prefer to acquire them from others through cunning. People are to be squeezed for all they are worth, and their value is judged according to their potential for exploitation. If this sort of manager is self-confident, captivating, assertive, and capable of great initiative, he is also inclined to be arrogant, seducing, conceited, selfish, and grasping.

The hoarding manager. Like Downs's conserver, the hoarding executive follows the motto, "There is nothing new under the sun. Let's leave things the way they are." Well structured, pedantically orderly, supercautious, and methodical, the hoarder is concerned not so much with acquiring new and greater status as with sitting tight and holding fast to what he already possesses. Although he may be quite bright, little in the way of novel or productive thinking is likely to come from him. He frequently dominates his own people, and closeness or intimacy constitutes a threat. His ideal is a well-ordered operation with a place for everything and everyone in his place.

The marketing manager. The motto of the marketing manager is, "I will become as you desire me." Quite common in our culture, this executive experiences himself not as a unique human being but as a commodity. His end is not happiness but salability. If he is successful, then he feels worthwhile; if not, he feels worthless. He will say and do almost anything that promotes his success and progress. His interpersonal relationships are transient, superficial, and impersonal. His sense of identity stems not from an inner image but from the opinions that others have of him. In a sense, he is a chameleon, ready and eager to please the highest bidder. He can be sociable, competitive, undogmatic, open-minded, adaptable, outgoing, and purposeful. But he is also unprincipled, uninvolved, aimless, hyperactive for activity's sake, and endlessly concerned with the problem of suppressing an underlying sense of insecurity and inferiority. What is worse, since he has no firm moorings in goals or values, he may experience himself as a thing, become selfless, and thus be alienated not only from others but from himself as well.

The productive manager. The executive with a productive orientation is far from perfect. He suffers from the same slings and arrows of outrageous fortune as any of his colleagues. Yet he has a relatively clear notion of who he is and what he stands for. He realizes that the two central tasks of life are to learn how to give and receive affection and to gain satisfaction from meaningful work. He does not merely exist; he is committed to life and living. His motto is, "I may not be completely master of my fate or captain of my soul, but I certainly am not merely the victim of mindless circumstances." Accordingly, he has a sense of balance and proportion and a resilience that enable him to experience ups and downs without overweening pride or despair. He has learned to come to grips with himself, with others, and with his environment. He seeks not only to actualize his potential but to contribute to the welfare of his fellow man and society at large.

Although there is no detailed scientific evidence to support the various classifications proposed by Downs and Dale, they have a ring of reality for the typical executive, who can readily supply names in his own firm for each of the categories. In fact, the average manager is likely to accept these descriptive types more readily than those produced by the tested research on leaders and leadership. Be this as it may, there are obviously no pure types, even though every executive's behavior is characterized by one or another major theme.

Charismatic Leaders

There is a frightening resemblance between the student "activists" of today, with their slogans of "idealism" and "sincerity," and the German youth movement just before and just after World War I. The resemblance even extends to externals, to long hair, to folk songs, and to such slogans as "Make love, not war." Yet the idealistic, antiauthoritarian

> *Wandervoegel of the German youth movement—who also did not trust "anyone over thirty"—became in short order fanatical, dedicated, unquestioning Nazis and idolators of Hitler. The youth want and need faith. And the demagogue is the specialist in sincerity."* [4]

Normally, one would give little thought to charismatic leaders. They go against the grain of a democratic philosophy of life. Yet they do arise from time to time. Accordingly, it is not so much the charismatic leader who should be the center of attention as it is the circumstances that produce him. What do we know about such leaders and the conditions that enable them to come to the fore? Robert Tucker [5] has summarized the genesis and characteristics of the charismatic leader along these lines:

1. The charismatic leader springs up during times of economic, social, political, or religious stress. He makes his move when long-established values are questioned or denied, when discontent with past traditions is painful, when customary ways of doing things fail, when a frustration-born desire for radical change is in the air, when disaster threatens.

2. A compelling magnetism and an overarching self-assurance are essential requirements for the charismatic leader. They enable him literally to cast a spell over his followers that prompts them to render him passionate allegiance, mindless enthusiasm, and blind obedience even when they may have doubts regarding certain ideas or actions he proposes.

3. He brings a message and a program that are evangelistic in their promise of salvation from the current impossible situation. His plan is simplistic and has great gut appeal. He is perceived by his followers as being almost mystically qualified to lead them out of their hopeless predicament, regardless of his objective qualifications to do so. It is this emotionalism that explains in large part an absurdity such as Hitler.

4. The magical message, which mesmerizes the unthinking (and which can often be supplied by skilled phrase makers), promises that things will become not just better but perfect. Charismatic leaders are experts at promising Utopia. Since perfection is the end, often the most heinous actions can be tolerated as seemingly necessary means to that end. In this sense, the extreme Right and the ultra Left form an unintended coali-

tion in their attacks on the more moderate groups of any society.

5. It helps greatly if the charismatic leader can set up a straw man as the sole and solitary cause of all the troubles suffered by his followers. This not only has the advantages of oversimplification but also allows the rank and file to vent their venom on a clearly identified target for purposes of catharsis, while distracting them from the mistakes and frailties of the leader. Any handy scapegoat will serve this purpose, be it capitalists, the money changers of Wall Street, imperialists, the establishment, or what have you.

6. The charismatic leader may be morally good or evil. He may be a mere visionary or a hardheaded pragmatist. In fact, he may combine elements of both in his personality.

If charismatic leadership can be utilized for ethically worthy aims, what is so bad about it? First, it makes the followers far too dependent than is good for them in the long run on the so-called indispensable man; this is especially true in a democracy, where those who govern do so with the consent of the governed. Second, such leaders rarely if ever provide for their own succession; they assume tacitly that they will be here forever. Additionally, much of the energy and thought of the followers is likely to be channeled not into improving the organization but into currying favor with the leader. As a bishop was heard to comment after his consecration, "Now that I am a bishop, there are two experiences I shall never have again. These are to eat a poorly prepared meal and to hear the whole truth."

In an era when no one in his right mind would try to predict definitively what the next two or three basic social or cultural changes will be, it is prudent to hold in mind the dangers of seeking charismatic leaders. Today, traditional values and principles are being subjected to exacting scrutiny. Young people no longer bow down before the ideologies to which an older generation gave allegiance. Much is made of the "age of anxiety," the "aspirin age," the "identity vacuum," and "existential dread." *Alienation* is a commonly used term. Copouts from society abound. Accepted customs and mores are considered at best meaningless, at worst hypocritical or deadly. The defects of the private enterprise system are held up to scorn in some quarters and its contributions passed over in silence. While one is hardly likely to press the panic button simply because a minuscule minority is angry with a system that has benefited more people in more ways than any other in the history of the world, it behooves executives to be aware of the attraction of the charismatic leader, especially when he sings a self-aggrandizing siren song to seduce the unwary and the uninformed.

Managerial Leadership as a Pattern of Traits

Tolstoy once remarked that all happy families are pretty much alike, "whereas each unhappy family is unhappy in its own way." As a projection of this observation, what would be more logical than to study the traits of outstanding leaders in the hope of gaining some insight into what differentiates prime movers from those who follow? Like many an idea that appears perfectly rational in the abstract, this has not worked out too well in practice, as we glimpsed in Chapter 1.

The first problem has to do with the number of qualities that are proposed as essential for leadership. The lists vary from 5 or so to 20 or more. One at times gets the impression that the lists tell more about the enumerators than about the characteristics of leadership. To make matters worse, we know from factor analysis that many traits named are merely variations of a common dimension. One investigation indicated that no fewer than 17,-000 one-word descriptions of leadership qualities were extant in the literature! Another reported that in 106 studies of leadership characteristics, only 5 percent of the traits appeared in four or more studies. And a close review of the literature concluded that numerous examinations of the personalities of leaders failed to produce any consistent pattern of traits. One can go on in this vein almost unendingly.

It is difficult to define traits that are mutually exclusive in operational terms. At times, contradictory qualities are included in the same listing, such as "forcefulness" and "tact." Even if the magical qualities were known, there would still remain the questions of what proportion of a set of traits is effective, how much of each is necessary, and in what situation a given trait is useful or harmful. The entire process is a fascinating exercise in frustration.

Even the most carefully done studies of leadership traits raise more question than they answer. First, it is extremely difficult to define qualities in a manner that all will accept, much less measure them accurately. Second, it is impossible to avoid considerable overlapping among the traits. Third, the entire problem of the "product mix" of the qualities considered necessary or optimal for on-the-job success is left hanging. The practicing executive is perhaps better advised to deal with observed behavior than with abstract traits that seem simple but actually represent a semantic quagmire.

The Situational Approach

Some espouse a "great man" theory of leadership; others find the idea of an elite group convincing. Then there are those who lean toward a deterministic environment over which a man has little or no sway. Since the pendulum syndrome is common in human affairs, it is not surprising that as the efforts to unearth the qualities that guarantee leadership success prove less than productive, a reaction takes place and the situation is assumed to be responsible for a leader's rise. It is not so much a matter of a person imposing his personality on a situation as of the situation making it possible for the leader to emerge. Without World War II, for example, Dwight D. Eisenhower would have lived and died a respected but relatively unknown military professional. With World War II, however, he went on to become president not only of a noted university but of his nation. In another context, where would Franklin D. Roosevelt have ended up without the worst depression this country has ever experienced? At a more pedestrian level, a man might well become head of a firm not because he possessed the *relevant* competence but rather because he was fortunate enough to have the *relative* competence, being the son of the founder. Thus, situationists stress not the characteristics of the leader but rather the group and environmental forces that enable a person to apply the qualities he happens to possess and thus exercise a needed leadership role. In a sense, it is much like making shadow figures by moving one's fingers between a light and a free-hanging sheet. Without the light and the sheet, the fingers would cast no shapes.

What Does It All Add Up To?

It seems clear from the discussion thus far that thinking of managerial leadership in terms of absolutes is largely futile. It is far wiser to think of it in terms of the interaction of several variables. The first is the personality of the leader. The personality structure of the typical executive is much too settled to alter radically. Whatever its configuration, it will make certain kinds of behavior easy for him to engage in, others hard, and still others impossible to carry off with finesse. This is evident from the analyses made by Downs and Dale.

As far as leadership characteristics are concerned, Bavelas summed up the matter neatly when he observed that there are *similar* qualities that tend to appear in a relatively broad spectrum of oganizations, but there are also characteristics that are *unique* to each organization. Accordingly, an either-or approach is inadmissible. Certain so-called universal characteristics, such as intellectual acumen, prudently channeled initiative, resourcefulness, sensitivity to the feelings of others, and the ability to motivate and to communicate with impact, are always assets. But the way they are utilized must be guided by a careful assessment of the setting in which they are exercised. The manager-leader makes this assessment to ascertain the unique aspects of a given situation so that he may engage in appropriate behavior.

The qualities that the manager possesses or lacks are not nearly so important as his understanding of what kinds of behavior and which characteristics are likely to attract or alienate the work group. The entire notion of relying on the qualities that the leader should have represents an egregious misemphasis. Since it is the group he would influence, he must take his cues not from abstract research but from the persons and personalities who constitute the work force. Finally, even the most outstanding personal qualities need a suitable arena to be exercised effectively. As the arena changes, together with the fields of force that it aggregates, the relative importance of this or that pattern of traits may be radically altered.

research guidelines

The general run of line managers find the results of research studies not only puzzling but frustrating. What they need and want is something definite, clear-cut, simple, and immediately applicable to their own real-life problems. What they usually get are complex statistical analyses, prolonged discussions of abstract points, and cautions that the findings will not necessarily apply to *their* work groups and *their* work contexts. Is it any wonder that Saul W. Gellerman became famous by taking the mystique out of motivation research and translating it into terms that made sense to the average manager? Is it any wonder that many operations people clutch at anything that promises them salvation without effort?

Yet some of the studies of managerial leadership offer useful concepts, distilling practices and relationships into success patterns that are germane to almost every management role. Far from the "dogmatically stated nonsense" Barnard criticized, these overviews serve as guidelines it would be profitable to examine even though they fail to provide complete or compelling answers.

The Earlier Studies

The Michigan Studies

Starting in 1946 and continuing to the present time, the Michigan studies, under the leadership of Rensis Likert,[1] reveal five major dimensions of a supervisor's effectiveness: (1) his definition of his role, (2) his orientation toward the work group, (3) the closeness of his supervision, (4) the quality of his group relations, and (5) the type of supervision he receives from his superiors.

His definition of his role. The research has discovered the obvious, namely, that if a supervisor fails to define his job and differentiate his role from that of the workforce, then a nonformal leader will rise, and the troops will take their guidance and direction from him. It has been found that the supervisor cannot be merely a member of the work group or act like one of the boys. Until he spells out his job as a manager, his people cannot define either their jobs or their relationship to him as the leader. This is a finding that managers who are more intent on being liked than respected might well take to heart.

His orientation toward the work group. From the Michigan studies have come the now famous terms *employee-centered supervisor* and *production-centered supervisor.* It has been found that usually, but not always, the former is associated with high-producing groups whereas the latter manages low-producing groups.

The employee-centered supervisor is generally more sensitive to the needs and feelings of his people. He is supportive of his subordinates, helpful to them, and concerned for their well-being. They perceive him as being interested not merely in the technical aspects of production but also in the human aspects of the work. He is likely to have three characteristics: a strong regard for employees as human beings, a commitment to high production, and a contagious enthusiasm for good quality of work. In contrast, the production-centered supervisor is inclined to perceive his people as mere hands to get the work out. He is noted for neither his concern for their welfare nor considerateness of their feelings and needs. In his view, technical work factors take precedence by far over human work factors. In sum, this kind of supervisor is a mere boss to whom working with machines equals working with people. It is not surprising that he is generally in charge of low-producing groups.

Closeness of his supervision. The supervisory styles of the two kinds of managers are quite different. The employee-centered supervisor tends to state what is to be done and why it has to be done and then allows employees a certain amount of autonomy in doing the job as they think best, as long as it meets organizational requirements. His opposite number more often than not gives detailed orders and demands strict adherence to specified procedures. Where the production-centered supervisor is punitive and destructive in his discipline, his counterpart seeks to be constructive and instructive. And so it goes. The employee-centered leader is a catalyst of cooperation and coordination. The production-centered boss is a mere expediter of work output. One engages in general supervision; the other hangs over his people's shoulders. One discusses matters with his subordinates at least now and then; the other throws his voice around. One exerts reasonable pressure for performance; the other uses unreasonable pressure to get results. One earns the confidence of his people while keeping friction down; the other encounters conflict largely because he has lost his subordinates' trust.

It is interesting that the employee-centered supervisor spends most of his time supervising the work of his group, whereas the production-centered supervisor is just as likely to pitch in and do the work himself. Where the former is open to suggestions and grievances, the latter reacts defensively. One seeks to clarify objectives and build a sense of personal responsibility for the work in his employees, but the other indulges in a kind of "Do this, do that, do it this way" direction. The employee-centered supervisor has confidence in the goodwill and ability of his work group. The production-centered supervisor distrusts his people and checks frequently for any deviation from the prescribed routines. In a word, one acts as a supervisor; the other acts as a snoopervisor.

His group relations. Leaders of high-producing work groups generally appreciate the importance of building group cohesiveness and pride coupled with a climate of mutual helpfulness. More often than not, as we saw, they adopt a supportive attitude toward their people and use group-centered methods of supervision; as opportunities present themselves, they allow subordinates to contribute to and participate in problem solving and decision making. Employee-centered supervisors seem to sense that a cohesive work group can influence the thinking, attitudes, and behavior of its members. If it is motivated to attain the goals set by management, then it will do so more efficiently than a less cohesive group. On the other hand, if the group is motivated to work at cross-purposes with management's aims, then productivity will not be so high. Over and beyond this, it has been discovered that, contrary to popular mythology, happy people, unlike happy cows, do not necessarily produce more: high morale may correlate with high, average, or low productivity. Although there is some tendency for productivity to be associated with morale, it is too slight to be predictive.

The type of supervision he receives. Again, the research has discovered the obvious: a man does not have to live with the president of his firm; he has to live with and please his immediate superiors. Supervisors of high-producing work groups report that their managers feel high production is *one* of the most important things about the job but not *the* most important. Supervisors of low-producing groups report that their superiors either act as if high production were *the* most important aim or overemphasize the output aspects of the work. In a word, the supervisor of a low-producing group seems caught in a web partly of his own making and partly spun by the type of leadership exercised on him by his manager.

The Ohio State Studies

Like the Michigan studies, the Ohio State studies, under the leadership of Carrol Shartle, aimed to discover the dimensions of on-the-job leadership.[2] They too came up with two dichotomous variables: *Consideration* and *Initiation of Structure*. A given supervisor might find himself anywhere along a continuum with regard to each dimension. *Consideration* does not mean such superficial attentions as the back-patting or first-name calling that so often masquerades as good human relations. It connotes rapport between the supervisor and his men, a mutual warmth and trust, a concern for the needs of the members of the work group, an attitude that encourages participative management and two-way communication. *Structure,* on the other hand, refers to efforts to insure that the work of the group is organized, coordinated, sequential, organizationally relevant, and effective in attaining the objectives of the department or section. In a sense, then, *Consideration* is geared to the needs of the employees, *Initiation of Structure* to corporate demands. The Ohio studies also uncovered three other factors requisite for on-the-job supervisory success: (1) *Maintenance of Membership*—leadership behavior that is acceptable to the workforce; (2) *Objective Attainment,* which involves setting goals, structuring activities, moving toward objectives, and representing group accomplishments to outside groups; and (3) *Group Interaction,* behavior that creates a productive climate, promotes a pleasant work environment, and reduces conflict among workers.

The Ohio State studies found, to the surprise of no one, that employees desire more in the way of *Consideration,* but the supervisors' superiors tend to emphasize *Structure.* In fact, the higher one goes in the organization, the greater the concern for *Structure.* Also, supervisors reporting to managers who emphasize *Consideration* are more empathic with their employees; the converse was also found to be the case.

Training foremen in human relations produces few or no lasting on-the-job changes in behavior *if* the attitudes of their superiors and the climate of the department do not change in a similar direction. In fact, the training creates additional difficulties *if* the superiors remain high on the continuum of *Structure.* It produces improvement only when the foremen's managers behave pretty much in accord with the principles taught in the courses.

A relationship was found between grievances and turnover on the one hand and the degree of *Consideration* or *Structure* on the other. They are lowest when *Structure* is low and *Consideration* is high. They are highest when *Consideration* is low regardless of the amount of *Structure* that is prevalent. Supervisors can compensate somewhat for high *Structure* by increasing their *Consideration* behavior. The obverse, however, is not true: low *Consideration cannot* be compensated for by lowering *Structure.* Interestingly, supervisors who are high on *Consideration* can increase their *Structuring* behavior with very little increase in grievances and no increase in turnover.

Some Observations

The findings of the Michigan studies are so familiar to the general run of managers that much of their initial impact has been lost. They nonetheless provide a helpful set of guidelines for any manager who would lead rather than drive his subordinates. In a sense, the Ohio State results, which have received far less publicity, are even more interesting. The fact that a manager who is high on consideration can increase his structuring behavior without incurring a backlash of resentment is an eye-opener that goes contrary to the happiness boys' concept of effective human relations. No less revealing is the finding that one can compensate for a relatively high degree of structuring by increasing his consideration, whereas lowering structuring will not compensate for a low degree of consideration. But perhaps the most important conclusion of all is that it is useless to expect human relations courses to improve supervisors and lower-level managers when superiors and the climate of the organization do not change. It might perhaps be wiser to devote more thought and effort to organizational renewal and the alteration of higher management's attitudes than to expect those who are low on the totem pole to fight City Hall.

Everybody is blessed with retrospective infallibility. Hence, it is no reflection on the Michigan and Ohio State studies to point out that they emphasized the wrong end of the organizational ladder. Were it possible, it would have been far better had they studied those at the top of the hierarchy instead of supervisors, who carry little or no clout. In addition, the dichotomy between employee- and production-centered supervision and consideration and structuring prompts one to think in terms of a saint-sinner model. Reality is rarely so simple as this. In fact, Victor H. Vroom and Floyd C. Mann have found that whereas workers who are organized into closely knit units do indeed prefer the employee-centered type of supervision, those who work largely on their own prefer a more directive approach. Moreover, those who have weak independence needs and authoritarian tendencies show no improvement in either productivity or attitudes as a result of a participative managerial approach, although those with strong independence needs do improve with respect to both criteria. Finally, the early studies were forced to deal with supervisors almost in isolation from the mainstream of the organization. Likert is much closer to reality, if not truth, when he speaks of "management systems." For it is the management philosophy permeating an organization that is crucial, not the re-

are obtained from the study of this or that group of
el supervisors and managers.

The Leadership Contingency Approach

Fred E. Fiedler has been wrestling with a theory of leadership for over 20 years.[3] The process by which he has tested out
just one hypothesis reads like an interesting mystery story.
Using the performance of work groups as his criterion, Fiedler
suggests that three variables are significant for leadership effectiveness: *leader-member relations, task structure,* and *position
power.*

Leader-member relations are the most important factor, since
the manager whom the group accepts, trusts, and likes does not
have to pull rank in order to get things done. Yet it is not the
only necessary ingredient, for the well-liked leader may not act
any more wisely than one who is disliked. *Task structure* means
the degree to which a given task can be programmed or done
by the numbers. Clearly, the more a job can be so structured,
the more power the manager has, regardless of his leader-member relations or his position power. The least important variable
is *position power*—the degree to which a position itself enables
the leader to get his group to comply with and accept his direction. It is of least significance because it is related more to reward and punishment power than to genuine influence.

These three factors interact with the leader's knowledge of the
group, his familiarity with the task at hand, the homogeneity of
the group, and similar particulars to define the *Favorableness of
the Situation.* This is the degree to which the situation enables
the manager to exert influence and control over the group process. It signifies the number of elements that the leader has
going for him. To speak in terms of extremes, the ideal situation
is that in which a well-liked manager who has great position
power deals with a structured task and leads a homogeneous
group which he knows well and which accepts him. The bleak-
est situation is that in which a disliked manager who has weak
position power tries to lead a heterogeneous group in the performance of a vague or ill-defined task.

Fiedler has come up with certain conclusions that go against the accepted stereotypes. Both directive, managing, task-oriented managers and human-relations-oriented, nondirective managers are successful under certain conditions. Also, in both very favorable and very unfavorable situations, the controlling, managing, directive leadership style seems to work best.

Moreover, both highly accepted and highly rejected leaders perform best if they are controlling and directive. Apparently the highly accepted manager *can* be forceful because he is accepted, whereas the rejected manager *must* be forceful because he has no alternative—if he tries to be nondirective, the group may abandon the task entirely. This agrees with the finding that structuring can be increased with impunity if consideration is high, but that lowering structuring does no good if consideration is low. Finally, leaders who are in the intermediate range, being neither accepted nor rejected markedly by the group, perform best if they are permissive and nondirective.

One of the greatest virtues of Fiedler's findings is that they avoid a polarizing either-or model. His theory provides for a range in leadership behavior, varying according to the practical situation the manager faces. It also allows for a change of behavior as the favorableness of the situation changes. It therefore circumvents the pitfall of rigidity, of adherence to a given approach regardless of the pragmatic circumstances of a particular group or task. Thus, as Fiedler notes, the head of a research team might adopt a consultative and participative approach at the outset for the simple reason that no one really knows for certain how to proceed. Once a given plan and appropriate strategies have been decided upon, however, he might become rather firm and forceful so far as any major deviation from the plan is concerned.

Organizationally, too, Fiedler's theory has much in its favor, for any firm has certain options open to it, as he points out. It can attempt to alter the personality of the manager, an estimable but generally fruitless task. It can train its managers in the various leadership styles, a worthy but time-consuming chore that promises no sure results. It can seek to place managers in situations that are best suited to their natural leadership attitudes and behavior, a realistic procedure but hardly universally applicable. Then again, it can change the manager's position power, making it more or less strong; it can alter the task structure, making it more or less programmed; it can modify the leader-member relations, making a group more cohesive. This three-pronged approach, according to Fiedler, is more realistic than any of the others.

How do Fiedler's findings fit in with those of the Michigan and Ohio State studies? It appears that they complement rather than contradict them. For as the latter researchers knew very well, employee-centered supervisors act at times in a dominant, if not domineering, way; in turn, production-centered supervisors act at times supportively. Also, as Joe Kelly points out, two different sets of perceptions are being compared. The Michigan and Ohio State studies asked subordinates to look up at their superiors. Thus, the effective supervisors were perceived as being considerate and supportive. In contrast, Fiedler asked superiors to look down at and rate their subordinates. The effective superiors saw themselves as rejecting the less competent. In this sense, Kelly comments, the comparison juxtaposes a worm's-eye view and a bird's-eye view. And worms and birds rarely perceive the same reality in an identical fashion.

The Human Dilemmas of Leadership

Abraham Zaleznik sets the tone for his examination of leadership in the very first paragraph of his book:

> *The most self-conscious people in the world are its leaders. They may also be the most anxious and insecure. As men of action, leaders face risks and uncertainty, and often display remarkable courage in shouldering grave responsibility. But beneath their fortitude, there often lies an agonizing sense of doubt and a need to justify themselves.*[4]

Adopting a psychoanalytic approach, Zaleznik states that the executive is both the beneficiary and the victim of his past psychological history. He is not a blank page that can be changed this way or that so as to fill all possible roles. At the risk of doing his theory the injustice of oversimplification, it might be said that Zaleznik proposes three major categories of managerial behavior, every executive being more or less comfortable with and geared to each. *Maintenance* behavior is vectored inward as far as the organization is concerned, and represents internally generated responses to internally produced problems. *Mediative* behavior marshals organizational resources to cope with stimuli or demands made on the firm by the external environment. *Pro-active* behavior is basically innovative in character and seeks to change the milieu in which the organization finds itself; good examples of such behavior are the inventions of the automobile and jet aircraft, which brought with them new ways of living.

The *person-oriented* manager tends to prefer activities of the maintenance type. He invests much energy in human relationships. Working with people comes naturally to him, and he not only is friendly and approachable but may even identify emotionally with underlings, if not underdogs. Radical changes and innovations are not his cup of tea, and he may be rather conservative and conforming for the sake of peace and organizational homeostasis. It is not surprising, then, that he inclines toward maintenance activities and avoids pro-active, with mediative actions assuming an intermediate position. In contrast, the *idea-* or *task-oriented* manager is attuned to competition and achievement and can be aggressive. He prefers vertical relationships based on authority rather than peer relations based on friendship. The fact that he bruises feelings or steps on toes does not bother him overly as long as worthwhile goals are attained. Small wonder that he likes pro-active functions and avoids the maintenance variety, with mediative activities again taking an intermediate position. The *fusion-oriented* executive relates best to operations of the mediative kind. He has the ability to work energetically while taking people into account. He can accept both aggression and intimacy, but he stresses their organizational context. On the surface, it would appear that this sort of manager has the best of both worlds, but this is not necessarily so. He may suffer from excessive conventionality. Hence, he identifies with pro-active behavior least comfortably and relegates maintenance activities to secondary consideration.

Zaleznik is not so naive as to assume that one can pigeonhole managers into discrete boxes. This given, his concentration on personality as a catalytic or constraining variable is enlightening. Despite the obvious fact that every manager has a range of possible behaviors on which he can draw, there is no question that different executives feel more or less at ease with different behaviors. It well may be, as Fiedler affirms, that it is easier to engineer the job to fit the manager's personality than to attempt to alter his psychic makeup to suit the job. In fact, there is an old saying, "If you cannot change the man, then change the man's environment."

Some Attempted Syntheses

W. J. Reddin, Paul Hersey and Kenneth H. Blanchard, and Robert R. Blake and his associates have tried to allow for combinations of managerial leadership behaviors along various continua or dimensions. All have built on the work of the Michigan and Ohio State research results. What they have attempted to do is package these findings in a manner that the average busy executive will not only understand readily but relate to easily. At times the nomenclature is eye-catching; at other times it is bathetic.

Employing a so-called 3-D theory that relates the effectiveness of managerial style to specific situations and divides a given situation into five manageable units, Reddin shows how the demands of each unit influence the style of behavior. A Management Style Diagnostic Test is used to help the manager recognize and be sensitive to his own behavior. Reddin [5] synthesizes four less effective and four relatively more effective management types. The dimensions involved in these styles are *task orientation, relationships orientation,* and *effectiveness.*

The four ineffective kinds of managers are

The deserter, who has fled the field as far as concern for either good human relations or achievement is involved.

The missionary, who sacrifices efficient production on the altar of popularity.

The autocrat, who sacrifices human considerations on the altar of mechanical efficiency and production.

The compromiser, whose stock in trade are ambivalence and a readiness to respond to the greatest pressure of the moment.

The parallel but increasingly effective management styles are those of

The bureaucrat, who feigns an interest in his people and is not really concerned about productivity but follows rules and procedures religiously.

The developer, who sees his task as essentially one of providing a work environment that maximizes individual satisfaction and motivation. His production is generally high, though he may at times overstress the importance of good relationships.

The benevolent autocrat, who is able to win obedience to his wishes without creating enough resentment to hurt production.

The executive, whose commitment is to both high production and good relationships.

Even though Reddin modestly avoids any extraordinary claims for his approach, some of his observations are interesting. He has found that more than half of the business students studied were either missionaries or developers. Whatever happened to the old entrepreneur? On the other hand, 20 percent of the engineering students embraced the autocratic style, one that was totally rejected by the business students. In a second study, of 800 managers at all levels in one company, Reddin found that only 8 percent utilized the executive style, whereas 62 percent employed one or another of the less effective styles! Perhaps it is just as well that top management did not have access to the results.

Hersey and Blanchard have also attempted a synthesis of the known research.[6] Like Reddin, they add a third dimension, *effectiveness,* to the well-recognized dimensions *task orientation* and *relationships* of the earlier research. This allows for various combinations along the continua in question. Crucial to their discussion is the distinction between *successful* and *effective* managerial leadership. An executive can be successful and yet not be effective. For instance, a manager might get his subordinates to perform up to the requirements of the organization through the use of threats, coercion, pressure, or what have you. Since he has attained the planned ends, he has been successful. But if his people are resentful and hostile, as is most likely, then he is not effective. Suppose, on the other hand, the same manager motivates and energizes the people in his work group so that they do willingly what they are obliged to do because they experience achievement or satisfaction in excelling or feel that their needs are being met as well as those of the firm. Then he is

not only successful but also effective. In this sense, concentration camps and prisons are successful, but one would hardly call
them effective.

Using their so-called Tri-Dimensional Leadership Effectiveness Model, Hersey and Blanchard, in much the same manner as
Fiedler, provide for leadership behaviors that vary according to
the realities of a given situation. Thus, in the operating room of
a hospital, a *high task–low relationships* orientation might be in
order. It might be completely inappropriate in the children's
ward. The leader of the crew on a moon shot, however, might
have to exercise a *high task–high relationships* approach, since
the crew must not only be extremely intent on achievement but
also work in a coordinated and cooperative way. In a voluntary
organization, where the authority of the leader may be at a minimum, since he is dealing with people who are donating their
time, a *low task–high relationships* combination might be the
most appropriate. Finally, a *low task–low relationships* style
might be best in a situation in which military officers supervise
civilian scientists, who know precisely what they are about, do
not require much structure or direction, and normally do not
look to their military superiors for a great deal of personal consideration.

An interesting story is told of Admiral King during World
War II. He was a brilliant, forceful navy leader who was
not easily swayed. The head of a scientific research team
came to him with a possible solution to a problem. Admiral
King is reported to have said to his civilian subordinate, in
essence, "Sir, this is a military matter and will be decided
on this premise. As a scientist, you are not entitled to an
opinion." Whereupon the scientist replied, again in essence,
"Admiral, this is both a military and a scientific decision.
And in the area of science, you are a babe in arms and as
such are not entitled to an opinion." It is to Admiral King's
credit that he took this from the scientist and worked well
with him. But even so fine a commander as he, on this occasion at least, failed initially to adjust his leadership behavior to the realities of the situation and the expectations of
his civilian subordinate, whose first allegiance was not to

the military but to his country, his profession, and his scientific specialty.

One of the most popular approaches to management development and, to a lesser extent, to organizational change is that of Blake and his associates.[7] Blake, using the now familiar Managerial Grid ®, helps the executive to become more aware of and sensitive to his managerial leadership style. Employing as his dimensions *concern for production* and *concern for people* and using a range of 1 to 9 on each, Blake derives five major styles and two minor variations.

Country club management (1,9) is soft management at its worst. The legitimate expectations of the organization are sacrificed to making people happy. Managers are liked, but there is no urgency to produce or improve.

Task management (9,1) is obviously the opposite of the style that sacrifices the rightful needs and expectations of workers to the wishes of management. People either shape up or ship out. Getting the work done is the supreme value. Tension and resentment exist, but they are squelched.

Dampened pendulum management (5,5) characterizes the kind of executive who knows that survival is the first law of human nature. Like the man caught between a tiger and a lion, he tries to keep both the workers and his superiors off his back. He pushes hard enough for production to keep management from becoming too unhappy with him. On the other hand, he keeps the troops from becoming overly restive or resistive. In essence, then, he is a compromiser and an appeaser. A variation of this style is *wide-arc pendulum management,* whose practitioner reacts to the latest and strongest pressure. When his superiors are dissatisfied, he tightens the screws on his men; then, when his people bristle, he eases off. In truth, he lives a swinging life but one with little satisfaction. *Paternalistic management* is a second variation of the dampened pendulum style. Here the *matter* is task-oriented but the *manner* country club. Operationally, rules and procedures are tight. Organizationally, much may be made of fringe benefits, a family atmosphere, and efforts to get the employees to identify with the firm. But the tone is one of buying peace and docility. Should the work group prove to be less than tractable, then there is an implied threat that the organizational sweets will be taken from them.

Impoverished management (1,1) is the style of the man who said "A curse on both your houses" and has fled the field. His attitude is that his superiors make impossible demands and the people are just impossible. Impoverished management is at times typical of the old Charlies of a company who have been passed over for promotion and have retired at full pay without having the courtesy to let the organization know.

Team management (9,9) is at once the most difficult, the most effective, and the most rewarding leadership style. The executive is concerned for both high production and the needs of his people. The building blocks, however, are not individuals but horizontally and vertically integrated work teams. The leader seeks to involve his subordinates in the work through consultation, participation, and joint problem solving. Tensions are openly admitted and dealt with. Attempts are made to make the work more meaningful rather than either hard or easy.

Implications for the Practicing Manager

In the brief summaries that have been presented, it has not been possible to do justice to the authorities who have devoted so much time and thought ferreting out factors in the leadership-followership process. The interested reader is urged to pursue the subject by reading the original sources. Even so cursory a review, however, provides the manager-leader with useful guidelines for his on-the-job behavior, some of which will serve only to reinforce the common sense of his own experience but others of which will run counter to popular conceptions.

The manager-leader must first and primarily define precisely what his job is. While this is a truism, more than a few managers would be hard put to rank their activities according to whether they are *essential,* as an engine is essential for the operation of a car; *important,* in the sense that a rear-view mirror or heater is important; or *incidental,* as the chrome and radio are incidental to the functioning of an automobile. The fact is that we do not even write job descriptions in this way. All duties and functions are treated as though they are equally important.

The manager-leader has only so much of his basic assets—time, thought, talent, and behavior. Unless he spells out, in his own mind at least, just how he should invest them, his leadership efforts will be hampered.

The manager-leader must define just what the jobs of his key subordinates are, preferably in a participative way. Unless they are committed to the achievement of commonly accepted goals, each will tend to fashion his own job according to his preferences and aversions.

It is clear from the research that the executive must be involved in certain basic types of leadership behavior. These include at least behavior that is geared to task performance and attainment; behavior that builds a spirit of mutual acceptance, respect, and helpfulness in his people in their dealings with each other; behavior that organizes the resources of his part of the firm so that what is done is accomplished efficiently; behavior that is sensitive to the needs and legitimate grievances of his employees; behavior that is supportive of subordinates in their desire to satisfy these needs; behavior that facilitates the efforts of his people to perform by providing them with the help they must have in their relations with other units of the organization; and behavior that is aimed at integrating the organization's requirements and the employees' expectations so that the two sides can identify with and take pride in each other.

If he is to avoid an abrupt comeuppance and frustration, the manager-leader must study not only the philosophy and mores of the company but also and especially the expectations of his superiors so that his behavior may be congruent with these realities. This, by the by, does not imply that he is to become either an organization man or a yes man.

The executive must appreciate the fact that his personality and his psychological history predispose him to engage in certain types of activities—maintenance, mediative, pro-active, or what have you—and make it difficult for him to carry out others. Hence, he must discipline himself to do what must be done rather than take easy refuge in what comes naturally or what he prefers to do.

Accordingly, he must think of on-the-job leadership as a pattern of strategies, each implemented by appropriate tactics. All talk about dichotomies, such as psychologically close versus psychologically distant leaders, employee- versus production-centered supervision, and consideration versus structuring, tends to ignore the permutations and combinations of things, events, people, pressures, and so on that characterize life in any firm. The manager-leader must be consistent, but he must avoid rigidity like cholera.

If the manager is to be effective as well as successful, then his attitudes toward his key people and the ways he interacts with them must be aimed not only at reinforcing their acceptance of him but also at satisfying the expectations they have of him.

The manager who would lead might do well to imitate the physician. Aware of the theory of medicine and having a wide spectrum of therapies available, the doctor adapts the indicated treatment to the personality of the patient as well as to the objective disease from which he suffers. Like the doctor, the manager-leader must be sensitive to side effects that may be extremely harmful, even to the point of undoing him.

macro factors

There are two major divisions in the study of economics—macroeconomics and microeconomics. The former spans the broad aggregate that is the overall economy and the principal elements that enter into it. The latter examines the components that make up the economy. Studies of leadership on the job have overemphasized a micro approach—focusing on the supervisor, his subordinates, his superiors—to the neglect of the effect that the macro aspects of the process can have. Evidence for this contention is derived from the fact that at times, when studies or experiments conducted in the United States have been replicated in other nations and cultures, the results obtained have been rather different. Hence, a managerial leadership model that gives due consideration to both the micro and the macro aspects is essential.

Leadership Is a Culturally Defined Variable

Culture is so pervasive that it is difficult to define precisely. The term denotes the shared values, the philosophical principles, the ethical concepts, the mores, and the patterns of learned behavior that are accepted by a given people and passed from generation to generation. Cultural differences are so apparent that they readily give rise to stereotypes, which may or may not be accurate. Cultural definitions can greatly influence one's idea of appropriate managerial leadership behavior.

European executives tend to be far more oriented toward the past and sensitive to the importance of tradition and established custom than are most of their American counterparts. The former are likely to have a regard for social and class distinctions; philosophical questions generally interest them, and they seek a balance among business, esthetic, and leisure-time activities. Most American businessmen, on the other hand, are oriented toward the present and future. They prefer rapid change to slow evolution. They entertain an affection for the self-made man; even people like Nelson A. Rockefeller, who couldn't count his money if he tried, seek to identify with the "common man" and the "average citizen." Although real distinctions exist, class distinctions are taboo. Know-how and getting things done often take precedence over theoretical or philosophical considerations. As often as not, authority is viewed not as coming down the chain of command but rather, as Barnard observed, as rising from the bottom up. People govern on the basis of neither heredity nor peculiar right but rather proven competence, and even then with the consent of the governed. In America, people do not so much know their place as carve out their place, earning their way up the ladder of prestige and power.

Multitudinous variations can be found within the European context. The *padrone* philosophy of small business in Italy, which follows what Clarence C. Walton calls a household model of social responsibility, is quite different from the impersonal approach of the British. The British emphasis on the "right" background, the "right" schools, and so on differs in turn from the authoritarianism that still prevails in Germany despite the modifications this tradition has undergone since World War II. And so one could move from country to country finding striking differences, although obviously similarities also abound.

The cast of mind with which managers approach their tasks as businessmen varies markedly from Japan to Latin America to England to America. Conventions and formalities that are the accepted norm in one social system seem odd in another. Latins are effusive, as any American who has been kissed by a male friend on his arrival in the host country has discovered to his amazement or amusement. Americans and British esteem the person who disciplines his emotions. The extreme courtesy of the Japanese is charming to the American visitor, although certain other customs are confusing. The British tend to be reserved, the Americans to be hail-fellows-well-met.

The way business is conducted likewise varies throughout the world. With Americans, it is a no-nonsense approach that says, let's get on with the matter and have done with it. In other nations, an interminable amount of time—in the American view, at least—seems to be wasted in preliminaries, protocol, and proprieties.

Subcultures and Subgroups

Subcultures within a given nation must also be reckoned with. New England is not the Deep South. In fact, G. K. Chesterton once observed that if one wished to discover old England, he should visit not New England but the South. An advantage of being transferred around the country is that one becomes sensitive to the different folkways and folklore that characterize each section. The denominator of Americanism remains the same, but the numerators are similar rather than identical. Nowhere is the variation of subcultures so evident as in Quebec, Ontario, and British Columbia, although all three are provinces of one nation.

Nor is that the end of the matter. Where the workforce is composed predominantly of representatives of a given racial, ethnic, or religious group, the supervisor or manager must have keen insight into the dynamics of this group. Historically, many organizations have been managed, especially at the top echelons, by native-born, college-educated, upper-middle- or lower-upper-class High-Church Protestants. Much of the workforce, however, has consisted of immigrants or first-generation natives who did not go to college, belonged to the lower middle or upper lower class, and were Catholics or low-church Protestants. With such disparities between rulers and ruled, conflict was predictable because it was inevitable. The differences—and the clashes—continue to this day; study the backgrounds of corporate executives and union leaders, for example.

Even in a much more narrowly defined context, cultural factors have their impact. The manager of a stevedoring firm in New York or San Francisco must contend with different subcultural traits from those his counterpart faces in a large bank in either metropolis. As a matter of fact, two bank managers, one in the Midwest with blacks constituting only about 3 percent of the employees and the other in Philadelphia with minority-group employees perhaps as high as 30 percent, will find that their managerial styles may differ rather widely in some respects.

A young black manager, during the course of a management development program, addressed his white peers in the following terms. "We can learn to live with you much more quickly and easily than you can with us. Because of our position, we have had to study you in order to find ways of getting along with you. But you white people have never had to study us or relate to us. You have known only one way, the way of being superior and making us do as you wished. Now that we refuse to be pushed around and deprived of our rights any longer, we are a puzzle to you. You don't seem to know what to do with us or how to deal with us. You are going to have to learn about us—how we think and feel—just as we had to learn about you if we are going to work together and respect each other." It is interesting that the group, which consisted wholly of Southerners, listened intently to the black manager and agreed that there was at least something in what he had to say.

Leadership Is an Ethos-determined Variable

Ethos is a favorite term in top management development programs in large corporations. It refers to the prevailing spirit— the dominant economic, social, philosophical, political, ethical, and religious views—accepted and esteemed in a society. It signals the kinds of ideas and behavior that will be highly regarded, tolerated, frowned upon, or considered impermissible in a given milieu. From the ethos come the norms of conduct, the rules of the game. For instance, one of the major principles in the American ethos is fairness; even small children resent anything that smacks of the unfair. Egalitarianism is another concept that is in the blood chemistry of almost every American. The scope and influence of a people's ethos are far greater than those of either religion or ethics; certain elements of the ethos may stand contrary to or completely apart from any ethical or religious considerations.

The Puritan Ethic and Its Challengers

Any American-born executive over the age of 50 has been reared according to the almost unalloyed tenets of the so-called Puritan ethic; a much more exact term would be Puritan ethos. Richard Henry Tawney and Max Weber have both summarized the major principles of this spirit.[1] A man worth his salt is supposed to be self-reliant, independent, productive, ambitious, hard-working, hard-driving, and energetic in his efforts to improve himself and move up the economic and social ladders. Laziness is the greatest sin; lack of willpower is an inexcusable weakness. Work is not something done to provide the necessities of life; it is the natural lot of man. In work, man finds himself, completes himself, actualizes himself. Failure to make the most of one's talents is a crime against the self and society. Failure to contribute to the amelioration of society's ills and to the well-being of one's fellow man is a dereliction of duty. Material wealth, advancement, power, and prestige are good in themselves; possession of them is a virtue.

Practically every person in this country is still molded to some degree by these ideals. Regardless of religion—Protestant, Catholic, or Jewish; regardless of national origins—English, German, Irish, Hungarian, or what have you; regardless of the schools attended—private or public, the fact is that the citizens of our country are more "Puritan" than Protestant, Catholic, or Jewish, English, Irish, or German.

North and South America were discovered at approximately the same time. South America contains far more natural resources than North America. Both land masses screamed for exploitation and development. Why are the countries of South America so far behind those of North America in technological and industrial progress? Although it is simpleminded to attribute a complex result to a single cause, much of the difference can be attributed to the different ethos that guided the people who settled in each section and channeled their energies in diverse directions.

Some years ago, William H. Whyte, Jr. popularized the term *social ethic*. This ethos represents an almost 180-degree turn from the Puritan ethic in numerous particulars. Instead of individuality, togetherness is exalted. Listening to one's own drummer is replaced by group think. Rather than being one's own man, the major desideratum is to become part of the corporate team. Pursuing one's personal career plan must give way to efforts to achieve acceptance and belonging. Thinking one's own thought is displaced by developing a company brain. Innovative tendencies are subdued in favor of conformity; mediocrity is more readily tolerated than excellence or creativity. Scientism is used to help everybody adjust so that no waves will disrupt the serene waters of organizational existence. Although Whyte obviously overstated his case, there is no question that his observations contain more than a germ of truth. Peter F. Drucker has implied and John Kenneth Galbraith has stated that we are moving in the direction of a postindustrial ethic, in which knowledge will indeed be power and, to use IBM's saying, men will think while machines work.

Leadership Is a Politically Determined Variable

That political structure influences leadership patterns needs no proof. Managers in a Communist society and those in a democratic society, even though they possess equivalent intellectual and technical skills, are likely to follow different philosophies of leadership on the job. Where the political apparatus is omnipotent, where deviations from the party line are ruthlessly crushed, where criticism is not allowed, where planning and policy are formulated by powerful bureaucracies, the manager's behavior will necessarily be different in many important ways from that demanded and expected in a democratic setting. For in the latter, free discussion is encouraged; every person has certain inalienable rights; criticism and dissent are tolerated; agreement and consensus are the preferred ways of getting things accomplished. It is safe to say that, in a democracy, it is far more difficult to be a manager-leader but far more rewarding as well.

Leadership Is a Societally Determined Variable

Every society willy-nilly proposes for the young the kind of hero it esteems. In the United States, the hero has been the achiever. In India, by way of contrast, it is the holy man. David C. McClelland and his associates have discovered that the achievement motive of countries like Russia and the United States is very high, although not so high in the latter as it once was.[2] England and Sweden at one time had a high achievement motive, but it later declined. McClelland and his colleagues pose this hypothesis: nations that have a high achievement motive make faster economic progress than those that are low in this quality. Their research indicates that achievers have certain characteristics:

1. They prefer situations in which success depends more on their personal talents and skills than on chance.
2. They seek out situations in which the risk is proportionate to their resources for coping with it. They avoid sure things and wild risks.
3. They need to operate under conditions that provide them with concrete feedback on their performance and knowledge of the results they have attained.
4. They have a tendency to think ahead in anticipation of future possibilities.

Despite the talk about the social and postindustrial ethos, the average executive still has a high regard for the Puritan ethos. He continues to pursue the status rewards and the increments of power, prestige, and authority that represent so much of the prize society bestows on those who excel. If the newer ethos have made certain inroads into traditional values, they have a long way to go before they become dominant in either the thinking of the public in general or the motivations of the average manager in particular. Society will smile for a long time on the individual or group that creates more effective organizations, that meets challenges and overcomes them, and that brings about progress.

Leadership Is a Philosophically Determined Variable

Although it is patent that everything a manager does is ultimately a result of his image of his fellow man, pitifully little attention is paid to this in the professional literature. One does not expect executives to be philosophers, much less philosophers to become managers. But one should be mindful of the truth that as a person thinks, so he becomes; as he thinks of his fellow men, so he will behave toward them. Surely both saints and Nazis have proved these truths.

Concepts of Man

In oversimplified terms, several views of the nature of man have prevailed throughout history and are now current. The manager-leader might analyze just where his views fit into these generalizations and what implications they will have for his on-the-job activities.[3]

People as evil. The notion that people are fundamentally evil is an ancient one that has endured for millennia. The Puritans picked it up by way of Calvin, who emphasized mankind's predestination. Its managerial implications are that one must consider subordinates as prone to loafing, cheating, and malingering. Any idea of goodwill or desire to do a good job on their part is a luxury of the incredibly naive. Since workers are inclined to be lazy, cut corners, and act unethically, then logically they must be boxed in by strict rules and threats of punishments. Controls must be infinite in detail and punitive in purpose. Examples are made of those who stray from the straight and narrow to prevent others from being tempted to wander down the primrose path of delinquency. Surprisingly, a few managers who would intellectually ridicule such a view of their fellow man behave toward him as though they were convinced of its validity.

People as good. The intrinsic goodness of man is of course the basic premise of Jean-Jacques Rousseau. Man is good; society is evil and corrupts him. Most utopian idealists proclaim the truth of these assumptions. No manager in his right mind maintains unreserved faith in the virtuousness of his people.

People as determined. The determinist approach would have the manager believe that man is but a meaningless mass of molecules being bounced this way and that by a chaotic, mechanistic world. He cannot act; he only reacts. He is the product of his heredity, past conditioning, training, and experiences. He sails through life now blessed by fair winds and now buffeted by storms, devoid of star, compass, charts, steering wheel, or rudder. The best he can hope to do is adjust to a malevolent universe. Again, no manager with any experience places much credence in such a dismal conception of human nature.

People as blank pages. "Give me a child for the first six years of his life, and I will make him whatever you wish" was the war cry of the old behaviorist psychologists with their overemphasis on conditioning. Heredity is not nearly so important as training. Nature yields to nurture. Goodness or evil can be inculcated with equal ease by prolonged conditioning processes. Man, in short, is a blank page on which those who control him can write anything they care to. This, of course, is the key concept in all totalitarian forms of government. The good Communist is not born; he is made. Whereas it can be readily granted that man is partially molded by his previous experiences, this is totally different from claiming that he is a mere blob who has no power of self-determination.

People as defined but changeable. In the view that man is defined but changeable, three factors are significant. *Heredity* provides the potential that is to be actualized while at the same time setting limits on this process of fulfillment. Man is not born an intelligent being. He is born with potential intelligence, which must be actualized. In this sense, intelligence is an achievement rather than a gift. Moreover, man has a drive to grow and mature. The *environment* affords each person certain opportunities to develop his inherited potential while at the same time imposing constraints on how far he can do so. The *individual's own efforts* determine the extent to which the original capacities will be actualized and the opportunities utilized. Within the perimeters set by his heredity and environment, a man can be changed or change himself. The limits are definite, but they are not predetermined as in a mathematical formula.

Cultural, political, and other forces can combine to dictate a concept of man that radically affects the quality of life in a given society for better—as was the case for many countries during the Renaissance and the Enlightenment—or for worse. The most extraordinary example in modern times of how such a synthesis worked to hurt not only organizations but an entire nation might be called "the rise and decline of Lysenko." During the 1930s, Trofim Denisovich Lysenko, a mediocre Russian agronomist, carved his way to absolute monarchy over biological science in that country. He rejected the laws of genetics established by such giants as Gregor Mendel and Thomas Hunt Morgan. Heredity was nothing; training and development were everything. What more natural when peasants had overthrown princes and the state was intent on fashioning citizens to its own image and likeness? The laughingstock of the rest of the world, Lysenko ruled supreme until 1964, thanks to the repression and persecution of demurring Russian scientists. The amazing thing was that even so objective and impersonal a field as biology could be prostituted to serve the current concept of man, irrational though that view was.

Concepts in Action

As far as managerial leadership is concerned, the first task of the executive is to reflect on what theory of man *operationally* governs his attitudes and behavior toward his superiors, peers, and subordinates. To what extent are his preferences for some and aversions to others based on evidence? To what extent are they rooted in biases? How does he see them—as gentlemanly cooperators and competitors, as foes who must be fought tooth and nail, as objects for exploitation who are to be manipulated to whatever degree possible? The manager might also profitably dwell on his own self-concept. Does he perceive himself as a reasonably well-adjusted, mature, and competent person, despite his human limitations? Or is he jealous of his prerogatives, insecure in his position, and wary of everyone whom he considers a threat? Again, he might now and then analyze his own beliefs about how people relate to one another in this vale of tears. Is it a system of dog-eat-dog or of the devil take the hindmost? Or is it a process of balancing out self-interests with a genuine concern for helping others? Finally, if people are limited but capable of growth, what is his personal program for improving his management effectiveness and leadership on the job?

Leadership Is a Technologically Determined Variable

A factor that tended to be ignored in the early studies of leadership was the technology that characterized the department or firm in which the research was carried on. Now that computerization, automation, and scientific advances are proceeding at a gallop, it can no longer be neglected. It seems logical—and there is evidence to support this view—that in a manufacturing operation, where machine pacing of the work and the need for a smooth flow of production couple with the built-in pressures of tight schedules, there might be a place for a forceful manager who puts considerable emphasis on organization and structure. This does not mean that the needs of the workforce are slighted but rather that they may be of secondary importance. By contrast, in a work environment where the pressures to perform are less taut, the need for good human relations may be primary. It is doubtful that the same mix of firmness and permissiveness would be equally effective in the management of salesmen, office clerks, and production workers in a factory.

Joan Woodward classified some 100 English companies into three production categories according to the technology employed: (1) small-batch or unit production, (2) large-batch or mass production, and (3) continuous process.[4] In unit production, such as sales or carpentry, much of the responsibility for insuring quality rested with the worker, who normally was quite skilled. But as the technology became more complex and integrated, the manager supervised not so much individuals or groups but a process. Other studies support the view that in unit production there may be a need for a friendly atmosphere and considerate behavior, whereas in mass production or continuous process these may be far more difficult to maintain. There is no question here of an either-or approach. The point is that the manager-leader must take into account the fact that the prevailing technology will have an influence on what he can and should do.

One of the classic examples of the effects of technological change on workers' efficiency and morale occurred in Great

Britain. Since the mining industry was sick, it was decided to switch from "short-wall" to "long-wall" technology. In the "short-wall" approach, men worked in small groups of two to eight self-selected men along a short length of the mine on a pick and shovel basis. They worked in close proximity, there was much job rotation, interaction among the men was great, and a given piece of work representeα a self-contained unit. The men were paid on a group piecework basis. All this changed under the "long-wall" system in which work teams consisted of 40 to 50 miners spread over some 200 yards of wall. Each did a specialized job. There was little rotation from job to job, and opportunities to interact with one another were limited. Pay was based on group output. What were the results? On the part of management, much more time and energy were expended in co-ordinating and supervising the work teams and dealing with operating contingencies. On the part of the workers, productivity did not go up, but absenteeism and grievances did. Finally, a compromise had to be worked out which combined the "long-wall" technology with small, cohesive work groups.[5]

Leadership Is an Organizationally Determined Variable

Not nearly enough is known about the day-to-day interactions of the typical manager with people upward, downward, and horizontally.[6] Mountains of words are written on what he *should* do; the information regarding what he actually *does* is a molehill by comparison. William F. Whyte presents a fascinating account of a character named Tom Walker.[7] At one time, Walker was considered an outstanding success. Two years later, he was a failure who had to be replaced! Whyte shows how certain types of relationships were critical for Walker's success or failure. These included (1) his vertical dealings with superiors and subordinates, (2) his horizontal interaction with his fellow foremen to insure a proper work flow without bottlenecks or pileups, (3) his horizontal relationships with shop stewards, (4) his diagonally upward dealings with the maintenance superintendent, (5) his diagonally upward relations with the union presi-

dent, and (6) his horizontal interaction with such staff units as inspection. As long as Walker handled these relationships effectively, he was outstanding. As soon as they deteriorated markedly, his fate was sealed. This case study is a strong counterpoise for any temptation to oversimplify the on-the-job leadership problems of the manager.

Glenn A. Bassett [8] has an interesting classification of the orientations of different companies. In the *failure-avoidance* organization, the main desideratum is to keep one's nose clean at all costs. Energy is expended in self-protective maneuvers and defenses. When something goes wrong, projecting the blame on someone else is taken up as the favorite indoor pastime. During the Civil War, President Lincoln became so annoyed at General McClellan's talent for procrastination that he once asked if he could borrow the army for a short time, since the general did not seem to have any use for it. The best example of a *maintenance* organization is any large bureaucracy. Drucker says that every corporation finds it difficult to abandon yesterday's tasks and stop doing the unproductive. In the maintenance type of firm, there is no desire to do so. Consistent mediocrity is prized over innovation. Energy is wasted defending the past and traditional ways of doing things. In the *change-oriented* organization, prudent risk taking is encouraged. Innovation is rewarded rather than lockstep conformity. It is assumed that the worst enemy of the best is the good enough. Finally, a *results-oriented* organization insists on the attainment of clearly defined objectives. Excuses are not accepted as substitutes for goal achievement.

Analyzing the Organizational Force Field

It is rather evident that a managerial leadership pattern that will work well in a failure-avoidance climate will be a bomb in a change-oriented atmosphere. It is surprising how sometimes even a seasoned executive can fall on his face simply because he tries to impose on one kind of organization a type of behavior that worked effectively for him in another company with a rather different philosophy. Instead of analyzing the new situation in which he finds himself, he assumes that it is identical to the one in which he has previously been successful. He would be better advised to imitate scientists, who are disciplined to study the phenomena that they would cope with before endeavoring to deal with them. Practically, this means that the manager-leader should make a series of analyses of the organization or department.[9]

Key people analysis. As has been said, the people who occupy key positions may be quite other than the key people in an organization. Power is unequally distributed throughout every corporation. The manager-leader must discover who casts the long shadows in the firm and who carries the clout. Power centers and power figures must be identified for the reason that they are in a position to assist or negate the leader's efforts to work effectively. Executive secretaries do not generally appear on organization charts. Were a power structure pictured, however, some would carry more weight than a few middle managers. A staff assistant may be a mere messenger or legman, but he may also be an *éminence grise.*

Nonformal organization analysis. In every organization, to quote the old ditty, "Things are seldom what they seem. Skimmed milk masquerades as cream." Things almost never get done as they appear to from the higher reaches of the firm. Since there is always some kind of nonformal organization, the manager-leader who would succeed seeks to answer questions of this sort: To what extent is the nonformal organization working at cross-purposes with the formal? To what degree do the objectives of the nonformal organization agree with those of the formal? How effective is the nonformal organization in achieving its goals? How effective regarding the aims of the formal organization? How does the nonformal organization get the work done? What are its dynamics? Who are its leaders? How can the manager-leader capitalize on the resources of the nonformal organization? How can he minimize its actual or potential harmful effects?

Interpersonal analysis. The ability to cross organizational lines without making the organization cross is a fine art. Even finer is the art of stimulating the system without irritating it. Every department is an arena of interaction—at times "seething caldron" would be a more accurate description—with a chemistry unique unto itself. Even though to an outsider a company may appear to be a static structure of men, machines, and money, all geared to productivity and profit, the insider soon discovers that it is a place where dreams are born and ambitions are buried. In it, friendships are built and jealousies are nourished. On its premises, competition and cooperation live cheek by jowl. The economic man lives hip and thigh with the psychological man. Team spirit and corporate discord wax and wane. Some advance in triumph while others retreat in defeat. Loyalties and antagonisms abide. Human frailties and fears are discovered, but human strengths and virtues are evident.

If he is to succeed, the manager-leader must scrutinize with the utmost care the interaction patterns of the organization or at least of his subunit. There is an old cliché that 20 percent of the people in any organization cause 80 percent of the problems. At the very minimum, the manager must be alert to the individuals and groups who can get him into hot water. He must be sensitive to the in groups and the out groups. He must be aware of the special rapports and special enmities that exist in any firm, not to mention the intra- and interdepartmental friendships and frictions that are the normal human experience.

Communications analysis. In any company, the rumors are roadrunners, the grapevine a hot line. They far outstrip all official pronunciamentos and pipelines. Accordingly, the manager-leader is sage to analyze how the word really gets around. Questions such as who listens to whom, who tells whom what, who tunes out whom, who speaks to whom and with what effect, and who does not speak to whom are of crucial importance. At best, the manager can develop strategies for making the most effective use of the formal and nonformal channels of communication. At least, he can try to lessen his vulnerability to their shrapnel effects.

Decision-making analysis. Everyone knows what is wrong with the City of New York. Trouble arises when one attempts to rank the values according to which the decisions will be made. The difficulty stems from the problem of establishing an order of priorities within the constraints of limited financial resources. Both the trouble and the difficulty are compounded by the reality that every fundamental decision must be by definition political. In his analysis of how decisions are made in the firm or department, the manager had best start with some evaluation of the values, principles, and philosophy that guide the decision-making process. He must be attuned to the priorities that his superiors think important. He should try to master the art of seeing a given problem or situation through the eyes of the key power people.

Navigating the Force Field

In philosophic terms, top management consists of rational animals. Amid the pressures of the general run of firms, however, the upper hierarchs may act as irrationally as do lesser mortals. Hence, the manager-leader, who frequently cannot change things on his own but must obtain the support of others, learns to work through and with not merely his subordinates but also his boss. It is a moot point whether anyone should "manage" his superior. But the leader who expects his boss or the organization to accept his ideas or make decisions wholly on the facts of a situation is destined to run aground on the rocks and shoals that spell disaster for the unwitting. His real task is to package what he has to offer in such a manner that the services, benefits, and advantages of a given proposal are evident to his superiors and the organization as a whole.

If it is essential that the manager-leader obtain a favorable answer from the higher-ups, it is no less necessary that he gain a favorable reaction to his decisions and actions from his employees, at least from those key people who represent make-or-break factors. The process of coming to a decision is often far less complicated than that of implementing it effectively. Pockets of resistance must be identified and strategies for dealing with them formulated. The manager must know in advance how he intends to cope with not only those who remain intellectually convinced that a given decision is less than wise but also those who will be resistant because their prestige or status may be threatened. Many an excellent proposal has come to ruin because of the ineptness with which it was implemented, to the dismay of the proposer and the embarrassment of his superiors. Even what appear on the surface to be a relatively simple and direct decision and an uncomplicated decision-making process can at times turn out to be filled with pitfalls.

The B-School, as its helpless critics and detractors are reminded, is a school of management rather than of business

*instruction. It has also become, like so many of the corpora-
tions that support it, an almost unmanageable structure.
There are its 1,500 students (all chiefs and no Indians, they
proudly admit). There is the faculty of 180 prima donnas
(some of them white-shirted tyrants enforcing obedience
through petulance and attendance checks) guarding their
individual prestige and considerable earnings from internal
as well as external threats.*[10]

A piece of automated equipment was purchased by one of
the largest newspapers in the world. It was highly satisfac-
tory from a technical viewpoint. It was shipped and set up
on the floor of the composing room. Naturally, it attracted
the attention of the chapel chairman, who had not been
consulted regarding its installation. When it was explained
that the new equipment was to be blended into the operations, he laughed and commented, "Never happen." In five
years, that equipment was not used for as long as one minute.

These two incidents, one about the most prestigious business
education institution in America and the other about a firm at
the rank and file level, suggest how troublesome it may be to
make even a relatively straightforward change or to implement
a rational decision. The manager-leader who would be prudent
as well as forceful might do well to bear in mind what are
called Murphy's laws: (1) if anything can possibly go wrong, it
will; (2) nothing is ever so simple as it looks; (3) it always takes
far more time than we thought it would. These negative criteria
will at least serve the purpose of preventing enthusiasm from
obscuring the need to evolve impersonal and practical measures
for dealing with resistance and obstructionism.

Leadership Is a Skill-Mix–Determined Variable

It is largely a waste of breath to state that the manager-leader
requires these or those skills. Considering skills in the abstract
without taking into account the nuances of the organizational
context in which they must be exercised probably does more
harm than good. Floyd C. Mann has brought this fact to light

very clearly in a series of studies.[11] Using a three-part classification of skills—into technical, administrative, and human relations—he found in a study of ten hospitals that every group evaluated its superiors highest on their technical skills and lowest on their human relations skills, with administrative skills intermediate. On the other hand, various groups ranked the skills in diverse ways. For instance, supervising nurses felt that their superiors' human relations skills were primary. In contrast, department heads perceived the administrative skills of their superiors to be most important, with human relations skills assuming a poor second position. The technicians were principally oriented toward the superiors' perceived technical and human relations skills. The results, derived from five groups representing different organizational levels, suggested that the skill mix desirable in a superior depends on the nature of the work and the groups doing the work. This conclusion is substantiated by a study Mann carried out of six power plants, including three levels of management. The plants ranged from almost obsolete to brand new. Foremen in the new plants distinguished more sharply between their managers' technical and administrative skills than did foremen in the older plants. Their satisfaction was more highly related to the administrative skills than to the technical or human relations skills they perceived in their managers. In the oldest plant, however, the satisfactions of both the workers and the foremen were associated with their estimate of the superiors' human relations skills.

In still another study, Mann observed the accounting department of a large electric company for four years as it changed over to a series of computerized operations. He found that supervisors had to draw upon various combinations of skills at different times. Before the change-over started, when the organization was relatively stable, much of the supervisors' energy was devoted to maintaining the department in equilibrium, and this required an emphasis on human relations and the pertinent skills. During the transition, however, the supervisors had to rely more and more on their technical and administrative skills. The problems were such that only these were equal to their solution. It is not that human relations skills were insignificant; they simply were not adequate to cope with the complexities involved in the change-over. Interestingly, the skill mix required at different levels also tended to change somewhat. Initially, top management was concerned about the implementation of the computerization from a technical and administrative viewpoint. At the same time, lower-level managers and supervisors were concerned with allaying the fears of employees regarding the implications of the change. Then as the change-over progressed, human relations problems which could not be handled adequately at the lower levels moved up the chain of command for policy decisions on the part of the higher echelons. As Mann says, "And so on almost cyclically."

In sum, then, the manager-leader must give serious thought to the macro factors that can greatly influence his on-the-job behavior. Some of these, such as the surrounding culture, ethos, society, and political structure and his conceptual view of his fellow man, are subtle and indirect in their impact. He would be well advised to bring them to the surface and confront them candidly. Others, such as the technology utilized in his part of the firm, the pertinent organizational factors, and the skill-mix requirements, are more obvious. In any case, the manager cannot succeed for long in his efforts to lead if he either seeks to impose his views on these realities or persistently ignores the effect that they can have.

micro factors

No manager is paid to lead; he is paid to accomplish organizational goals with and through his people, and leadership is but one of the instruments that he has available for doing so. Leadership and management are not interchangeable synonyms. As one subordinate said of his boss, "He's a wonderful person and a fine leader. If he were only a good manager, we'd be in clover."

The Leader's View of the Management Process

As a matter of fact, most descriptions of what managers do have only some direct relationship to leadership as such. John K. Hemphill, for instance, reported a study in which 93 executives completed a questionnaire indicating to what degree each of 575 job elements, which had been derived from the use of a job-activity inventory, applied to their positions.[1] A factor analysis procedure suggested that the common dimensions of their positions were as follows: (1) providing a staff service for nonoperational areas, (2) supervising others' work, (3) exercising internal business control, (4) overseeing technical aspects of products and markets, (5) attending to human, community, and social affairs, (6) formulating long-range plans, (7) exercising broad power and authority, (8) maintaining the firm's business reputation, (9) responding to personal demands, (10) preserving the company's assets. It is clear that only some of these have anything to do with leadership per se. Other studies have produced similar results.

Strategies in Managing

A fact of life that any experienced manager is aware of is that he rarely can manage in the manner that is described in textbooks on the subject. The array of diverse viewpoints is so broad, the lack of mutual respect so common, the clash of personalities so prevalent, the voice of each special interest group so insistent that it would be strange indeed were an executive able to manage by the book. What he needs is a spectrum of strategies for coping with the numerous pressures to which he must respond. According to the contingencies of a given situation, he may employ any or all of the following.

Unlimited conflict. The no-holds-barred strategy is at once the easiest and the most dangerous. It is the easiest because people seem to have an inner compulsion to make others submit to them. It is the most dangerous because it commits all one's resources, which involves a real risk that all may be lost in a single confrontation. Although there may be rare instances when it is necessary to adopt an unyielding position, such an approach should be employed only when all other strategies have failed.

Partial conflict. In carefully selected situations where the ends are limited, partial or limited conflict may serve some useful purpose. It may be necessary if the manager is to maintain his status, prerogatives, or prestige in the face of aggression from a peer or another department. Even so, it has certain inherent dangers. First, the executive may win battles only to lose wars. Second, limited conflict usually leaves residues of resentment that may later haunt him even when he wins.

Guerrilla conflict. A basic maxim in boxing is that the pugilist who makes an opponent carry the fight will always win. This is the heart of guerrilla conflict. The United States has learned this lesson the hard way in Vietnam. Guerrilla conflict assumes that the manager can choose the site, the conditions, and the tactics that will be most effective.

Compromise. Warfare is to be avoided whenever possible for the reason that it entails a win-lose outcome. Compromise leads each side to yield on points that it considers less important in order to prevail with respect to those that are considered essential. This give-and-take process enables both parties to arrive at a solution they can live with, even though compromise inevitably leaves each somewhat unsatisfied. Given their druthers, most people would rather dominate than compromise. But the realities dictate that if they are to get on with the business at hand, compromises are in order. It goes without saying that the weaker party is always the one that is more amenable to compromise.

To compromise intelligently, the manager-leader must divide the issues into four classifications. He must clarify the *essentials* for himself. These are elements on which he will not yield. At the opposite end of the continuum are the *unlivables*, factors so repugnant that any decision or action containing even one of them must be rejected. The essentials and the unlivables, in a word, constitute those positive and negative areas in which no movement is possible. Any course of action must give the leader all of the essentials and none of the unlivables. Somewhere in between these extremes are to be found aspects that can be categorized as the *palatables* and the *unpalatables*. Obviously, one seeks to secure as many of the palatables as he possibly can and avoid accepting the unpalatables. What is more important is that they define the limits within which one is willing to compromise. If the manager can maximize the palatables he can garner while minimizing the unpalatables he must swallow, then he has gotten the best possible outcome. It requires real skill to trade off certain desirable elements for essential ones. But if he has clear ideas on the four categories discussed, he is in a good position to compromise.

Accommodation. When the light is bright or dim, the lens of the eye adjusts to the unusual intensity. The person sees regardless of the accommodations that must be made. Analogously, the manager-leader must at times accommodate himself to certain people or situations when he cannot sway them directly. Accommodation requires that he adapt to, adjust to, or meet the needs of other people. Flexibility within the parameters of values and convictions is the key to using this strategy intelligently. Accommodation goes on all the time—to the organization's philosophy, tempo, and climate; to authority figures, peers, and subordinate work groups. Skill in accommodating gracefully and graciously often makes it much easier for others to relate to the manager-leader, provided his action is not interpreted as a sign of weakness or indecisiveness.

Persuasion. A persuasive approach implies a deliberate attempt to modify the thinking, attitudes, and behavior of another person or group in order to bring them into conformity with those of the persuader. Only fools would deny the advantages of being persuasive. But it does involve certain difficulties that should be avoided. First, some people will never learn the difference between being truly smooth and merely slick. The unctuousness of their manner is alienating. Second, when one seeks to persuade another, he inevitably adopts a manipulative approach. Again, since the aim of persuasion is to reduce the opposite party's available options to the single one that the persuader is interested in, persuasion often prompts the vis-à-vis to react defensively. In the face of the persuasive attack, he looks for outs and battles to keep them open. It would be absurd to contend that persuasion does not have a genuine place in the management process; the more persuasive the leader, within limits, the better. But he should remember that persuasion connotes a suggestion of superiority that another person may resist. Moreover, persuasion is basically a me-versus-you strategy in which the me is going to coax the you to do as the me wishes. In short, persuasion seeks to satisfy the persuader's needs, not those of both parties.

Negotiation. Negotiation is a process of mutual bargaining whose aim is to arrive at an agreed-upon objective. Actually, most managers carry out their functions and play their roles not principally by the use of authority but through an almost endless process of negotiating with their superiors, peers, and subordinates. True negotiation begins with an attitude of you-and-me but seeks to end with one of us-and-our. It cannot take place unless the climate is fundamentally one of sincerity, mutual confidence, and honesty. Its basic aim is to integrate as much as possible the needs, wants, and interests of both parties and to reach objectives that are mutually satisfying. This satisfaction need not be and rarely is a 50-50 proposition. At times, the manager-leader will give more than he will receive because he is concerned with long-term results; at other times, he will place his own needs first and foremost. To negotiate successfully, he

require tactics appropriate to the problems and the people
lved. The following may prove helpful, depending on realities with which he must contend.

Meet the other person's needs. In all negotiating, the opposite
party has two questions in the back of his mind: (1) What's in it
for me? (2) How will the solution affect me and my position?
Effective negotiating activities must honestly seek to help the
person answer these questions.

Negotiate benefits, not obstacles. No one really buys logic (especially someone else's), facts (especially as presented by someone else), or reasoning (especially when it is based on someone
else's premises). Self-centeredly—and this is not to be confused
with selfishly—one buys advantages, benefits, and services to
himself. Hence, the task of the negotiating manager is to help
the other party see that he will gain more than he will lose if a
given decision is made.

Build support. Only people with a Joan of Arc complex like
to go it alone. This fault is at times seen in the young manager
who falls in love with his own ideas and expects the world to
meet him on his terms. This is not only self-defeating; it can be
self-destructive. The broader the base of support, the easier it is
to negotiate.

Get a group involved. The research shows clearly that when
a group perceives some advantage to itself as a whole, it is
likely to be more amenable to change. Despite all that has
been written about fear of change, it is not change that disturbs
people but uncertainty. The job of the negotiating manager is to
allay undue concern about uncertainty. When a person or group
becomes involved and has a stake in a decision or change, then
not only are its chances of success augmented but fear of uncertainty and any accompanying resistance are much more easily
handled.

Seek limited objectives. Desirable though the ideal is, often
the manager-leader must tailor his goals to what is possible in
the circumstances. After all, a general in the field does not have
to win the war; this is merely an ambition. His first job is to win
a battle; this is an objective. People will often go along with
limited objectives when they would mightily resist grandiose
ambitions. With success, it will be easier for both the executive
and his counterparts to move ahead together to further goals.

Stress agreement, not disagreement. It is a perverse human tendency to emphasize differences rather than similarities, to stress what divides people rather than what unites them. On the other hand, a basic principle of negotiation is that the wider the areas of agreement become, the less nettlesome areas of disagreement appear. The duty of the negotiating manager is not to impose his will on the "enemy" but to seek out ways in which he and his opposite number can profit from the relationship.

Seek preliminary criticisms. Asking the advice of a potential adversary and, as far as possible, incorporating his suggestions into a decision or course of action is one of the best ways of preventing needless opposition.

Build a state of psychological readiness. There is an old saying that an idea whose time has come is irresistible. The reason for this is evident. An idea is compelling when people are ready for it and open to it. When conditions allow, the manager-leader is well advised to invest time and energy building a receptive climate for whatever he has in mind. Moving too fast or at the wrong time has destroyed many a good program. At times, making haste slowly is the better part of prudence.

Make lemonade out of the lemon. Consistent success is the lot of no one on this earth. When the manager-leader encounters defeat or rebuff, he is shrewd to analyze the reasons for the mishap and then regroup his forces and try again. The Phoenix rises from its own ashes rejuvenated and able to go on to a new life.

Be prepared to yield. Negotiation by definition leads the parties concerned to make a mutual adjustment in the process of mutually satisfying their needs. Unless they seek out opportunities to yield on minor matters so that the major needs of each may be relatively well satisfied, then the entire process degenerates into a tug-of-war, with each trying to outwit the other. It is integration on significant matters that is needed, not unconditional surrender.

It would be pleasant if corporations were populated by angels. Unhappily, they are not. The people in them come in all sizes, dimensions, and personalities. While the majority may be basically decent and gentlemanly, the fact is that every company has its share of the overly ambitious, the unethical, the back-stabbing, and the pole-vaulting, all eager to seize power by climbing over the bodies of less resistant contemporaries. If the altruistic are numerous, the connivers will always be with us, not to mention the self-serving plotters. Accordingly, rather than go lamblike to his own destruction, the manager-leader must on occasion resort to one or another of the strategies and tactics that have been outlined. Although he can always endeavor to negotiate, accommodate, persuade, or even compromise, the fact remains that someone who typically goes for the jugular cannot be handled with kid gloves; in such a case, the iron fist may be much more in order.

The Manager-Leader's Concept of His Role

The head of an engineering department has on his desk a sign that reads, "Director of Change." This man's view of his role is quite different from that of the manager who merely gets today's work done in a neat and tidy manner with no thought of innovation or improvement. Each manager brings to his task certain perceptions, expectations, values, and priorities. Each will focus on different aspects of the same position; each will go about attaining organizational objectives in his unique way; each will place greater or less stress on the diverse factors that make up his overall responsibility. The new broom will perceive his role rather differently from the timeserver who is really waiting for the blessed day of relief when he retires. It is surprising how few executives ever frankly face up to the question, "Just what am I being paid to accomplish?" If they did, it is certain that some major changes would take place in their day-to-day behavior.

Mutual Perceptions and Expectations

How the Manager and His Superiors See Each Other

Every superior has definite expectations of his subordinate managers. Executive A, in spite of what he says, actually wants a rather docile, efficient hewer of wood who with great dispatch attends to the more mundane aspects of his delegated responsibilities. Executive B wants a manager who gets tomorrow's job done yesterday with innovative verve. Executive C would like to work with his subordinates in a close and informal manner. Executive D prefers a more formal and socially distant climate and relationship.

What can the manager do when his superiors have neither the time nor the inclination to spell out for him exactly what they require as appropriate behavior? The following suggestions may help.

1. He can develop what sociologists call a sensing ability. As a good host or toastmaster must learn to sense what is fitting and becoming, so too the manager must look constantly for clues to what his bosses are looking for, no matter what has been said or left unsaid between them.

2. He can accept the fact that his real task, regardless of what his position description may say, is to seek out every reasonable opportunity to make his immediate superior and the organization come up smelling like a rose while fostering his own advancement in the process.

3. He can avoid like the plague bending a superior's ear, twisting his arm, stepping on his toes, and wringing his heart with sad stories of a woeful lot.

4. He can study his superiors, as a scientist studies any phenomenon that he would deal with, to get a reading on their preferences, aversions, pet peeves, sore spots, sacred cows, preferred methods of operating, idiosyncrasies, and so on. It is important that he avoid all moral judgments or criticisms in this analysis. His job is to comprehend, not evaluate.

5. He can, again like the scientist, experiment prudently with different approaches to his superiors until he discovers the style they respond to most positively.

6. He can be wary of competing with his superiors, perhaps unconsciously. His duty is to supplement their limited resources with his strengths, not to endeavor subtlely to supplant them.

7. He can take the initiative and write up what he thinks his immediate boss expects of him. Then, at a suitable time and place, he can present his assessment to the superior, requesting him to review it and make any observations or corrections that are needed. It is difficult to see how any executive could take such a procedure in the wrong spirit if it is done tactfully and

with a view to making their cooperation and coordination of effort more effective and cordial.

How the Manager and His People See Each Other

The attitude of some top managements used to be, "The machine belongs to the company; the worker is made for the machine; ergo, the worker belongs to the company and exists to satisfy its needs." Entertaining such a perspective today would border on lunacy, although managers can be found who act as though they still prescribe to it. The simple fact is that no employee works primarily to satisfy the needs of any organization. He labors first and foremost to meet *his* needs, wants, desires, and aspirations. Only secondarily is he concerned for the welfare of the firm. Additionally, the leader soon learns to accept his people as he finds them rather than as he would like them to be. Even if he is unhappy with their performance, he knows that the only possible starting point for improvement is where they are and as they are at a given time.

Five facts are at the heart of any mutual perception process. First, initial impressions tend to be lasting as well as erroneous. It is necessary not only that the manager-leader perceive his people accurately but that he make it easy for them to see him as he is without sham or flimflam. Second, a person perceives what he looks for and very little else. This means that the manager should emphasize the positive in sizing up his people. If he is aware of their limitations, he is also conscious of the fact that he will not make much progress with them by focusing on deficiencies. Far too much time is squandered in most organizations on attempts to eradicate defects. It would be wiser to concentrate on capitalizing on assets and building strengths. Third, needs govern perceptions. At the outset of any relationship, there is bound to be some uncertainty on both sides. If he is an unframed picture to his subordinates, the manager realizes that they are not sure just how to go about relating to him. His responsibility is to be authentic in his dealings with them and open to interaction with them. Authenticity and openness in dealing with his subordinates will help them satisfy their need to know where they stand, how they should relate to him, what kind of person he is, and how he intends to manage. Then they will get a true picture of him and how he operates without wasting time second-guessing and playing games with him. The fourth fact is that attitudes govern perceptions. A positive, supportive attitude is readily sensed by employees, who, even if they are school-dull, are generally life-bright. Finally, perceptions are really transactions between the people involved. As the leader must allow his people opportunities to interact with him, so he must also interact with them. In this way, both will make the getting-to-know-you process efficient and rapid.

How the Manager Sees His Lateral Relationships

One of the more popular misconceptions about leadership is that the manager works mainly as a thinker, planner, decision maker, and problem solver relating vertically to his subordinates and superiors. The fact is that in large organizations the typical manager is fortunate to spend as much as 30 percent of his time dealing with his employees directly. Much of his day is occupied with other departments that have a lateral or oblique effect on his ability to get his job done. To quote a mechanical superintendent in a huge newspaper, "Those damn people in sales and editorial wait till the last minute. Then, when the paper hits the street late, we catch hell from top management."

The modern manager realizes that he is but one element of a tightly knit system. For this reason, in Likert's terms, he serves as a linking pin between his department and other organizational units whose cooperation he needs. Personnel, industrial engineering, production, planning and control, inspection, quality control, and employee relations are just a few of the staff services that can make his job easy or a hell on earth. The major functional areas are also crucial. Sales, engineering, and accounting may be in a position to facilitate or hamper his operation. The work flow plays an important role: if he does not negotiate adroitly with those who supply him with work and those who receive it from him, then he will inevitably be plagued by bottlenecks and pileups.

It behooves the manager-leader, therefore, to adopt a panoramic rather than a tunnel-vision approach to his work and its relationship with other parts of the organization. In any system, one must be aware of the impact of his action on cognate and affected sections of the firm. Tunnel vision is bad enough, but perceiving other departments as adversaries is worse. Reducing interdepartmental jealousy, friction, and wrangling would almost surely improve many a company's profit and loss statement.

The Manager's Self-Concepts

Every manager sees himself in a unique way. So important is this self-concept to organizational success that Eugene E. Jennings says bluntly, "The executive's view of himself is his most crucial tool [in] developing and maintaining a productive and satisfying administrative career." [2] And in another context, he observes, "The self-image of the executive is his psychic center of gravity. . . . A career crisis is basically a crisis of the self." [3] The executive's self-concept is probably the most fragile element in his psychological makeup. When it is threatened ever so slightly, he will mobilize all his resources to defend it. Let it be assaulted and his career may suffer a partial or complete reverse.

By the *self* is meant one's sense of identity. It is concerned with such questions as these: Who am I? What do I stand for? What kind of human being am I? What do I feel I must become and do? How worthwhile am I as a human being? What do I think of myself as a unique person? How much do I respect myself? What are my values and convictions? The manager's self-concept has evolved throughout his life, beginning in his early childhood. It has been fashioned chiefly by his interaction with the key people in his life and by the evaluations that they have made of him. Successful and unsuccessful past experiences also play an important role. A record of failure produces a diminished self-concept and lessened self-esteem; inevitably, his level of aspiration and expectation must be lowered. A history of periodic success, on the other hand, stimulates him to lift his level of aspiration and expectation while at the same time engendering a more robust sense of adequacy and self-regard.

It is a mistake to speak of *the* self-concept, for it has many dimensions. One has a physical, intellectual, social, psychological, and ideal self, among others. Witness the variety of underlying self-images of the three men in the following descriptions.

Jones is assertive and self-assured. In a work situation, he assumes authority easily and directly. Although he does not tolerate fools with any degree of graciousness and at times is rather insistent, he is open to divergent points of view. Socially, he can hold his own, even if one would not call him adept. Intellectually, though not brilliant, he is sharp and catches on quickly. Ethically, he lives according to acceptable norms, if not by the golden rule. His relations with others are formal and cordially proper rather than friendly or intimate. He at times is not overly impressed by the talents of some of his superiors, but he rationalizes authority well. Though he tends to be more critical of his peers than is perhaps prudent, he gets along with them reasonably well. He is quite ambitious and has a carefully considered career plan that he is determined to carry out. Emotionally, he is devoid of any noticeable quirks that might hamper his efficiency. He seems rather well adjusted though hardly free-spirited and uninhibited.

Brown is outgoing and gregarious and makes a special effort to make people feel at ease. He seems not only to be liked by superiors, equals, and subordinates but to need to be well thought of by them. Bright beyond the average and extremely skilled socially, he invests his energy principally in considerateness and pleasantness. As a result, his managers find him most cooperative, and he is regarded by his people as "one of the very best bosses in the company." He avoids confrontations whenever possible; he is quick to accommodate himself to another's viewpoint; he can adjust to all kinds of personalities. Ethically, his behavior is beyond reproach. Emotionally, he is very well adjusted and free from eccentricities. He is, however, not very ambitious. He expects to make progress, but he is inclined to balance out organizational advance with a richly varied off-the-job life.

Smith has excelled since high school. Extremely bright, he is condescending to those who cannot hold to his intellectual pace. He is quite firm-minded and strong-willed; he has little taste for accommodating his views to those of others. His managerial and ethical convictions are so strong that his relations with others tend to be more than a little rigid, and he drives himself and his subordinates very hard. Insight into people and ability to relate to them easily are not his strongest assets. His excess of virtue at times prompts him to go it alone, although he is not a true loner. He is very ambitious but is most at ease when dealing with highly structured situations. Emotionally, he suffers from no disabling difficulties, but his inclination to see things as either black or white causes him to have more confrontations with his peers than need be. Most of his people respect him, but few like him or can get close to him. No blithe spirit, he, he keeps a tight control over his emotions and feelings, a habit that prompted one key subordinate to remark, "He's a logic machine but pretty decent if ever you get to know him."

The physical self-concept. In a culture that speaks of such things as body language and is sensitive to such nonessentials as the stereotyped height, weight, good looks, and energy of "the man of distinction," it would be surprising if the typical person were not responsive to himself as a physical being. Despite the fact that effective executives come in all sizes, shapes, and physical characteristics, he who is an approximation of the man of distinction starts with an initial advantage over his counterpart who is short, pudgy, and plain looking. As one manager said, "I've gone about as far as I can go. I'm too short. I look too Italian. I just don't fit their idea of what an executive should look like." A cruelly unfair assessment, and perhaps indeed the organization's attitude. On the other hand, it may reflect only the man's own appraisal of himself. Clearly, it is not the possession of certain physical traits that is important but how the possessor reacts to them. These self-reactions are crucial. The manager-leader who can come to grips with himself and say, "I am what I am—now, let's make the most of what I have," is in good shape. But his peer who pines after this or that attribute will waste much of his energy in psychic friction, which is never productive.

The intellectual self-concept. Brown is bright beyond the average, Smith is brilliant, and Jones is sharp. In a society in which knowledge indeed is becoming synonymous with power, it would be exceptional if each of these three managers did not react differently to their self-images as intellectual beings. One can be brilliant but humble, like Einstein, or very intelligent and somewhat arrogant, like Smith. Again, it is not the amount of intellectual acumen a person has but rather how he reacts to it and applies it. One can take intellectual gifts in stride and use them to plan, solve problems, and help others succeed; or he can utilize them to be patronizing and bitingly critical of his equals. Moreover, there is a difference between being bright as measured by academic work and intelligence tests and possessing a practical intelligence in dealing with life's problems and opportunities. There is a well-known lecturer on management, one of the most erudite authorities in the field, who will rarely translate what he has to say into terms that most executives can readily grasp. As a result, he splits his audiences in half. One group thinks that he is insightful and penetrating; the other is convinced that he is on cloud 9 and finds him incomprehensible.

The social self-concept. Man by nature is a social animal; the more he lives in himself, the less a man he becomes. Moreover, as Alexis de Tocqueville shrewdly observed more than a century ago, the American people are the most sociable on earth. Parents are often as concerned that their children be popular as that they be good. The valued skills are those of an interpersonal nature. In David Riesman's [4] terms, Brown is "other-directed" in the sense that he needs people and must be liked. He has a "radar" that tunes him in on how others feel about him. He is agreeable, conforming, and adaptable. Smith, however, is likely to be "inner-directed." Instead of a radar, he has a "gyroscope" that enables him to keep his balance without too much regard for what others think or feel. Jones really does not get involved with people to any noticeable degree. He can go through the expected paces but listens to his own drummer and has an eye on the reactions of others largely because he is intent on executing his career plan.

The psychological self-concept. Pierce the executive mask and penetrate beyond the manager's carefully cultivated facade, and as sure as fate, one will discover his self-image as a human being. It does little good to deal in such extremes as introversion and extroversion or dominance and submissiveness. It does even less good to launch into a litany of desirable or undesirable qualities, such as forcefulness, persistence, and resilience or overcontrol, tentativeness, and lack of confidence. What is important is that the manager-leader have some degree of insight into why he acts as he does, that he recognize his strengths and make the most of them while admitting his deficiencies and endeavoring to improve them. But what is essential is that the manager-leader avoid indulging in self-deceptions as much as is humanly possible. It is common knowledge that the majority of executives fail not because of a lack of technical or administrative finesse but because of personality and social defects. "To thine own self be true" is still a valid adage.

The ideal self-concept. Socrates once remarked that the unexamined life is not worth living. Every manager has some ideal conception of the kind of person he should become—a kind of "the me I must be." The moral Hun is unacceptable in modern business. But so too is the moralistic tyrant who seeks to compel himself and others to adhere to unrealistically high standards of ethics. Sooner or later, every executive must learn to live not only with himself but with his ideals and values. Neurotic guilt can be the result of frustrated attempts to live up to ethical standards imposed by a punitive superego that are not meant for this imperfect world with its fallible inhabitants.

Of all the self-concepts, this is by far the most important. When a person lives according to his convictions, he has an inner peace that is obtainable in no other way. When he disregards them so that a marked discrepancy habitually exists between what he should do and what he does, then he lives a hell on earth. For no accuser is more doggedly persistent than one's own conscience, no judgment more cruel than that passed on oneself by oneself. On the other hand, the manager is not expected to be either more or less perfect than any other human being. Suffice it to say that if he strives to abide by principles that are rational and ethical while seeking to improve the moral quality of his life as he does the technical aspects of his competence, then he has done all that can be expected of him. No one knows what his reward in the afterlife may be. But he will receive a reward of satisfaction and gratification in this life for which there is no lasting adequate substitute.

The Manager-Leader's Attitudes

An attitude is a readiness to feel about, act toward, or react to an idea, situation, or person or group in a favorable or unfavorable manner. It is a predisposition to think, feel, and behave in a given way. It is a mental set that conditions action. Unfortunately, very little has been written in business literature about the importance of attitudes, apart from endless attempts to measure them. What is known about attitudes and their influence?

1. They are learned and acquired, regardless of whether they are positive or negative in nature.
2. They are remarkably stable and very difficult to change.
3. They are often more or less impervious to rational evidence and valid information. In a conflict between data and logic on one hand and strong attitudes on the other, the attitudes will generally prevail.
4. They can vary greatly in intensity, and a person may have even contradictory attitudes in his makeup.
5. They are basic to all motivation and determine our perceptions.
6. They may be either logical (based on evidence and consistent with reality) or illogical (contrary to reality).
7. They are often adopted from key people or groups.
8. Inevitably, they consciously or unconsciously translate themselves into behavior.

Since attitudes, like emotions, make wonderful servants but dreadfully tyrannical masters, the manager-leader must be aware of his own, be they laudable or unworthy. If they are unworthy, then not only will they get him into hot water, but his shrewder subordinates will learn to play on them—and him—like a piano. If they are laudable, then inevitably they will be communicated to his people with beneficial results for both him and them. Apart from this, the leader must be sensitive to the attitudes that employees have toward the organization, him, and each other. No one carries a neon sign openly declaring his attitudes. The executive must be alert to the ways in which attitudes are displayed—through language and behavior. Once he is attuned to his own attitudes and those of his superiors, peers, and subordinates, he can use his common sense to formulate effective methods for coping with them. To ignore them is to cop out. Once one cops out, he can never learn to cope with reality.

organizational realities

The systematically arranged organization charts, the policy manuals, the position descriptions, the standard operating procedures, and the rules and regulations with which every company is equipped do not make up a true statement of corporate actualities. At best, they represent an idealization of the way things should get done as perceived from the eagle's viewpoint of top management. They spell out the channels and boundaries that the executive group hopes will facilitate the work flow while restricting those who would overstep the limits of their authority and responsibility. Unhappily, they almost never depict how things really operate in the zoo; they tell little of the ways in which people carry out the transactions that are necessary for achieving goals. This is so true that were one to draw up the most accurate organization chart possible, it is safe to say that, within three to six months, changes in the human system would have taken place which would render the chart less than a precise picture of the true state of affairs.

This is not to minimize the essential importance of such official documents. Without them, it would be impossible to build a desirable degree of rationality and coherence into the firm's activities. But once the incumbents in a series of positions begin to act, react, and interact, things never take place as envisioned by the upper echelons. The boxes of the typical chart are logical, meaningful, and orderly. Unfortunately, most of the action tends to take place in the white spaces *between* the boxes. The manager-leader soon finds that he must contend with a system that is not provided for in the dicta of the executive peacock alley. He must wrestle with a pattern of roles that can be only partly defined authoritatively. He must learn how to cope with many systems. If he does not succeed in this task, not only will his competence be ineffectual but his tenure in office may well be short.

The Authority System

Corporations, as Harold Leavitt has pointed out, consist of pyramids and people. The pyramids take care of the distribution of necessary authority and accountability throughout the company. The people are those who both exercise and are affected by this distribution. As a results-oriented entity, every company requires integration of inputs that have a thrust in the direction of planned goal attainment. Anything as essential for survival and growth can scarcely be left to the mutual benevolence of corporate citizens. Whether the advocates of permissiveness like it or not, no society can long endure without authority. As Thomas Aquinas averred, even in a society of saints in heaven, there will be a need for order, and order stems primarily from authority.

Authority, in its simplest definition, is a right to obligate subordinates to carry out assigned tasks, execute legitimate directives, and generally perform as required in justice. No organization has lasted without acting upon the need to assign the few the right to determine objectives, make crucial decisions, define relevant behavior, and reward and punish according to the demands of those who have been entrusted with the welfare of that organization. When President Harry Truman said, "The buck stops here," he was referring not merely to ultimate accountability but also to ultimate authority.

Three points are worth making with regard to authority. It should never be absolute; it should always be relative in the sense that no manager should have more than he needs to carry out his duties. If he has more, then someone else perforce possesses less than he needs, since the amount of authority in any company is limited. Second, the authority appertains not to the person who occupies a given position for a time but rather to the office itself. When a few South American students threw rocks at President Nixon, the affront was not so much to Nixon as to the presidency. Third, authority is legitimate when it conforms to the norms of society, particularly the criterion of justice, and to the corresponding rights of those who must defer to it. Otherwise, it degenerates into tyranny at worst and mere coercive power at best.

Authority has no meaning unless it is answered with obedience. Barnard once claimed that the question of whether or not an order had authority resided not with the person issuing the order but rather with those to whom it was addressed. This, of course, is sheer nonsense. A person may have a perfect *right* to issue an order without having either the *means* of compelling obedience or the *influence* with subordinates to lead them to accept and abide by it. To get things accomplished with and through others, however, does entail a willingness on their part, at least in a democracy, to obey just and rational commands. In this sense, Bertrand de Juvenel was correct when he maintained that "authority ends where voluntary assent ends." The crux of the matter for the manager-leader is that his mere right to exact obedience on the part of his people does not guarantee him the means for insuring compliance with his demands. As Douglas McGregor once remarked, the consent of the governed is more than a pious phrase. Therefore, the executive would be prudent to appreciate the fact that subordinates tend to establish their own zones of acceptance—areas in which they are open to and accept authority. But they also establish zones of resistance—areas in which they resist or rebel against authority. Knowing just where one ends and the other begins takes a fair bit of insight. There is an old saying that at times the best way to save face is to shut the lower half of it. The manager-leader who gives an order that he knows will not be obeyed is a fool.

The Manager-Leader's Attitudes Toward Authority

An adage in all religious, business, and military organizations has it that he who cannot learn to follow must never be given leadership. In fact, one observation of the experienced regarding a few of the more activist young would-be leaders is that they have an ambition to be alpha fish when they have not yet learned to work within the school; no wonder their solution to all ills is destruction of the system. One learns to lead by following, by mastering the art of being sensitive to the cues sent forth by the group. Accordingly, before the manager-leader begins to exercise authority over others, he must give some thought to his reactions to the authority exercised on him by his superiors. Jennings, on the basis of rich and varied experience in counseling seasoned executives, maintains that the authority-centered crisis is one of the three major crises that trip up a manager.[1]

Mark Whiting, vice-president of marketing, had trouble with authority figures throughout his career. Since he felt inadequate and insecure, he compensated by being cocky and aggressive. With superiors, he learned to mask his inclination to lash back by cultivating a deferential attitude. As he grew more successful in his work, he developed an inflated concept of himself. When the president reprimanded him for the selection of an incompetent subordinate, "Whiting nullified all of the accomplishments that he had so carefully achieved for his career's success. He mobilized his forces to prove that he was a bigger, better man than the president." To the surprise of no one, the president put him down effectively.

Albert, an executive vice-president, overidentified with authority figures, had a naive trust in them, modeled himself after them, and committed himself to their service. He had never really defied authority, or stood up to it when reasons were available, and could not do so even if he were prodded. "He had no clear concept of his own identity and had no emotional reservations about his superiors. The president took an extended trip to Africa, and Albert was placed in charge. Three months later, he was known as 'table-it Albert.' He could not make a difficult decision."

Arthur became a member of the executive group at the age of 40 but was passed over as the successor to the president. He was incapable of handling authority figures when they acted negatively toward him. His path to success lay in his becoming a master of strategies for attaining organizational goals. But he kept authority figures at a distance emotionally and was cautious not to grow too intimate with them. As a result, they felt that he could not be completely trusted. When he was passed over, his covert hostile feelings became overt, to his regret. "Arthur's case illustrates a common executive difficulty—how to develop and maintain positive but moderately reserved attachments to authority figures."

There are at least three attitude patterns toward authority that are calculated to get the manager-leader in warm water with his superiors. The first is a dependence that exceeds the bounds of moderation. Obviously, every subordinate is by definition dependent to some extent on the favor of his superiors. But when it reaches the point where the manager becomes passive, ultra-conforming, and devoid of assertiveness, then he is reduced to a mere No. 2 man who will be treated as a messenger. At the opposite extreme is the person who so prizes what he calls independence that he forgets he lives in an interdependent society. His chip-on-the-shoulder attitude bruises sensibilities unnecessarily. What superior has either the time or the energy to wrestle with a porcupine five days a week? Worst of all, possibly, is the man who swings from dependence to hostility because his attitude toward authority is ambivalent. Deference and opposition succeed each other cyclically, to the confusion and annoyance of all concerned.

The research is positive in indicating that the effective manager-leader accepts authority as a necessary fact of organizational life, even when he finds it nettlesome. He justifies it well. He expects it to be used fairly by his superiors. He expects in turn to utilize it fairly and impersonally with his people. One suspects that both those who overemphasize the need for authority and those who are unduly concerned for human relations suffer from variations of the same basic problem. The former may be hiding their insecurity behind the mask of authority. The latter may be expressing negative attitudes toward it as well as inability to cope with it under the guise of preoccupation with their fellow man and his fate. Be this as it may, if the manager-leader does not come to grips frankly with his own emotional reactions to authority, he will find it difficult to employ it prudently and productively.

Organizational authority is distributed. Organizational power is grasped. It is natural for any human being or group to endeavor to enlarge his or its spectrum of power; it is human to maximize one's power at the expense of weaker elements in the firm. Since the authority system and the power system are likely to rest in different hands, it behooves the executive to gain as much information as possible about the focuses of power.

Power is naught but the ability to impose one's will on others whether or not they like it, resist it, or what have you. It is the capability of making the flow of events go in the direction that the power wielder wishes. It connotes the number of options from which he can choose without bothering to give anyone else so much as a by-your-leave. It is related to the number of constraints on free action that are absent. Unlike authority, which is merely a right, power is always more or less productive of results. Like authority, however, it is always limited. Generally, power assumes one of two forms: power *over* or power *to act*. Power over, as Herbert Goldhammer and Edward Shils have pointed out, may be exercised by coercion or manipulation through orders and directives. It may also take the form of seduction or threats. At times, a union can attain its objectives merely by threatening to strike; a key person may rearrange a situation to his liking by threatening to join a competitor. When the shareholders sued Henry Ford because he gave them what they felt to be an unjust return on their investment, he changed their minds by threatening to organize a new company. It is common knowledge that huge users of the products of packaging firms keep their suppliers "honest" by threatening obliquely to manufacture their own containers.

Types of Power

Among the more significant forms of power in any large organization, according to John French and Bertram Raven,[2] are the following.

Position power. Position power is Fiedler's concept of the power that is vested in a given position, regardless of who its incumbent is. Some positions have much power, others relatively little.

Reward-punishment power. Some managers still have incredible faith in the perennial carrot-and-stick approach. While no one would deny the need for coercive power and the ability to distribute organizational goodies, the manager would be wise to bear in mind the following facts of corporate life: (1) Such rewards are in very short supply in the average firm. (2) Punishment may get only short-term results and alienate those punished. (3) The manager is not the only distributor of rewards or punishments; at times, a person would much prefer to be punished by management but rewarded by his peer group than to have it the other way around. (4) The dichotomous reward-punishment approach, especially when the reward takes the form of money, ignores all the intervening ways of obtaining desired behavior from employees. (5) This is how one trains a dog, not develops a human being.

Expert power. Drucker rightly claims that we are entering an era in which the knowledge worker will have a great deal of clout in organizations. More and more, the key question is not who has the relevant authority but rather who has the needed expertise. The corporate citizens who possess essential knowledge or know-how are at times in a position to carry great weight with their superiors, regardless of differences in compensation or authority that may exist. Many a manager finds himself, to his discomfiture, supervising some key subordinates who are better educated than he, who have an expertise that he can never hope to possess. Within the limits of their competence, they may exert considerable power.

Referent power. Referent power, as Etzioni has stated, connotes power *with* rather than *over*. It is personal rather than position power. It involves emotional identification and affiliation with the manager. The man who is liked by his people has much of it; the mere figurehead or boss has little.

Social power. As a social animal, every person is sensitive to the approbation of the reference groups with which he identifies. Only the extremely inner-directed person, the zealot, the isolate, or the radically deviant man acts as though he cared not a farthing for the opinions his peers have of him. The pressures that a desired group can bring to bear on the thinking, attitudes, and behavior of a manager are enormous.

Handling the Authority and Power Systems

What can the manager-leader do to keep his balance in the authority and power systems in the real order?

1. He can begin by taking his objectives and actions seriously, not his authority or himself. His task, akin to that of the conductor of a symphony orchestra, is twofold: to educe from each prima-donna instrumentalist the very best that he can offer, and to blend the individual contributions into a unified impact so as to attain with excellence the results he seeks.

2. Since neither the bull of the woods nor the Milquetoast evolves by happenstance, the executive can candidly confront his attitudes toward authority. This applies with equal strength to his relations with superiors and his exercise of authority with subordinates. Authority and power are pretty strong medicines. They should be used only when needed. No physician prescribes penicillin to cure a scratch. Yet when they are requisite for the attainment of goals, they should be employed without hesitation or reluctance.

3. No leader can be expert in all areas. Hence, in this regard, the manager again has a twofold task: to be open and available to the inputs of his subordinates who may be more knowledgeable than he in this or that field (far too many managers act as though they were jealous of the expertise of their key people), and to learn the art of asking the right questions of the right people at the right times so as to secure straight answers rather than a snow job.

4. It would be ideal if the leader possessed position, reward-punishment, expert, referent, and social power. In this less than best of all worlds, however, his resources in these sectors are likely to be uneven. He will be tempted to regress to the familiar and resort to a stereotyped approach to his people. He has the developmental task rather to program himself to capitalize as fully as possible on what he has going for him while planning to actualize his potential more largely in areas where he is anemic.

5. The manager-leader must be very cautious with respect to the behavior that he rewards and punishes. After all, one learns less what he is told, taught, or shown than what he is rewarded for. It is not the discipline or the reward that is important. What are significant are the learning results secured by their application.

6. The manager who would lead rather than drive his employees might be more sensitive to his personal than his position power. Too much reliance on the latter inclines one toward the use of coercion. On the contrary, the greater the executive's personal power, the less need he has to resort to force to get things done.

The Group System

Every mature manager appreciates the fact that the unit at work is not the individual but the group; the relationship is akin to that between a sentence and a paragraph in writing. Fiedler speaks of interacting, coacting, and counteracting groups. The designation depends on whether the members have a face-to-face relationship, work relatively independently of each other, or are opposed and yet must reconcile conflicting viewpoints, as happens in labor-management relations. On the basis of his studies, Leonard Sayles discusses apathetic, erratic, strategic, and conservative groups. Any manager could easily add to this nomenclature from his own experience. He is familiar with the hypersensitive group jealous of its rights and prerogatives; the arrogant group, which demands that every other bow down before it; and the conflict-ridden group that is torn apart with its own inner dissensions.

The Impact of the Work Group on Its Members

Justice Oliver Wendell Holmes once remarked that when the meaning of the facts was understood, the facts themselves might safely be forgotten. Much the same sort of thing applies to the manager-leader and his dealings with groups. Itemizing every possible kind of group is an exercise in frustration. What is required is that the manager gain some insight into the dynamics of his work unit and that he realize the impact it can have on its members.

> *Watts after some weeks desiring to have me in the composing room, I left the pressmen. A new sum for drink, five shillings, was demanded of me by the compositors. I thought it an imposition, as I had paid below. The master thought so too, and forbade my paying it. I stood out for two or three weeks, and had so many little pieces of private mischief done me, by mixing my sorts [letters in a font of type], transposing my pages, breaking my matter, if I were ever so little out of the room, and all being ascribed to the chapel [printing house] ghost, which they said ever haunted those not regularly admitted, that I found myself obliged to pay the money; convinced of the folly of being on ill terms with those one lives with.*[3]

The charm of this delightful anecdote from Benjamin Franklin's early work history derives from the amusing way it illustrates the powerful pressures that a work group can exert on employees. Long before Kurt Lewin and other researchers showed that the group was a forceful influence for good or ill, Franklin had learned this lesson the hard way.

As often as not, it is not management but the work group that determines what constitutes a fair day's work. Violations of this norm by so-called rate busters is met by punitive measures ranging from needling to outright ostracism or even physical violence. It is noteworthy that, even with the support of his superior, who forbade him to pay the drink assessment, Franklin was ultimately forced to conform to the established practice. Nothing has changed since his day. The executive should not be surprised if the employee, given the alternative of rewards from management or those the work group can provide, often prefers those proffered by his peers. Additionally, it is a common observation that subordinates are at times not at all reluctant to evade or break rules established by the higher echelons; they rarely, unless they are loners or isolates, act contrary to those ordained by the work force. The authority of the manager may be rather anemic when compared with the power exercised by desired reference groups.

Whence comes the power of the work group? The group provides a sense of identity and unity for its members. It gives them what the Communist Party always promises and never delivers—a sense of solidarity and some protection from the impositions and incursions of management, since no manager wishes to alienate the only people he has to get the work done. He may trifle with this or that individual, but he will think twice before stepping on the toes of the group as a whole. The group can not only defend its members but also cover up for them and offer assistance in coping with management's requirements. And, as has been stated, it has its own reward-punishment system, its own power system, its own pecking order, and the means of enforcing its will.

The Effect on Productivity of the Work Group

Likert and others have shown that cohesive groups with high peer loyalty show less variation in productivity than do those with less cohesion. If their goals are in line with management's, then production will be superior; if not, then it will tend to be below standard. Such groups also have more favorable attitudes toward the high-producing individual. Additionally, a cohesive work group, when properly motivated, is likely to produce well in the absence of the manager or supervisor, and its problem solving and decision making are often superior to the average individual's. As a corollary, it will often set higher targets than the manager or the average member and, perhaps more importantly, will work more perseveringly, harder, and with less strain to attain them. When people belong to work units with which they identify, there are fewer unexcused absences. Assuming some congruence between the members' common aims and the organization's, the employees will have better attitudes toward their jobs and the enterprise. Finally, to belabor the obvious, any work group helps the employee satisfy his social needs, as management never can, by offering him opportunities to feel accepted, to belong, to communicate, to interact with his peers in a rewarding way.[4]

The Implications of Group Influences for the Manager

How can the manager-leader capitalize on the potential for good that is inherent in any group of subordinates while counteracting its potential for less than desirable productivity? Although no list of do's and don'ts can be offered, the following suggestions may prevent him from making his own task more onerous than it need be.

1. Whenever possible, the leader can try to involve his people in problem solving and decision making when they are competent to make meaningful contributions. Yet he must bear in mind that group decisions are never better than those the *most gifted* member can come up with. Groups by definition tend toward mediocrity in seeking a decision that everyone can live with; this, of course, is the curse of committee decision making. Accordingly, the manager must determine to just what extent he intends to rely on group resources. At times, he will do far better to accept a decision that is only 50 percent perfect but that the group will push through with 90 percent of its enthusiasm than one that is 90 percent technically effective but that the group will embrace with only 50 percent of its enthusiasm. At other times, he will do well to rely on his own expertise or his own coupled with that of a handful of very competent subordinates. There are few things so sad as to see a manager trying to utilize a so-called democratic process when the group members lack the necessary skills to grapple with the problem effectively. It may give employees good feelings of being involved, but it also foredooms any decision or solution to the ordinary. Deciding when the group may be in on the act, when a few key subordinates will participate, and when he should go it alone is one of the most taxing tasks of any executive.

2. The manager needs to be mindful that his primary job is not motivating individuals but building cohesive work teams that are committed to the attainment of objectives. He must be aware of the need for group rewards in addition to his recognition of the accomplishments of stellar performers, who often stand out at the expense of the group's productivity. Many managers are convinced of the merits of forcing subordinates to compete with each other. Except in extraordinary conditions,

this is probably the worst form of competition since it usually works to the detriment of group morale and cohesion. A man should measure himself against his past performance and record; here he has the optimum chance to succeed and raise his level of aspiration. Group competition, especially between geographically separate units in the same line of work, may also be beneficial at times. But intramural competition introduces a him-or-me climate that is destructive of *esprit de corps*. It is simple justice to reward individuals who excel. It is the better part of diplomacy to also reward those who help others perform, who facilitate the work of the group, and who build cooperation and team effort.

3. The leader must be wary of becoming jealous of the group's power over its members. Except when basic principles are at issue, he must avoid head-on confrontations. A painful illustration of the difficulties involved in such power matches is given by the experience of Frederick W. Taylor, of all people, the father of scientific management.

Before becoming a foreman, Taylor had been an excellent machinist and was well liked by the men. But he also knew that production was only about one-third of what it could be because the men were deliberately restricting their efforts. First, he asked the men to step it up—no results. Then he operated a lathe himself to show that increased production was possible without undue stress—no results. Deciding to fight fire with fire, he brought in some of the more intelligent workers, taught them how to operate the equipment, and got a promise from them to do a fair day's work. Under group pressure, they soon cut production to an acceptable group level. Taylor then cut their pay rates. The men complained to management, to no avail. They started to produce at a fair day's rate, but at the same time resorted to a new stratagem to do Taylor in. To prove that he was driving them too hard, some of the machinists deliberately broke their machines. But Taylor had been shrewd enough to forewarn management that this might happen and had its full support. He responded to this tactic by letting the men know that anyone whose machine broke down would be disciplined. *It was only after three years of struggling that Taylor, who liked the men and had been liked by them, prevailed!* [5]

There are obviously times when the manager can hardly afford to bow to the pressures of the work group. But this three-year battle shows that confrontations should be resorted to only when all other means have failed.

4. The manager should avoid embracing a human relations approach as though it were a universal solvent. There is much more to management and productivity then merely motivating, developing, and communicating with subordinates. On the other hand, the importance of these activities must not be underrated. Surely one root of Taylor's confrontation was a break in communications: what appeared to be logical and reasonable from his standpoint may very well have been perceived as whimsical or imperious by the workforce. A group tends to have a logic of its own and is not likely to be persuaded by any other.

5. The leader should therefore be attuned to what the work group is trying to tell him by its behavior and its reactions to his managerial activities. The vigorous and committed group is no more an accident of fate than the apathetic, conflicted, arrogant, or hostile one. In either case, treating symptoms will do little good. What is necessary is a diagnosis of why the group's attitude has come into being.

6. The executive should be alert to the dangers of developing team spirit among his own people in ways that alienate other departments or sections. While such tactics undoubtedly make the work of the manager easier, they do so at the expense of the total productive system. Instead of concentrating single-mindedly on organizational losses that can readily be counted, top management might well give serious thought to the less definable costs of lack of loyalty, failure to cooperate, jealousy, friction, and empire building.

The Role System

Shakespeare once observed that in his lifetime a man plays many parts. For the sociologist, these parts are roles. A role defines the functions and activities to be performed and the behavior that is considered appropriate in a given position.

The manager's *organizational role* spells out the firm's perceptions and expectations of the incumbent in a given job. For better or worse, however, every person brings his own expectations to the job. These constitute his *perceived role*. They comprise at least such fundamentals as the autonomy he wants to have, the prerogatives he will enjoy, the way he will operate, and the status he will be entitled to. The leader's subordinates also get into the act. They have their own views of how he should act and how they will relate to him. This *nonformal role* and his ability to fulfill it successfully may well have much to do with his ultimate success or failure.

As the executive interacts with superiors and peers, he soon discovers that they perceive him in ways that may bear little resemblance to his official position, as we saw. They put pressures on him; they look for certain reactions from him; they have their own ideas about just how he is to fit into the overall cooperating and coordinating pattern. The leader must contend not only with these *imposed roles* but also with the needs of his wife and children. At times, society itself has its own concept of how the executive should behave. These *extraorganizational roles* are becoming more and more significant as the social responsibility of the corporation becomes a more sensitive and nettlesome area.

It would be a miracle if the manager-leader were able to balance out these diverse demands with aplomb. In fact, he may spend many a sleepless night trying to adjust to these role expectations, which are so frequently conflicting. Certainly, among the more painful dilemmas with which the executive must come to grips are the following.[6]

Role ambiguity. When higher management has failed to spell out specifically the authority, accountability, priorities, objectives, and autonomy of the manager, his role is ambiguous. Not too surprisingly, in such a situation he tends to become frustrated, tense, uncertain, and lacking in confidence.

Role overload. A consultant once walked into a large plant and asked one of the foremen, "Who is your boss?" Sighing, the man replied, "Anyone you can see wearing a coat is *my* boss and gives me orders." When the leader is faced with conditions in which he must but cannot satisfy the expectations of diverse people or groups that are important to him, he is in a quandary. He would like to please everyone but cannot. He is damned if he does and damned if he doesn't.

Role conflict. As the name implies, role conflict occurs when the leader must simultaneously fulfill two incompatible roles. The role overload of the foreman just described resulted from a not uncommon type of *intersender conflict.* Another classic illustration is the executive who must devote so much time and energy to satisfying organizational needs that he feels guilty about neglecting his wife and family. *Intrasender conflict* arises when the manager must deal with divergent expectations that come from the same source. The testimony of some of the defendants during the infamous electric company trials was based on this very conflict. In their view, at least, higher management insisted on robust profits produced in ethically acceptable ways, while at the same time it was common knowledge that big-profit contracts were obtained in a way that smelled of collusion and had been so obtained for years. Interestingly, even upper management did not avoid this dilemma. General Electric, which had a written policy covering such an eventuality, legalistically demoted or fired those caught in the act, although some critics contended that it was in its own way as guilty as the defendants. Westinghouse, on the other hand, took no such extreme punitive action since it felt that some of the blame stemmed from its failure to press hard and consistently for ethical behavior. *Person-role conflict* is generated when organizational demands are at variance with the convictions of the executive. This phenomenon was also encountered in the electric company case. One of the men involved refused to go along with the allocation system because it compromised his values and beliefs.

Handling Role Pressures

As McGregor pointed out long ago and as every executive has learned from his own experience, the leader is not a passive victim of the forces that press down on him. He does his utmost to define his own role. He accommodates himself to important demands and pressures while ignoring others. He adjusts to significant requirements, but he also endeavors to bring them in line with his own perceptions. He works to set his own order of priorities. In sum, he negotiates with his environment to get the best deal possible for himself so that he can perform most effectively. This granted, he takes to heart two facts: (1) as but one element in a field of forces that is ever in a state of change, he will have to define and redefine his role as these forces rearrange themselves; (2) his role is determined not by abstractions such as position descriptions, organization charts, or policy manuals but rather by insight into and interaction with corporate realities. Any executive of a smaller firm that has been merged with a larger company understands these facts in a way that no M.B.A. possibly can.

The manager can often deal with *role ambiguity* by carefully blueprinting achievement targets, accountabilities, and autonomy limits in conjunction with his superior. As suggested in Chapter 5, he might write up his job as he perceives it, asking the boss to review and amend it as necessary. On occasion, he may have to carve out his own mission, a perfectly legitimate procedure when the job is new or lacking in precedent. At the very minimum, he can sift the bits and pieces of his day-to-day work with the intention of concentrating on activities that are relevant to his responsibilities and will enable him to achieve satisfactorily while minimizing the amount of time and energy squandered on mere administrivia.

Role overload is inevitable in any organization for the simple reason that everyone would rather have someone else do his work than attend to it personally. It is a good management principle that a person *report* to one superior as a matter of course. Unhappily, he must generally *respond* to many people in authority or key positions.

Intersender conflict can best be handled by a prudent process of accommodation and negotiation. Explaining *why* one cannot satisfy the demands of different people who make divergent requests can at times jolt the opposite party out of his parochial insistence on getting what he wants yesterday. It may on occasion be necessary for the manager to stand up to unreasonable requirements tactfully; if he does not, he may end up as the organizational doormat. A third strategy is to express unemotionally one's willingness to conform with the demands made by various parties while explaining the impossibility of so doing.

This throws the problem into the laps of those creating it for them to resolve. When all else fails, the manager may be forced to satisfy the expectations of the individual or group that has the greatest power to enhance his effectiveness; survival, after all, is the basic principle of organizational as well as organic life.

Two additional observations are in order. More often than not, the executive suffers from role overload because he has not multiplied himself and his efficiency through delegation and participative management. A lack of trust in the abilities of his people, a failure to develop them, or a habit of clinging to what he likes to do rather than what he should be doing creates many needless problems. Second, although it is essential that the leader *react* intelligently to the pressures of others, his main task is to *act*. If he spends excessive time reacting, he will find that other people in the organization will keep him very busy indeed; in fact, he may never get around to his true job.

Intrasender conflict can be difficult to cope with. The superior is subject to his own field of changing forces. He, too, must react to the pressures imposed on him. It would be nice if he were perfectly consistent and predictable, but this is not typical of most humans. The first step for the manager-leader, therefore, is to try to understand the position of his boss. Some seemingly inconsistent or contradictory demands are practical reactions to altered conditions; the American presence in Vietnam was at one time widely approved of, only later to become just as widely disapproved of. Whatever the reason for the conflict, the task of a subordinate manager is to shore up his superior's weaknesses with his strengths, to work with him so as to help him perform optimally; the manager has not been given the privilege of criticizing or denigrating his superior. With this attitude established, the manager can simply ask the higher authority to clarify the relationship. Intrasender conflict can be avoided only if both parties keep attuned to each other's expectations. The superior-subordinate relationship remains constant, but both people change—slightly or markedly—throughout their association. Unless it is periodically reconsidered and redefined, trouble is predictable; this is as true of corporate as of married life.

Person-role conflicts must be handled on the basis of conscience. When the expectations of others violate the executive's moral convictions, he has several courses of action open to him. (1) He can seek to persuade his superiors to change their demands; securing a call girl for a buyer has never been written into anyone's position description. (2) He can make his objections known and request that someone else who is not so affected be given the chore to perform. (3) He can simply refuse to do what he finds unacceptable, explaining his reasons for taking such a stand. In the final analysis, the manager who is not his own man soon becomes the servile pawn of another man, especially when convictions are involved.

The Status System

Although novelists and sociologists poke fun at status and the symbols thereof, the fact is that managers work very hard to attain a higher perch on the totem pole. Objectively, status is a necessity in every organization. It goes along with titles, ranks, privileges, prerogatives, freedoms, and authority. To its seeker, status denotes the way he expects to be treated, the badges of office to which he is entitled, the behavior he feels he should adopt, the behavior that will either please or affront him. Thus, from the firm's viewpoint, status represents both an incentive and a form of earned recognition. From the individual's perspective, it is a goal and an achievement.

Anything so personal and psychological in nature as status is bound to create problems in any organization; even Jesus' disciples argued about who would be first when the Kingdom came, despite his continued reminders that the first would be last. Jealousy of status has probably hurt more companies than lack of technical competence. Efforts to increase one's status at the expense of others can easily do more harm than a competing firm. Status anxiety, status fluctuations, and status loss can cause any manager-leader a great deal of emotional damage.

Accordingly, the executive should take his job seriously, not his status. If he is overly concerned about his status, this will guarantee friction among his people as they, too, struggle to increase their status at the expense of their fellows. Having given an example by taking his status in stride, the leader can then press subordinates to produce, not merely strive to increase their personal positions by maneuvering. More importantly, he can use status as a powerful incentive to stimulate employees to perform *if* he treats it as a form of earned praise and recognition. Finally, the manager can learn to share status with his people. Delegating, inviting consultative management, giving special assignments, allowing the subordinate to do his job as he sees fit as long as it meets organizational requirements, and asking for advice and suggestions are all ways of increasing both the organizational and the subjective status of a subordinate. One manager rotated the chairmanship of his weekly meetings among his key people. Another used a "planning and review committee" composed of selected subordinates to help him plot out the next month's work and then to appraise the results attained. Still another had an "advisory board," this, too, composed of his more experienced people, to whom he submitted new ideas for their consideration and from whom he accepted suggestions and recommendations. A knowledgeable manager can find a multitude of ways to use status as an incentive.

The Map versus the Reality

Organizational documents are the embodiment of blueprint-like precision, orderliness, coherence, and rationality. As such, they can readily lull the manager-leader into assuming that the map is the reality. Once on the job, he finds that he is caught in a tangle of authority, power, group, role, and status systems—none of which ever appears as such in any official pronouncement. He finds that he is enmeshed in a web of relationships spun from cooperation, jealousy, friction, coordination, and competition that he must learn to cope with adroitly. Failure to gain understanding of and insight into these organizational givens may mean that he will be shot down before he ever tries to get his activities off the launching pad. This Khrushchev, as we saw in Chapter 1, discovered to his chagrin.

selecting a managerial leadership pattern

It is imperative that the concepts of management and leadership be kept distinct; they are discrete, though related, ideas. As David Ewing has succinctly said, "Great leaders do not always leave strong organizations. Great managers do." [1] A man may be an outstanding leader, especially if he has charisma, and mismanage his workforce into disaster. On the other hand, an executive may be a sophisticated manager and yet not be regarded as a striking leader by his subordinates.

Manager First—Leader Second

In the ideal world of theory, the skills of management are combined with the talents of leadership. In the world of the practical, as pointed out several times, the executive is judged primarily on his success in satisfying organizational requirements, among which the present and future economic goals of the firm are uppermost. To attain these goals, leadership ability is important, but management finesse is essential.

Chapter 1 and other sections touch on some of the common elements of the manager's job and the crucial roles he must play. Aggregating and expanding them here will display the foundation for selecting a congruent managerial leadership pattern.

The manager adds value to the resources of the company. It takes no managerial skill at all to get ordinary work from ordinary people. Machines will run whether the manager is present or not. The challenge of professional management is to administer the animate and inanimate organizational resources so as to secure the greatest possible return on the firm's investment in them over the long run. Estimates of the index of efficiency at which people work in industry range from 10 to perhaps 25 percent. Whatever the index may be, the manager's job is to raise it. This he does by expertly planning, organizing, directing, and controlling activities aimed at achieving objectives with maximum efficiency and a minimum waste of talent, time, money, and effort.

The manager is a prime mover. The term *prime mover* far more accurately describes what the executive is supposed to be than does the pallid word *manager.* Saint Paul once asked, if the trumpet sounds an uncertain note, who will rise up to battle? The executive asks himself the same question periodically. The prime mover determines just where he is to go, and he must be vigorous in getting there. He pursues the ends for which he strives with single-minded intensity, whether he receives them from his superiors, arrives at them in conjunction with his key people, or evolves them himself. The means he uses must be flexible; strategies and tactics must accommodate situational realities. The prime mover may resort to authority or participation, encouragement or command, forcefulness or persuasion, depending on which approach is most likely to get him where he wants to go.

The manager energizes his people. To say that the manager must know what makes his people tick and what ticks them off is a bit too slick to be of much practical use. But it is a fact, and one he must accept at gut level, that his day-to-day behavior motivates or demotivates subordinates. In this regard, the title of Saul Gellerman's fine book *Management by Motivation* is a misnomer. A more accurate title might be *Motivation by Effective Management.* If the executive manages adroitly, the benefits of motivation follow naturally. Attempts to energize subordinates in the absence of good management will do more harm than good.

The manager builds a committed and cohesive work group. The executive inherits some subordinates, has others thrust upon him, and hires still others. His major duty is to build a cohesive and committed team from the sometimes ill-fitting parts that his people represent. Historically, there has been far too much talk about dealing with individuals, but relatively little stress has been given the importance of team building. One can rather readily manage people so that the work progresses in a coordinated way, as, for example, in a concentration camp. It is a far cry from this to managing them so that they are stimulated to cooperate willingly with each other, to offer mutual help spontaneously when needed, and to have pride in their workforce—to think of themselves as damned good.

The manager promotes need satisfaction. Astonishingly, many executives seem able to live with a contradiction between their view of their own reasons for working and their perceptions of others' reasons. On the one hand, a manager will frankly admit that he has joined a firm because it will serve as a suitable vehicle for implementing his personal career plan. Further, he intends to remain with the firm only as long as he receives a reasonable degree of satisfaction of his needs and aspirations; given a better opportunity both to carry out his intentions and to enhance his need satisfaction, he will feel no pangs of guilt in pursuing it. Yet, on the other hand, he may act as though his subordinates were born to live and work first and foremost for the honor and glory of the company. Such a naive double standard is not meant for this world.

Realistic managers assume that any person takes a job for about as self-centered reasons as the organization hires him. Each perceives the other as a means of meeting his or its needs and requirements. Every employee will therefore be more concerned with getting as much need satisfaction as he can from the work situation than with meeting organizational demands. Since the employer acts on the same premises, the executive has the responsibility of trying to change these self-centered stances to attitudes of mutual interest. In fact, if the firm is unwilling to make the first gesture toward building common cause between itself and the employee, it is ingenuous to expect the employee to take the initiative. If the executive fails to realize that some integration of interests and need satisfactions is essential, he will waste much of his energy wrestling with cross purposes and conflicts of aspirations. Adam Smith pointed this out in 1776.

The manager is a model. Executives often do not appreciate how much subordinate managers look to them for examples of appropriate behavior. Identification, to use a technical term from psychology, is an almost universal phenomenon. Unhappily, as Harry Levinson has pointed out in *The Exceptional Executive,*[2] identification may take a destructive form. The middle manager who works for a fear-producing, threatening boss may identify with him and imitate his behavior, and thus in turn will tend to frighten his people; he has "identified with the aggressor" and passes fear-producing stimuli down the line. "Identification by consent," on the other hand, is the reaction of subordinate managers who admire their superior and selectively assimilate certain aspects of his management behavior and his values because they are convinced that they are effective.

Every executive is giving examples—whether good or bad—of management in action. This is the fundamental justification for consultative management, delegation, coaching, counseling, and other recommended forms of functional sharing. The subordinate manager who has been the beneficiary of these activities is likely to follow the model that has been set for him. The manager who has been allowed to sink or swim on his own will most likely behave similarly toward his own key people.

The manager is a resource expert. There are three kinds of executives: locked-door, swinging-door, and open-door. The first maximizes the distance between himself and his subordinates. He is physically and emotionally unapproachable. He defends his remoteness on the specious ground that it separates the men from the boys. The second, usually a mindless practitioner of phony cordiality, boasts that anyone can come to him anytime with any kind of problem. Instead of acting like a manager, he serves as a convenient crutch for lower-level employees who enjoy circumventing their immediate superiors to spend a few minutes in the throne room.

The manager with an open-door policy avoids the extremes of excessive availability and impersonal aloofness. He makes it clear that he is more than willing to help, but only after his people have exhausted their own resources for coping with their problems. Although his attitude is supportive, he realizes that the muscle of competence, like any other muscle, is best developed through use. He is aware that if mothers always carried their young around in their arms, the children would never learn to walk; even birds nudge the fledgling out of the nest, for there is no other way for it to learn to fly. As a resource expert, the executive serves as a problem-solving catalyst, helping subordinates to fly on their own, encouraging them to work their way through their own difficulties, and offering his greater experience only after they have done their homework.

The manager is a tension inducer. One of the most widespread misinterpretations of psychological theory is the nonsense that the absence of tension is an indication of happiness. More often than not, it is a sign of death. There are two kinds of tension. The first is at gut level; it is irrational and chaotic. This, of course, is to be minimized as much as possible. The second kind is intellectual tension; it produces a restive discontent with the good enough, the worst enemy of the best. Corporations suffer most not from occasional setbacks or reversals but rather from complacence with past success. The purpose of inducing tension is to challenge employees to extend themselves.

The manager is a change agent. Change for the sake of change or merely in imitation of another organization is self-defeating. As we saw, the executive has the job of bringing about changes in a profitable, productive direction that would not happen in his absence. If they would occur without him, then he is a mere overseer or overpaid clerk. Anyone under the age of 30 today will live approximately 20 years longer than his counterpart in 1900. This is mainly the fruit of repeated small advances; medical progress has inched along the road of life lengthening far more often than it has leaped forward with seven-league boots. Too many executives still cling to a childish faith in a baptism-by-immersion or a break-the-record approach to improvement. A more realistic model is mountain climbing. The mountaineer knows where he wants to go; he realizes that the strategies he has evolved will have to be modified to overcome unforeseen obstacles; when he falls down, he gets up again, persevering in his efforts to conquer the mountain; and he usually achieves his objective.

These analogies from medicine and mountain climbing indicate that the executive should not expect dramatic breakthroughs or take needless risks with imprudent change but should commit himself to the hard work of planned, practical programs of improvement that are geared to measurable results.

The manager is a link pin. The link-pin concept, originally introduced by Likert, pictures the executive's job as extending beyond his vertical dealings with his superiors and subordinates to include his lateral and diagonal relations in the firm. If he fails to mesh the work of his subordinates with the efforts of other groups, his people will suffer from a certain degree of isolation. Parallel to this idea is the need for the manager to shield his people from unfair demands or incursions by other departments. If he must support the views of top management, it is equally necessary that he defend and communicate his group's views to the higher echelons. To deprive workers of an effective spokesman topside is unjust. Finally, the perspective of most employees is inevitably confined to the perimeters of their own department or section. This not only prevents them from becoming concerned with the success of the total operation but gives rise to provincial loyalties and interdepartmental frictions. The manager seeks to keep his people filled in both on what they *want* to know and on what they *need* to know if they are to coordinate their efforts with those of other work groups.

The manager influences his superiors. Subordinates who seek to "manage" their superiors are courting career suicide. Yet the manager who cannot influence the thinking, attitudes, and behavior of his bosses at times is useless to himself and his workforce. Employees sense the amount of power their immediate superior has with higher management, and what they do not sense the grapevine quickly makes known to them. Research indicates that it is useless for a lower-level manager to go to bat for his people if he does not have the necessary influence to get favorable action from those he reports to. In the subordinates' view, having an organizational doormat or a powerless nonentity on their side is hardly an asset.

The manager is a developer. Rather than ruling his empire with an iron hand, the modern manager is more likely to be a subtle leaven in the organizational loaf, undramatically building a climate for and a relationship with his key people that stimulate them to work with him and one another to achieve and improve. As a professional, the executive espouses a commitment to his calling, a rigorous insistence on polishing the professional skills he has, and an obligation to acquire those he does not have—to grow and become more proficient in his craft.

In the light of these observations, it is inane to organize development programs for lower-level managers if the prime mover does not bestir himself to abandon the status quo. Openness to new ideas and approaches and receptivity to the influence of his people are basic to both the executive's and his subordinates' development. The manager, as we saw, serves as a model to his subordinates. If he is more power- than achievement-oriented, what right has he to demand that his people take improvement activities seriously? If he is unwilling, as James L. Hayes, president of the American Management Association, has said, to eat crow—feathers and all—once a month by admitting he has made a mistake now and then, how can he expect subordinates to learn from their errors? In development, as in everything else, actions speak louder than exhortations. Companies throw money away on management development programs if the day-to-day behavior of superiors contradicts the training. When the behavior of top management reinforces the principles taught, all benefit. When it negates them, lower-level managers will be frustrated in their attempts to implement the new insights and techniques.

Leadership Is the Lever

Leadership has two major facets: *style* and *behavior patterns*. A leadership style devolves from the personal needs an executive seeks to satisfy as he carries out his leadership functions. Behavior patterns are the characteristics that habitually define his daily actions. If the style is autocratic, for instance, then the behavior will be domineering and stringently directive. It is a moot point whether an executive chooses a particular leadership style or whether the style selects him. He is neither the helpless victim of his psychological history and needs, nor is he wholly autonomous in preferring one style over another. This is the defect of exhortations that urge him to be firm, or permissive, or democratic, or nondirective. What the manager needs is some insight into the reasons why he selects a given leadership style and why he feels more comfortable with it than he might with another. Realization of the kinds of behavior that are likely to stem from a given style, coupled with the benefits and disadvantages of such behaviors, will help him become more sensitive to his actions without becoming self-conscious about them. In turn, this realization will make it possible for him to modify those behaviors that are calculated to lessen his effectiveness while he concentrates on those that will augment it. In this sense, the selection of an appropriate leadership pattern is a process of evolution and development.

The discussion that follows summarizes the major leadership styles that are open to the executive, together with the customary behaviors that are likely to accompany each style. It is obvious that no manager adheres tenaciously to only one behavior pattern. But as an identifiable major theme in a symphony rises above minor themes and variations, so, too, a given leadership style will express itself in a specific pattern of behavior.

Unproductive Leadership Patterns

As is apparent from the listings in Table 1, unproductive leadership styles range from the merely ineffectual to the downright destructive.[3]

The domineering manager-leader. The poor domineering stereotype has been so booed and tabooed in the literature that there is little need to add lashes to his back. He abuses his authority and power. He considers his people simple minions whose duty it is to be subservient. Although few if any executives act consistently in this manner, there are some who at times forget that firmness is not to be equated with arrogance. In a democracy, subordinates do not long follow a self-centered and overbearing boss. Small wonder that when the leader squelches his people, they develop ingenious ways of sabotaging him.

The pseudo-democratic manager-leader. At the opposite extreme is the pseudo-democratic executive. Phony familiarity, togetherness, and belonging are his hallmarks. He sees his role as

Table 1. Unproductive leadership patterns

Variable	Domineering	Pseudo-Democratic	Accommodative	Paternalistic	Bureaucratic
Basis of leadership	Coercive power	Popularity with the group	Talent for avoiding waves	Personal loyalty of subordinates	Position power
Customary behavior	Arrogant	Hand holding	Undemanding	Protective	Ritualistic
Leadership climate	Despotic	Ultrapermissive	Retiring	Avuncular	Protocol-conscious
Leader's role	Driver	Group sustainer	Figurehead	Shepherd	Overseer
Subordinates' role	Obey the boss	Adjust to the group	Go their own way	Please papa	Follow the rules
Achievement orientation	Do as told	Avoid conflict	Compromise	Demand filial responsiveness	Foster consistent mediocrity
Decision process	Dictatorial imposition	Group think	Expedience	Benevolent imposition	Adherence to official policies
Leader-subordinate relationship	Hostile	Mutually ego building	Mutually indifferent	Parent-child	Politely formal
Control method	Threats and punishments	Group tyranny	Noninterference	Conditional love	Application of bureaucratic regulations
Subordinates' reaction	Resentment and sabotage	Other-directedness	Contempt for the leader	Anything for the Old Man	Apathy
Conflict resolution method	Suppression	Denial of conflict	Agreement to disagree	Oiling over of conflict	Legalistic appeals system
Communications	Downward and insistent	Free flowing but not authentic	Intermittent and tension-releasing	Downward and reassuring	Downward and impersonal
Motivation process	Force and flogging	Fear of alienating the group	Inconsistent incentives	Emotional manipulation	Official rewards and punishments
Morale indicator	Subservience	Group contentment	Absence of trouble	Compliance with leader's wishes	Lack of grievances
Subordinate needs met	Survival and avoidance	Affiliation	Pseudo-independence	Dependence	Security

that of a mothering (for which read: smothering) hen intent on building a unit in which everybody is happy. The workforce, in turn, becomes a therapy group that wastes much time breast baring, analyzing feelings that are not occupationally relevant. Thus, though communication is free flowing, it lacks authenticity. Critical thinking and new ideas are rejected for the sake of harmony. Despite all the manager's claims of honesty with and among subordinates, he is emotionally dishonest in that he stifles disagreement and conflict and precipitates avalanches of mutual ego building and reassurances that everyone is "loved." Pseudo-democratic leadership behavior is often confused with sensitivity training, but this is a gross misinterpretation. Sensitivity training, under the right conditions and expert direction, can make substantial contributions to the executive's insight and his skill in interpersonal relations. The pseudo-democratic manager, however, gains only shallow popularity. He does not realize why he is being paid. No wonder that such adventures in amateur psychiatry end up as unprofitable exercises of the incompetent leading the ignorant in dealing with the inconsequential to achieve the unimportant.

The accommodative manager-leader. Lacking in purposefulness, decisiveness, and ego strength, the accommodative manager is caught between the devil and the deep blue sea. Anxious to please his superiors and yet fearful that his subordinates will dislike him, he bends before the greatest current pressure. As Blake has pointed out, he puts the screws on the troops when management puts the heat on him, and when subordinates become restive or resentful, he eases off even if this involves sacrificing the organization's rightful requirements. Thus, he sways back and forth like a reed, earning contempt on all sides. He has a talent for not making waves; he is skilled in balancing divergent pressures for the sake of survival. He stands for nothing, and he frequently gets no satisfaction from his managerial role.

The paternalistic manager-leader. The silken threads of emotional dependence bind more tightly than bands of steel. This the paternalistic executive has learned well. He does much for and to his people while cutting them off from doing much for themselves. He forgets that a satin-lined prison is no less a prison for all its comfort. Interaction with subordinates is sometimes unctuously friendly and other times condescending and patronizing. When the manager is well liked by employees, he controls them first by extending to them conditional love and subsequently by making them feel guilty for having "let the Old Man down." He treats them like children who have to be protected by a benevolent father figure who knows what is in their best interest. T. S. Eliot once observed that the greatest sin of all was to do the right thing for the wrong reasons. This is probably the greatest fault of the paternalistic leader. He ignores the fact that men develop better from workouts than from handouts. Moreover, he is horrified when employees, who should be dutifully grateful, bite the hand that feeds them. At such times, his benevolent veneer peels off and he threatens to withhold or take away the organizational rewards that he uses to buy compliance and docility. He can often count on personal loyalty and even personal affection from his employees, but these are not admirable traits when they are demanded rather than earned. If people in a democracy do not respond favorably to arrogance, they take even less kindly to shepherding that requires them to be servile.

The bureaucratic manager-leader. The larger an organization grows, the more formal its procedures become, the more impersonal its interactions and the more standardized its routines. Policies, rules, and regulations turn into a way of life. The zest and adventure that are associated with young enterprises yield to a more sedate pace and a stricter regard for protocol. Preventing hardening of the arteries becomes one of the most taxing tasks of prime movers in a ponderous corporation: organizational inertia constitutes a deadly threat and organizational renewal a major requirement in the company's struggle for relevance to society's demands and opportunities.

In such conditions, it is not surprising to find more than a few executives adopting the bureaucratic leadership style. They do not cause the firm egregious damage over the short term, but neither do they do it any outstanding good. They merely oversee an ongoing operation, maintaining a persistent resistance to innovation and change. The hand of precedent weighs heavily on them. As often as not, their achievement orientation is contentment with mediocrity. Subordinates respond by becoming apathetic, since all that is expected of them is dependable, lack-luster behavior. Energy that bureaucratic managers might invest in creativity is squandered in jealously defending their status and prerogatives, for most are ultrasensitive about their rights.

Productive Leadership Patterns

Table 2 synthesizes leadership styles that are generally pro-ductive and the behavior patterns that usually stem from each.

The directive manager-leader. Because the directive type of executive does not easily fit into a single research category, there has been a tendency either to overlook him or to lump him with the domineering manager. However, many singularly successful superiors fall into this classification. They win respect rather than affection. They can at times be demanding, bother-some, and even angering. They are hell on wheels toward foot shufflers, though they often reward excellence richly.

Executives of this ilk arouse ambivalent feelings on the part of subordinates. Their forcefulness and dominance, even when they are wrong, can be irritating; yet their obvious talents earn them grudging admiration. The directive manager tends to overpower his people. His leadership is task-oriented and has a no-non-sense air about it. Hence, he is not easily swayed, though he will listen to subordinates' suggestions when they are supported by sound evidence. Too firm-minded and strong-willed for his own good in the long run, such an executive at times fails to de-velop a suitable understudy. Yet often, except when faced with slack work, he can be very considerate and generous. It is not surprising that he is an enigma to all but a few close subordi-nates.

The cultural changes that are taking place make it more and more difficult for a man to manage in this style. Very few can carry it off over the long term. Neither society nor well-edu-cated subordinates will sit still for overdirection. Yet his people and his competitors generally respect his sense of fairness and justice, and he can motivate his workforce to perform in high gear.

The collaborative manager-leader. The difference between the paternalistic and collaborative types of managerial leadership is

Table 2. Productive leadership patterns

Variable	Directive	Collaborative	Collegial
Basis of leadership	Competence and force of personality	Acceptance by group	Recognition by peers
Customary behavior	Task-oriented	Consultative	Catalytic
Leadership climate	Exacting but fair	Supportive	Egalitarian
Leader's role	Energizer and compeller	Team builder	Integrater
Subordinates' role	Perform as expected	Contribute to group goals	Share the leadership
Achievement orientation	Shape up or ship out	Cooperate to achieve objectives	Work for team success
Decision process	Adjudication by the leader	Consensual decision making	Acceptance of competent judgment
Leader-subordinate relationship	Psychologically distant	Psychologically close	Mutually respectful
Control method	Close supervision	General supervision	Self-supervision
Subordinates' reaction	Pride in group; respect for and annoyance with leader	Involvement in group success	Personal responsibility for team success
Conflict resolution method	Solution by leader	Integration of views	Productive confrontation
Communications	Downward and directive	Free flowing and relevant	Authentic and multidirectional
Motivation process	Challenge and reward or clobber	Participation	Self-motivation
Morale indicator	Efficiency: taut ship	Attainment of group goals	Improvement and innovation
Subordinate needs met	Pride, competence, and growth	Affiliation and ego satisfaction	Ego and self-actualization

well illustrated in the following statement by an employee quoted by Robert Ford.[4]

> *In the other district I worked very hard, but no one ever really appreciated me. Although they didn't give me the responsibility I needed, I received a great appraisal at the end of the year, and I thought I was patted on the back too much. A half-hour after the appraisal, nothing was changed. I was working at the same level and getting none of the achievement and recognition I needed. I felt that the appraisal in the old district wasn't worth anything and that management didn't think much of me. Now I'm evaluated as the month goes by, and I know where I stand because I'm responsible for things. And when I make a mistake, I'm the first to know.*

The collaborative manager finds all the verbiage about "hard" and "soft" management rather wearisome. Although he is committed to the practice of consultation, participation, and delegation, he is not hung up on human relations. He does not hesitate to be forceful when circumstances require, but he does not resort to directiveness as a matter of course. He prizes self-discipline over imposed discipline and constructive suggestions over submissive conformity. Viewing authority as based on competence rather than position, this leader interacts with his followers in a process of mutual influence. As a team builder, he realizes that his objective is to help employees satisfy some of their needs while achieving the goals of the group and the firm. Communication is free flowing, constructive, and directed to the purposes for which the group exists. Finally, if possible, conflict is resolved by the synthesis of diverse views. Subordinates learn to build on the contribution of others rather than shoot them down; when this is impossible, they disagree agreeably rather than split the group into antagonistic factions.

The collegial manager-leader. Organizational Renaissance men are conspicuous by their absence. Despite all the palaver about specialists, generalists, and generalists with specialties, the demands of modern business require sophisticated competence in each member of the top management team. What is required is coordination and cooperation among talented "corporateurs," rather than entrepreneurs, who have a total systems view of the firm. This concept, often identified with the president's office, or the presidents' office, is akin to that of collegiality. Collegiality connotes a collective sense of responsibility for a firm's success on the part of its prime movers. A common concern unites executives who have different areas of expertise. Each person is presumed to possess special knowledge without which the organization cannot function well, and thus to be superior in some ways and inferior in others to fellow members of the group. Accordingly, even though the leader has the right to the last word, he is virtually as dependent upon his people as they are upon him. Strong-minded men who are proud of their expertise and firm in their viewpoints are likely to communicate frankly and openly; confrontations can be tolerated and are productive; rigorous critiques of ideas are the rule rather than the exception. A shared sense of commitment to the team's success creates the centrifugal force in the group.

While a collegial approach to leadership is attractive, it does not often work out successfully. Perhaps it will become a widely adopted style at a future time, but the typical company is hardly ready for such a radical departure from accepted management practices. Despite the existence of task forces and venture forces in some organizations, most still adhere to the concept tersely enunciated by Ulysses when the Greeks were bogged down in factional disputes before the walls of Troy: "One let the leader be!"

Insuring the Goodness of Fit of a Leadership Pattern

Tables 1 and 2 are intended not to force those who manage into contrived classifications—human nature is far too individualistic and eccentric for such pigeonholing—but rather to help the practicing executive realize how a particular leadership style with its corresponding behavior pattern is likely to affect his day-to-day behavior.

Nine elements have a bearing on the choice of an appropriate managerial leadership pattern.

1. *The personality of the manager.* Since he is the product of his past experiences, the executive will find it easy to engage in certain types of behavior, difficult to carry off others adroitly, and impossible to feel comfortable with still others.

2. *The manager's life philosophy.* The executive's values are the rudder that guides his behavior. Obviously, the ethically callous can do things that the ethically sensitive would find unthinkable.

3. *The characteristics of the work group.* The workforce is no more a blank page than is the manager. Its members have their own traits as individuals, not to mention the group as a group, which has distinguishing characteristics of its own.

4. *The manager-workforce relationship.* The chemistry between the leader and the followers is crucial. One handles sodium and water quite differently from hydrogen and oxygen.

5. *The manager's influence with his superiors and others who have organizational clout.* Without relatively consistent backing from his superiors and cooperative support from other key organizational personnel, the manager's efforts to lead may well miscarry.

6. *The manager's interaction with other departments.* In complex companies, negotiation, accommodation, and adaptation are the order of the day.

7. *The mandates of the work and the work environment.* Opportunities for and obstacles to effective leadership necessarily vary from one situation to another.

8. *The requirements of the firm.* The organization's philosophy, climate, and tempo and the pressures on it dictate the types of managerial leadership that will be rewarded.

9. *The type of leadership esteemed by society.* No executive can fly in the face of his society for long. "The public be damned" was never good business sense; today, such an attitude would be fatal.

Selecting the Proper Leadership Behavior

Even a cursory examination of the nine factors listed indicates the futility of seeking a universal leadership model. What the executive needs is a spectrum of available behaviors, ranging from the most forceful to the most permissive, that he can choose from and tailor to his unique circumstances. Such a spectrum has been suggested by Robert Tannenbaum and Warren H. Schmidt.[5]

Leadership Behavior	Type of Situat
1. The manager makes a unilateral decision or determines a course of action and announces it to his people.	1. Any emergency situations in which employees are demoralized or perplexed, and situations in which the work group is split into cliques; the timid group, which often reacts well to firmness, and the balky group, which may initially have to be dealt with forcefully if it seeks to sabotage the manager.
2. The manager makes his decision or determines a course of action and then tries to persuade his people to do as he wishes.	2. Situations in which the workforce has implicit confidence in the manager and his judgment. If the "telling and selling" are mere manipulation, however, more harm than good will be done in the long run.
3. The manager makes his decision or determines a course of action and then explains his reasoning in the hope that his people will find it as persuasive as it is to him.	3. Situations in which the manager and his subordinates have generally seen eye to eye on most problems over a long period, and situations in which employees have a high regard for the expertise and competence of the manager.
4. The manager makes his decision or determines a course of action, explains his reasons, perhaps tries to win over his work group, and then asks its help in exploring and resolving problems and obstacles in advance that he may have missed but subordinates may foresee.	4. Situations in which the manager wishes to avoid unanticipated consequences, and situations in which he wishes to avoid the appearance of ramming his decision down his people's throats.

Leadership Behavior	Type of Situation
5. The manager makes a tentative decision or determines a tentative course of action and makes it clear that he is willing to change his mind only if subordinates produce convincing evidence that he should do so.	5. Situations in which the workforce possesses knowledge, competence, or experience the manager lacks, and situations in which subordinates are capable of thinking on their own. This approach should be used only when it will not be misinterpreted by employees as a sign of indecisiveness or weakness.
6. The manager defines the problem, encourages subordinates to contribute, and makes it clear that his objective is to reach the best course of action possible.	6. Situations in which subordinates have a stake in any decision or action that is taken and are competent to analyze and cope with problem; situations in which they represent make-or-break factors in implementing the decision, and situations in which subordinate acceptance of and enthusiasm for the decision are significant.
7. The manager makes it clear that he will accept whatever decision or course of action the group comes up with as long as it meets the criteria set by the manager, his superiors, or organizational policies and procedures.	7. Situations in which the group can be allowed complete freedom as long as the decision or course of action remains within the set parameters.
8. The manager makes it clear that the group is free to decide in its own best interests.	8. Situations that may be of interest or importance to the group but do not involve the firm or its operations.

With some such spectrum of possible behaviors as this, the manager can begin to experiment carefully on the basis of his insight into the significant variables in his work environment. As his group sends him feedback, he will gradually learn which type of behavior is most appropriate at different times and in different circumstances. As he develops flexibility in adjusting to each situation, he will overcome the natural human tendency to act out of habit or according to a fixed and rigid prescription.

understanding subordinates

Some managers who have a positive itch to motivate and communicate with their people do not see that they must first lay a sound basis of principles and procedures for understanding them. The result is great activity but little comprehension or empathy. Yet, as every sales executive knows, the principal difference between a salesman who makes $10,000 a year and one who earns $30,000 or more lies in the fact that the former possesses merely product knowledge, whereas the latter also possesses people knowledge. Perhaps no manager should try to interact with superiors, peers, or subordinates until he has digested Donald Laird's comment that not one person in ten thousand really tries to understand another. Gaining insight into why human beings act as they do is further complicated by the fact that most people have an almost obsessive desire to be an expert critic of the key people with whom they must cooperate. Moreover, one's understanding of others filters through his trained incapacity—the inability to perceive something except through the keyhole of one's own expertise or perspective:

To the economist, man is a money animal anxious to maximize his monetary status, power, and prestige.

To the sociologist, man is made for the group as the ant is for the anthill, eager only to fit in and be accepted.

To the theologian, man is an imperfect child of God.

To the classical philosopher, man is a logical, rational being.

To the psychologist, man is a behaving animal who is inclined to act irrationally as well as rationally.

To the physiologist, man is a bag that consists largely of water and is supported by two legs.

To the systems analyst, man is the most perfect system ever devised.

Each specialist concentrates on his limited view of man, a luxury that no executive can afford.

The manager often finds his job made harder through no real fault of his own. However varied his experience with people may be, it is necessarily restricted. Even so, it will color his perceptions and generalizations about his fellow man. From it he will evolve his theory of human nature, which inevitably will affect everything he does in the leadership area.

Understanding Human Needs

The laws of genetics being what they are, even twins are custom-tailored to unique specifications. This would seem to make the task of understanding others almost insuperable. The saving truth is that although men vary in every possible way— physically, intellectually, and ethically; in their personalities, social skills, and adjustment—they are more alike than different. As James L. Hayes, of the American Management Association, has said tersely, everyone is a fraction. The denominators are the same, but the numerators are diverse. To use Fromm's concept, in every man there are constants that he shares with all other men and variables that represent his individual differences.

All men have the same basic nature, the same human needs. In a given culture, they are likely to have very similar or even identical desires and aspirations. They differ in the quantity, not the quality, of the factors in their makeup. People can be compared with rugs whose threads are identical but whose patterns vary. This antithesis of sameness and diversity the executive must accept not only at the cerebral level, where it does little good, but at the gut level, where it can be all important.

A need is a potentiality, requirement, or capacity inherent in a person that must be reasonably satisfied or actualized if he is to develop into a relatively complete and integrated human being. Most managers are by now familiar with Abraham H. Maslow's hierarchy of needs—those geared to survival, safety and security, sociality and affiliation, ego and esteem, and self-fulfillment and self-actualization. Other psychologists present no fewer than 28 psychogenic needs over and beyond those that Maslow called the physiological. If we leave aside such needs as the physiological, which are relatively unimportant in our discussion, and the economic, which require no explanation, the human needs that are of primary importance in business are either psychological or social in nature.

The Psychological Needs

It is not possible to enumerate all of man's psychological needs, but certainly the following are among the most significant.

The need to be different. Organizations have typically pressured people to conform to their concepts of how employees should think and act; this is a natural human tendency. Executives, too, have a way of forcing subordinates to conform to their perceptions and preconceptions of them. One is reminded of the answer a reporter received when he asked an Ivy League undergraduate why he dressed and acted up as he was doing: "After I graduate, I'll have to work in a bank where my father is a top executive. I want to do my thing now, before I have to join the system." This anecdote illustrates the fact that to encroach unduly on a person's right to listen to his own drummer and to be his own man is one of the best ways to arouse undesirable resistance from him.

A worker is paid to perform. As long as he performs, while abiding by the prescriptions of society in general and the nature of his job (no one expects to tolerate a maître d'hôtel who wears overalls at work), then neither the firm nor any executive in it can rightly force him to comply with requirements that represent nothing but the personal whims or eccentricities of those in command. Every employee is entitled to his differences, as he is entitled to his unique name, as long as they do not interfere with his or others' performance. With the advent of the so-called knowledge worker, companies will perforce broaden the parameters of the behavior and decorum they find acceptable. In an article with which the reader may or may not agree, Samuel A. Culbert and James M. Elden give the following translations of certain student activist terms into the demands the students will make on corporations.[1]

Strike.	*I want to influence those in power in my corporation directly.*
Revolution.	*I want to work for a company that adapts to the changing needs of its people.*
Liberation.	*I want to have a job that allows me to do my thing and discover what is uniquely mine.*
Commune.	*I want to work with others in a way that emphasizes my human qualities.*
Power to the people.	*I want a voice in regulating my activities. Also, I want others to respect my autonomy.*
Relevance.	*I want to work for a company that is relevant to pressing needs.*

Companies will have to accommodate themselves to knowledge workers who act far more like prima donnas than their superiors would ever have dreamed of doing, even as these employees will have to adjust to the legitimate requirements of the organizations. There is nothing wrong with a prima donna if she is paid to sing and sings exceptionally well. But no firm has an obligation to put up with pretenders who act like prima donnas, expect to be treated like prima donnas, and take unto themselves the prerogatives of prima donnas—but cannot sing a note.

The need for independence and self-expression. It is noteworthy that the need to be different and the need for autonomy run all through the interpretations presented by Culbert and Elden. Even infants have an urge to express themselves, and it waxes stronger throughout life. There is no more woeful figure than the subordinate who has had his self-assertiveness squelched. Like most impulses, the need to express oneself is a two-edged sword. It can be the taproot of creativity and innovation; it can also be the source of much harm. The young manager who is intent on promoting his own views without considering those of others is courting needless trouble. But so is the executive who curbs his people unduly. Walking the fine line that separates dependence from independence and interdependence is a most difficult art for both superior and subordinate to master. Since the desire for self-expression and autonomy varies markedly from person to person, the manager-leader must take definite steps to define limits *before* employees test them.

First, he can make certain that there is a true meeting of minds between him and his key people regarding their job content, duties, and accountabilities. This usually requires considerable accommodation and negotiation and can never be obtained through such instruments as position descriptions alone.

He can also make sure that the achievement targets of the subordinate are not only clear to him but accepted by him as far as possible. Priorities must also be established in terms of the essential, the important, and the routine results that are expected.

> Most executives fancy that they do a superior job of setting performance standards. Unhappily, the research does not always bear them out. Maier and his colleagues asked a series of vice-presidents in several organizations to choose immediate subordinates with whose work they were familiar and to define their expectations of them. The subordinate picked by each vice-president was asked independently to define what he thought the executive expected of him. The degree of agreement was in the neighborhood of 35 percent.[2]

He can clarify for the subordinate the areas in which the latter is free to decide and act without getting permission, informing anyone, or consulting with this or that peer. He can spell out the areas of freedom to decide and act where the subordinate must inform either the boss or another department *after* the fact, and he can do the same with the areas of freedom where the employee must consult appropriate parties *before* the fact because decisions and actions in these areas can greatly affect their work. Finally, he can outline the areas in which the specific agreement of affected groups or permission of the manager must be obtained *before* any decision or action is taken.

Unless the manager-leader implements some such guidelines

as these, confusion will result. Self-assertion and autonomy are subjectively perceived factors. Some subordinates will not even use the freedom that is granted them, whereas others will assume a measure of independence that is wholly at variance with their job status and accountabilities.

The need to experience success, adequacy, and self-esteem. When texts talk about the "feeling" or "sense" of success, achievement, or competence, they are unwittingly distorting the need. Why is it not possible to give subordinates the chance to experience the genuine article? Why can they not experience their own competence so as to realize their own adequacy? Self-esteem can never be infused from without; it is ever internally generated, the product of knowing that one is a human being who, despite occasional failures, is effective and likable. It stems from a self-awareness that makes a person conscious of his deficiencies but more sensitive to his strengths.

What can the manager-leader do to help his people, even those performing the most menial tasks, experience success, adequacy, and self-regard? He can first seek out opportunities that will enable subordinates to have these self-reactions. This is the whole idea of delegation, consultative and participative management, earned recognition, and increased responsibility. He can also give each employee a job of his own. It is interesting that in Robert N. Ford's studies both an engineer and a woman who volunteered for a dumdum task reacted with the comment that at last they had a job of their own. Most important of all, the executive can start to do some people-thinking rather than mere thing-thinking.

The need for development. People who visit the Rockies are sometimes surprised to find spindly trees struggling to grow out of barren soil. To grow is rewarding. To be continually frustrated is killing. How well the need to develop and its obverse, the damage done by constant thwarting, are illustrated in the following experiment.

A pike was put into a tank with some minnows. To no one's surprise, the pike ate the tiny fish. Then a transparent shield was inserted between the pike and the minnows. When the pike swam toward his dinner, he was rudely rebuffed by the barrier. Again and again, he flung himself against the shield. Finally, overcome with frustration, he retired dejectedly to a corner of the tank. The shield was then removed, and the minnows—not known for their intelligence—swam all about the tank. The pike, however, was so apathetic as a result of his frustration that he died of hunger! It might be truer to say that he died of frustration.

The urge to grow—to learn, to achieve, to develop—is inborn. Job enlargement, job enrichment, job rotation, and special assignments all provide challenges to employees to stretch themselves and develop.

Many managers find, contrary to the theory of need satisfaction, that some of their people are unmotivated and passive. Why are the theory and the observed reality so much at variance? For one thing, lack of initiative is a result, not a cause. For another, there is a saying that the only difference between a flower girl and a lady is the way they have been treated. There is an even more popular old saw about the loose girl in the small town: having the name, she felt she might as well play the game. No one is born passive or apathetic. People become that way because of how they have been treated.

It would be absurd for the manager-leader to expect employees to get a new lease on life simply because he has gotten the religion of people thinking. One cannot turn an aircraft carrier in the same distance that it takes to turn a rowboat. One learns to toddle before he walks, to walk before he runs, and to run before he races. Every work group, as has been said, has its own personality, mores, folkways, attitudes, and reactions to work and authority. The manager-leader has the task of establishing a climate in which achievement is expected and rewarded. Rather than fearing that his subordinates may let him down, the executive would be better advised to weigh them down gradually and prudently with real jobs, genuine responsibility, and true opportunities to work out their own salvation. Such an approach will not work well with everyone or equally well with different people; even the most effective medicine will not be beneficial to all patients. But unless the manager-leader has a basic trust in the majority of his employees, who have a fair amount of good will, he will never know what they *could* do under the right kind of leadership; he will know only what they *have* done and *are* doing.

The need for defense. Every human being has not only an impulse to enhance his self-esteem but a corresponding drive to avoid any affront to this precious feeling. Isaac Newton determined that a body in motion tends to remain in motion. A subordinate offended tends to remain offended, regardless of his visible demeanor. The greater the authority an executive possesses, the easier it is for him to use it as a quick resort for getting results or simply his own way. Managers who are abrasive might well remember that in human affairs manner is ordinarily far more important than meaning. It is not the discipline so much as the way it is administered that often alienates employees. It does not appear too much to ask that the manager who would be a leader show the same kind of consideration to his people as he would a stranger in his home. No one is requiring him to be a paragon of virtue; he is human and subject to the same temptations to lash out as other men. But the manner of even the most painful action, such as demoting a person, will change if the executive will ask himself, "Is my intention to alienate the person and thus make it harder than ever to reach him when this is over, or is it to make our relationship a bit more cordial?" This question will safeguard him against the natural tendency to vent venom or ventilate nasty feelings in a cathartic burst of temper against a vulnerable subordinate. It may seem a bit old-fashioned to some, but a decent civility toward others is the lubricant that prevents undue friction in human relations.

The Social Needs

"The idea that men are created free and equal is both true and misleading; men are created different; they lose their social freedom and their individual autonomy in seeking to become like each other." [3] This observation by David Riesman points up the power of the social needs inherent in every person.

The need for attention and approval. "Love me if you will, hate me if you must, but don't ignore me" goes an old Irish saying. It illustrates the truths that attention is food for the ego and approval fuel for motivation. Neurotics go to ridiculous lengths to monopolize the center of the stage. Normal people would soon shrivel without the periodic watering of attention. Strangely enough, this aspect of the need to be considered a unique human being generally requires little in the way of time or effort. A compliment, a thank-you, a word of constructive criticism, an ear to a subordinate's legitimate grievance or suggestion—none of these acts consumes much energy.

A consultant was doing some work for a very large publishing company. One of the managers, whose behavior toward his people was so prim, proper, and stiffly formal that he had all the friendliness of an undertaker, asked for some help in relating better to them. It was suggested that he experiment with such activities as showing his teeth now and then in a smile, taking time for a brief conversation focused on the other person, sprinkling *earned* compliments *prudently,* and making opportunities for employees to approach him if they so wished. "I cannot do such things," was his impulsive response. "I would feel like a hypocrite." After some discussion, he agreed to give it a try. About three weeks later, the consultant and the manager met again. On being asked how his program of human relations improvement was going, he replied, "It all works so easily —the girls are so responsive to such little things that I feel more like a hypocrite now than I did before." It took some time before he could accept the fact that the way to reach human beings is to act humanly.

The attention the manager pays must be sincere. Compliments that the recipient knows he has not merited do more harm than good. Far too many managers endeavor to be manipulative when all they need to be is gracious. They are merely slick when they should be smooth. Most employees would prefer to receive negative attention from a superior whom they respect, even in the form of stringent discipline, than to accept contrived praise from a phony.

The need to belong and conform. Man represents a strange commingling of opposites. The psychotic espouses independence at the expense of all other human conditions. The jellyfish esteems acceptance by others over having a mind of his own. Most of us engage in a continual struggle to define the proper limits of each desirable quality. Man is a togetherness animal, and the need to fit in with and be liked by others is the social oxygen of his existence. Deprived of rewarding interaction with others, he will either go insane or die—literally.

Given this, the manager-leader has at his disposal a tremendous force for either good or ill in his work group. Any effort that he invests in helping his people pull together rather than apart is well spent. His task is not to live off his people but to work for and with them so that individual inputs can be multiplied by cohesive contributions. It is peculiar that, having this powerful resource, so many supervisors and managers look upon the work group as a necessary nuisance, especially if it is composed of women, instead of seeking ways to make its potential energy kinetic.

The need to be accepted has a vertical as well as a horizontal dimension. There are managers who vacillate, procrastinate, or speak with a forked tongue. They are so intent on being liked that they forget the importance of being respected. When the organization is right, these managers are spineless in facing down subordinates who happen to be in the wrong. They fail to realize that to be disliked by some people for the right reasons is more important than to be liked by other people for the wrong reasons.

On the other hand, there are managers who act as though the need to belong did not exist. Instead of helping subordinates meet this need in legitimate ways, instead of formulating means for the organization to capitalize more fully on the productive potential of this need, they seek to deny it in themselves and ignore it in their employees. As a supervisor of nurses shouted during a development program, "I didn't join this hospital to be popular. I came here to do a job. I couldn't care less what they think of me." (The only comment the writer could think of at the moment was, "Then why are you raising your voice?") Simple acceptance of the fact that the executive has the same need for belonging and conforming as everyone else is a good beginning.

The need to participate and contribute. There never has been a parent whose children did not at one time or another say,

"Dad, let me help" or "Let me do it." Whether such volunteering will continue even for a short time depends largely on how the parent reacts to it. Much the same thing is true in any firm. Bottom-up management is not mere pious benevolence; neither is coaching, counseling, training, or seeking the advice or suggestions of employees. They are rooted psychologically and socially in a basic need that all men have to be involved in something worthwhile. In fact, to pour out energy in a cause that is meaningful and important is one of the best therapies ever discovered.

"Sending up suggestions in this company," a lower-level manager once remarked, "is like playing handball with a cloud. You hit the ball and off it goes, but nothing ever happens. It's enveloped in a monstrous void." The manager-leader appreciates the fact that four of the most important words in the English language are, "What is your opinion?" Subordinates do not have to be very bright to sense whether or not a superior is really interested in their ideas. If the organizational climate is not conducive to upward communication, then all the downward exhortation to offer suggestions will be sterile. The manager-leader who wants to help employees contribute and participate must first answer the following questions honestly:

— How willing and able am I to listen to, not merely hear, a point of view that I find personally distasteful, as long as it is based on evidence?

— How easy is it for my subordinates to disagree with me when they have evidence or the experience to support their position?

— How comfortably can an employee at any level bring up an idea, method, or change for discussion that at first blush appears to be rather far out?

— To what extent do I welcome suggestions that might well rock the boat but have real possibilities of improving the operation?

— How ready am I to change my mind or position when the evidence adduced by subordinates is compelling?

— Am I guilty of subtly endeavoring to manipulate my people into agreeing with me, even though they are not persuaded by my evidence?

— When a point at issue is under discussion, do I make my views so strongly that my people yield too rapidly, despite their convictions to the contrary?

Unless the executive can give candid answers to these questions, all talk about participation and contribution is idle. Attempts to involve employees will be nothing more than a game of pseudo-democracy, a parody of tolerance, in which opinions are exchanged without being tested.

It is not sufficient that the manager-leader welcome employees' suggestions and constructive criticisms. He must know who is capable of making what kinds of contributions. One person may be knowledgeable about technical matters; another may be skilled in packaging a new idea so that it does not run aground on organizational rocks and shoals; a third may be adept at preventing the people from running animatedly in all directions at once; a fourth may be a gifted devil's advocate who can keep the group from going off halfcocked. It is not necessary that everyone be creative; in fact, no organization could function if it had only creative types. People who are less innovative can serve very useful purposes helping a fellow employee present and sell his novel ideas to those in authority or preventing them from being shot down out of jealousy.

Two major enemies of organizational health are corporate ossification and pigeonholing, boxing people in so that they lose all zest for performance and achievement. No executive is expected to give ear to someone who thinks that the earth is flat. But there is nothing so disheartening as to see an idea that a subordinate has worked out in painful detail meet a blank management wall. It is a sad fact of life that managers who take pride and appreciate the fun in innovating at times obstinately refuse their people any chance of securing the same fun from their work.

Making the Most of Human Needs

In any sizable department, there will be a wide range of individual differences in any variable the manager chooses to consider. What can he do in the practical order to cope with human uniqueness and human needs?

Avoid playing God. Everyone in authority is tempted to remake others according to his own likeness, a privilege that the good Lord reserves unto himself. Treat the other fellow as you

would like to be treated is the counsel of the golden rule. As a
guiding principle, it is perfect, but it can get the executive into
difficulties if put into practice mechanically. It can mislead him
into assuming that the other fellow is a mirror image of himself,
that he not only has the same needs but places the same order of
priority and emphasis on their satisfaction. The wise manager
sees his superiors and subordinates as similar to himself but also
different from him in very important ways.

Discard stereotypes. A stereotype is a picture in the mind that
we carry about regarding people—"hippy," "government bureaucrat," "ivory tower professor." Stereotypes are dangerous because they are rarely based on adequate evidence, they are almost always unconscious, and they are firmly ingrained. They
substitute labels for thought. What is worse, they prevent us
from thinking of people as individuals, from discriminating
among them, from judging each man on his merits. There is an
old saying that the more we learn to discriminate *among*, the
less we are tempted to discriminate *against*. Stereotyped thinking about subordinates may harm them and will surely blind the
manager to their undeveloped potential.

Accept people as they are. Parents and executives find this
very difficult to do. The reason is simple: we are all born re-
formers of our fellow man. But the fact is that the leader's employees are not going to change their behavior overnight; nor
can they change their personalities or past experiences at his be-
hest. Related to dealing with people as we find them, not as we
would like them to be, is the practice of looking for the right
things in people. The French maintain that one sees only what
he looks for. Any human being, as a composite of strengths
and weaknesses, will provide ample evidence for any opinion
the manager wants to form of him, positive or negative. If the
leader makes an effort to perceive what is good in subordinates
while remaining aware of what is wrong, then the good is what
he will evoke. The physician is attuned to a person's illness but
concentrates on his potential for health and development.

Act like a scientist. Scientists adopt as a fundamental principle that all behavior is a result; it is caused. They see it as directed toward the attainment of some goal, the satisfaction of
some need. And scientists know that analysis must precede prescription and prescription must precede action. Accordingly, the

manager's first challenge is to gain some insight into his subordinates. This can be done rather easily—certainly no M.B.A. or degree in psychology is required—if the executive will study his employees with a view to coming up with specific answers to the following questions:

What stirs their interest and causes them to prick up their ears?
What arouses their enthusiasm?
What tends to bother or annoy them?
What makes them so blind with anger that they become almost irrational?
What leaves them cold and unresponsive?

Writing as objective a paragraph as possible under each of these headings, starting with superiors and then continuing with key peer and subordinate figures, will do the manager more practical good than all the reading in the world. A problem-solving, analytic approach is far superior to one that is fault-finding and critical. Einstein once remarked that one should never endeavor to impose his views on a problem; he should rather study it, and, in time, a solution will reveal itself to him.

Observation alone is of course only the first step. The manager should continue to use the scientist as a model by being experimental in his approaches to others. Prudent experimentation is the key to increased knowledge because it enables the executive to test out his hypotheses about his people, his attitudes toward them, and his perceptions of them. He who will not experiment will not learn. This is as true of understanding human beings as it is of mastering physics. One of the most enduring myths ever perpetrated on a naive public is the nonsense that one learns by trial and error. This is no doubt the worst and most painful way to learn anything. One learns by observation, prudent experimentation, and discovery.

Be sensitive to feedback. The average manager gains far more job-related knowledge from feedback than he does from books. After all, every supervisor or manager has a built-in laboratory of human relations right under his nose; he needs only to learn from it. People are interacting as individuals and as groups throughout every working day. This does not mean that the manager should put people under his amateurish psychological microscope. All that is required is that he be alert to how they react to each other and respond to his efforts to lead and manage them. As he sifts through this behavioral feedback, he can modify his views of employees and superiors and adjust his actions in conformity with it.

Be wary of delusions of difference. It is at times astonishing how some managers behave as though their subordinates lived in an entirely different world from their own. This layer-cake concept of organizational life devolves in questions like "All this may work well with people at the management level, but will it really work with the troops?" Dividing the world into two classes, those who ride herd on others and those who are ridden, is the most effective technique available for fostering mutual misunderstanding. If one were to put the president of a firm and a sweeper in a sauna, it might be difficult to tell who was who. In a steam room, they would be stripped to one quality, which they would share in common—human nature. This is not to say that a company president and a sweeper are identical, for they would probably place varying degrees of emphasis on the same human needs. But the sweeper is no less a person than the president.

Catch himself in his own behavior. Examining one's own behavior is a fascinating and rewarding exercise if it is not overdone. Among its chief proponents was Karen Horney, one of the outstanding psychoanalysts that this country has ever had. It requires a person to be sensitive not only to the feelings and behavior of others but to his own. For instance, when he loses his temper, he asks himself, "Why did I react as I did? Was it worth the anger I spent on it?" The manager can do this in a variety of situations: when he finds someone irritating, when he hesitates to say something to the boss, when he imposes his will on another, when he allows himself to be flattered. The aim is twofold: to become a little more cognizant of one's own dynamics and to cope with one's feelings more objectively. Self-analysis can be very helpful when one is passed over for promotion or is slighted or disciplined. It will never change the feeling—this would be asking too much of human nature—but it will help one cope rationally with his feelings.

It is interesting to observe psychoanalysts acting just as human as the rest of mortals at times. During World War

II, Dr. Horney was scheduled to travel by air from a certain city. At the last minute, she was bumped off the flight and a noncommissioned officer was given her seat because he was traveling on a priority basis. She was furious. Then she applied her own principle and came to the conclusion that, although she was superior in many ways to the military man, he was more essential to the war effort. She was still disappointed, but she was better able to deal with her disappointment.

Launch his own understanding program. Nations are constantly gathering data on other nations. Companies scrutinize and analyze the competition unendingly. No professional ball team would dream of playing an opponent without first going over reports and films of its past games very painstakingly. When intelligence gathering is so widespread, it seems strange that so few executives seem to do it. A simple method the manager may use is to make a dossier on each key person in his work life, starting with his immediate superior and working his way out from this central point according to the dictates of common sense. Taking a sheet of paper for each, he writes down what he *thinks* is the case under the following headings: (1) strengths, (2) weaknesses, (3) preferences, (4) aversions, and (5) ways he likes to be treated. These categories may each be broken down into subheadings, such as technical, managerial, and human relations. Then he puts the papers away for a few weeks and lets experience take its course. When he takes out his record, he compares what he has observed during the past weeks with what he committed to paper, noting the changes and adjustments that should be made in the light of his experience. Naturally, this should be done in a relaxed, self-instructive manner—never compulsively or mechanically. It is obvious that people observe all the time, but inattentively and haphazardly; the method suggested here is planned and systematic, and can hone the manager's powers of understanding to a keen edge.

motivating subordinates

"Anyone who meets a payroll knows that people who really want to work for you are about the scarcest thing in industry." These words of Jeno Palucci's sum up the importance of motivation in managerial leadership. To get employees to do mediocre work, one need only *drive them,* using coercive and reward power in a manipulative way. To elicit their top performance, one must get them to *drive themselves,* and this requires a skill that relatively few executives master. Small wonder, as Dean Acheson once remarked, that good men can run the worst kind of organization, and poor men can't run the best. The manager who has no insight into his people soon squelches the will to work of even the most enthusiastic; the one who is adept at energizing subordinates gets them to achieve more than they thought possible. After all, any caretaker can get ordinary work from ordinary people; the manager-leader gets above-average results from ordinary people. The point bears repeating: better for the executive to have two people who work *with* him than five who labor *for* him. The former will multiply his productivity; the latter will merely drain his resources.

Why the Gap Between Theory and Practice?

Behavioral scientists have observed, studied, and experimented. They have produced new ideas, evidence, and valuable suggestions. Personnel specialists and training directors have welcomed these new views of perennial problems. Line managers have at times been less than persuaded that they work on the firing line. Yet the contributions of behaviorists have a long way to go before they permeate the workaday activities of the general run of managers and supervisors. Since it takes two to tango, this lack of penetration can be attributed to both parties —theorists and practitioners.

The Manager's Side

Line managers have failed to capitalize fully on behaviorists' findings for a number of reasons.

Some executives have scoffed at the ideas proposed because they appeared to contradict common sense or personal experience. Others have first swallowed incomplete research data whole—and found shortly that their naive faith was but a prelude to disaster. Still others have endeavored to implement the proposals of the experts mechanically, without tailoring them carefully to the unique circumstances of their own work situations. Their initial enthusiasm has quickly been displaced by an attitude of once burned, twice shy.

Some executives have failed to foresee that a commitment to the idea of people-thinking would involve a greater change in their roles and relationships than in those of their subordinates. When this realization has dawned on them, they have quickly regressed to old, familiar patterns of management.

On occasion, the implementation of human relations principles has taken the form of tinkering with this or that group. Since higher management has neither become involved in nor supported such programs, opposition and erosion have soon undercut the well-intentioned efforts. In other cases, concern for human relations has been relegated to such staff departments as personnel. Since line managers take their cues from their superior, they have given mere lip service to staff programs.

Even a healthy transplanted heart will be rejected by a body, which has its own peculiar way of functioning, unless the body's whole defense mechanism is adjusted. Patching bits and pieces of human relations onto the system that every firm is has often provided the production of antibodies, which cast off the grafts. This failure to adjust is partly the doing of executives who think of behavioral precepts as mere additions to their primary responsibility to perform, as parsley is a garnish for a steak or a vitamin pill is a supplement to one's regular diet. On the contrary, these precepts are oriented toward a philosophy and system of management that dominates almost everything top managers do. One reason for this piecemeal approach is that they have too often looked for easy, inexpensive solutions for human relations problems. They have rarely devoted either the financial resources or the energy to their human system that they have to their technological system. Until upper management is as committed to the development of people as it is to that of machines, little of lasting worth will be forthcoming.

The Behaviorists' Side

It is the nature of a profession to develop an aura of mystery and a jargon. These hallmarks keep even those whom it would help at a respectful distance and indeed tend to alienate them. No one in his right mind would contend that behavioral scientists as a group have translated their thoughts into terms readily understandable to the busy manager.

Moreover, scientists often have a tender ego, at least in their professional capacity. Proud of their expertise and demanding respect for their profession, they tend to be overly sensitive to the legitimate—or anyhow well-intentioned—objections and criticisms of line managers. They have now and then worsened the situation by seeming to talk down to the operations people.

On the other hand, human relations people are viewed by line managers as outsiders who have never held command positions. Some have tried to have the best of both worlds—influence without accountability. Since this is a luxury granted to no manager, it is natural if he is both suspicious and jealous of the role that some experts have sought to carve out for themselves. Behaviorists have at times contributed to this estrangement: far too often, because of an allegiance to their discipline, they have shown themselves to be staff- rather than line-minded.

Another point of friction arises from the fact that behavioral scientists, by training and experience, like the give-and-take of questioning, debate, and disagreement. The endless challenging that they take for granted causes confusion for many executives.

The former seek a fuller truth. The latter need a reliable input-throughput-output process that is realistic and practical. But there is not a single aspect of all of behavioral science about which the expert can guarantee results in the practical order, even though in many areas the cumulative evidence is quite persuasive. This realization is sufficient to make the prudent manager cautious. What is worse, at times some experts have promised more than they could deliver.

Worst of all, managers have occasionally found themselves faced not with honest error or failure but fraud. Charlatans exist in all fields. Behavioral science is no different. Despite the efforts of such organizations as the American Psychological Association to establish and enforce criteria for the education, admission, and functioning of competent practitioners, there is no question that people without extensive training or experience have set themselves up as experts.

The stresses encountered in management and behavioral science differ radically, and behavioral experts have seemed at times to lack understanding of the critical problems with which the average executive must wrestle to survive. Behaviorists have a high frustration threshold in their specialty; they can wait patiently until the evidence is in. The manager must meet deadlines; he must live up to production schedules; he must cope with stringent controls; he must deal with many people in trying to get his job done. Again, scientists like experiments. If one fails, then another can usually be undertaken. The situation of the executive could hardly be more different. When he "experiments" he commits organizational resources and perhaps his future—every survivor of the Edsel realizes this truth. Once committed, he must succeed. Reversing his program is at best painful, at worst impossible. Having put his hand to the plow, the manager, unlike the scientist, can rarely turn back successfully or with good grace, perhaps even when he should.

One more reason for the gap between behaviorists and managers should be noted. It is a natural human tendency to project one's value system on others, even though its components have neither the same meaning nor the same valence for them. At times, behavioral scientists have fallen into this error. It well may be that not every worker seeks autonomy, self-development, and creative freedom in his work. To assume that all employees are motivated by the goals theorists list may be a tragic mistake. Value judgments regarding how managers should behave must come from additional sources, beyond research.

Bridging the Gap

Even if every word that fell from the tongues of behavioral scientists were true, the real work of implementing the research findings would remain. The reasons are multiple.

First, many features of the work environment cannot be changed. They represent givens with which the manager must contend. Similarly, most organizational factors—philosophy, customs, traditions, mores, values, jealousies, sensitivities, tempo, stresses, climate, pressures—cannot be altered quickly. In addition, the demands and expectations of a manager's superiors are not normally subject to either his command or his persuasiveness. And it is much too late to change the psychological histories of his subordinates; for better or for worse, they are as they are.

So is the average manager. It is a bit naive to imagine that he can or will alter his own personality structure radically. Although he can certainly grow and improve within limits, most of his strong and weak points he will carry to his grave. His relationships with his peers, although again subject to improvement, are really beyond his immediate control. Finally, such unalterable circumstances as the presence of a union, the financial state of the firm, the condition of the economy, and the nature of the competitive market are facts of existence to which he must adjust.

It is obvious from these observations that the practicing manager is more constrained than autonomous. He can achieve little of lasting worth unless he allows for the impact of his situation on the contributions of behavioral science. A questioning attitude toward the research evidence is prudent. Cynicism can be harmful. Awareness of and openness to other evidence must replace an impulse to adopt formulas that have only a surface practicality. Because a research study has worked well in one environment does not mean that it will be equally effective in the manager's. A valid idea may be operationally inapplicable to a given set of corporate circumstances. The prevailing climate and philosophy may make it impossible to introduce an otherwise sound procedure. A patient making haste slowly and resistance to the beguiling come-ons of easy solutions are prerequisites to genuine progress.

The gap between the world of behavioral research and the industrial firing line is greater than many admit. The ideal specialist would be one who has a foot in both worlds—who possesses practical managerial experience and behavioral expertise. Since few can meet this criterion, it behooves the specialist to think of himself as an organizational behaviorist rather than a clinical, social, or industrial psychologist or a sociologist. It is the organization in which he moves and has his being. The farther he steps away from this reality, the less effective he is likely to become. Certainly he is expected to have his own convictions, to be a devil's advocate, to act as a constructive irritant questioning accepted ideas, procedures, and attitudes. If he but parodies the "party line" he degenerates into a mere sycophant. He must take his stance, however, at that rim of the horizon where professional expertise meets the legitimate expectations and needs of the company. The firm is not merely an arena in which he can carry on his research or put his pet ideas into practice; it is an enterprise intent on growth and increasing profitability. Independent in his profession, the behavioral scientist must espouse a correlative allegiance to the future fortunes of the firm. If he cannot or will not do this, then he should withdraw with good grace.

The Miscellany That Is Motivation

In any discussion of the motivations of people at work, modesty is a far more desirable posture than certitude for various reasons. First, there are more theories than universally applicable data. Although significant gains in knowledge about the subject have been made in the last 20 years, the perimeters of the unknown still greatly exceed those of precise information. The new insights are stimulating; the unanswered questions are frustrating. Second, many managers have only a limited familiarity with the contributions of behavioral science. Third, almost every major finding has been anticipated by the shrewd perceptions of philosophers and poets. The difference, of course—and it is no mean difference—is that where they had insight, the scientists have been accumulating evidence. Fourth, neither outside observers nor people themselves at times understand why they act as they do in a given set of circumstances. Theories and after-the-fact explanations abound. In *some* situations and with *some* work groups or individuals, it may be possible to analyze the patterns and predict future behavior more or less accurately. The manager-leader, however, always deals with probability in this area, never with certainty.

In view of these observations, it would seem well to limit the next sections of discussion to prescientific methods of motivation, some major contributions of behavioral science, and practical suggestions for the line manager.

Prescientific Motivation Techniques

The history of man's efforts to motivate his fellow man can be summarized in four terms, each of which begins with a *c*.

Coercion. The pharaohs and the Roman emperors had little use for insight into human nature. They possessed the necessary power. All they required were enough slaves and enough whips. When one has overwhelming power, there is no need to trifle with such niceties as human understanding. It is safe to say that this country was built largely through motivation by coercion. The ethos of the culture supported it, and the workers were ignorant immigrants whose first aim was survival. Those who managed did so on the assumptions of the divine right of ownership and private property. Interestingly, all this took place within the context of a democratic political philosophy.

Conniving. Since Newton's law applies in human affairs as in physics, to management's arrogant action there was a reaction, which took the form of the countervailing force of unionism. With its power circumscribed by the legal shackle called a contract, management at times sought, and still does remarkably often, to manipulate employees into doing as it would have them do. Unhappily, this approach generally won battles and lost wars. It gave short-term results on occasion but usually at the expense of long-term cooperative relationships.

Compensation. In a materialist culture, it is predictable that those in power will tend to look to money as the prime motivater. Man *is* an economic animal and money *is* the major means for satisfying his material needs. Somerset Maugham once called money the sixth sense, without which the other five cannot be enjoyed. The logic, as far as it goes, is persuasive. But man is intent on meeting more than his bread-and-butter requirements. He endeavors to "satisfice" many needs in a balanced manner. This balance is dictated by his—not management's—values, aspirations, and wants and the pressures that bear down on him.

It has been fashionable in some quarters to put down the importance of money. This is fatuously naive. For better or worse, society still measures and rewards success largely in terms of the things that money can buy. Saint Francis of Assisi may be admired by many businessmen; he is imitated by few indeed. Hence, to minimize the incentive aspect of money is to deny reality. Money in the form of inadequate pay is a devastating demotivater. The motivational power of money in itself, however, is rather limited; its status power is considerable. It represents earned recognition; it is an outward sign of the firm's appreciation of an employee's contributions; and it reinforces his self-image as a valued worker.

Cuddle and coddle. There was a time when some organizations acted on the proposition that if they paid fair wages, offered superior fringe benefits, provided excellent working conditions, and so on, employees would be grateful. Because of this gratitude, they would be motivated to do more and better work. History gives ample testimony that doing things for people rather than allowing them opportunities to do things for themselves has generally borne little fruit. It is not that employees did not expect and appreciate these things; they did. The mistake lay in expecting that such extras alone would suffice to motivate them.

Some Contributions of Behavioral Science

Brief summaries involve selection, and any selection involves an element of injustice to those who are omitted. Although many behaviorists have made substantive contributions, surely the names of McGregor, Maslow, Herzberg, Argyris, and Bennis stand in the forefront.

Douglas McGregor

McGregor's [1] key concept is that every executive relates to his subordinates on the basis of a set of assumptions. Theory X includes the traditional postulates regarding the typical worker in America—that he is by nature indolent and averse to work, lacks ambition and avoids responsibility, is passive and prefers to be led, is gullible and easily duped by charlatans, must be molded to fit the needs of the organization, and must be persuaded and pushed, punished and rewarded, tightly supervised and controlled if he is to perform as expected since he is indifferent to organizational needs and incapable of self-discipline. Theory Y operates on quite different assumptions. Work is as natural as play; it can be satisfying or punishing depending on circumstances. People not only are capable of assuming responsibility but in the right conditions seek it. They are also able to exercise self-direction. Motivation does not involve what the manager does to his people; the motivating forces already exist in the workforce. Ingenuity and creativity do not exist solely at the managerial level.

McGregor readily agreed that indifferent workers abound. His contention was that they become this way because of how they have been treated. He also admitted that few if any managers hold totally to either theory; he set up the dichotomy for purposes of clarity. He rejected the concepts of "hard" and "soft" management. Rather, the task of the Theory Y manager is to build such a climate and so organize working relationships that employees can best attain their goals by directing their efforts toward corporate aims. Common objectives, frankly admitted interdependence, and collaboration are the key instruments. Where Theory X counsels management by imposition, Theory Y proposes management by involvement, contribution, and commitment.

Abraham H. Maslow

Emphasizing need satisfaction, Maslow [2] theorized that human needs stand in a hierarchy of importance, the lowest being the most pressing:

Physiological needs are geared to survival.

Safety and security needs are concerned with economic, physical, and mental well-being.

Social, or affiliation, needs appeal to man's social nature in that all normal people want to be liked, to be accepted, to belong.

Ego needs have to do with such desiderata as knowledge, independence, achievement, and self-confidence along with status, recognition, appreciation, and the respect of others.

Self-actualization needs refer to an inner urge to actualize one's potential—"What a man *can* be, he *must* be."

Certain guidelines for managerial behavior stem from this theory. Needs are driving forces. Opportunities for subordinates to satisfy their needs are the most effective motivational devices. On the other hand, a satisfied need is not a motivater; if a person is content with his salary, adding to it is not likely to have any lasting effect. However, appealing to higher-level needs when those at a lower level are unsatisfied is useless; this is the reason so many calls to company loyalty have had a less than atomic impact. As the needs at one level are reasonably well met, people strive to satisfy higher ones. The needs are not discrete but overlapping and interactive. Man is multimotivated, and his yearning for need satisfaction is insatiable. The lower-level needs are more demanding, but those farther up the hierarchy are more enduring and effective as motivaters.

Frederick Herzberg

Traditionally, according to Frederick Herzberg,[3] management has acted on the belief that merely removing the causes of job dissatisfaction and low morale will automatically result in improvement in these areas, and that motivation and demotivation are but opposite ends of the same continuum. This view is false, Herzberg maintains. In its place, he substitutes a two-dimensional model, since motivation and demotivation are distinct phenomena. The *hygiene* or *maintenance* factors appeal to man's avoidance mechanisms or tranquilize complaints and grievances. These maintainers make the job congenial and the person comfortable in his work. Largely environmental in nature, they include such elements as company policies and communications, security, fringe benefits, working conditions, supervision, and interpersonal relations. The *satisfiers* or *motivaters*, on the other hand, are geared to making the job challenging. They appeal to a person's drives for growth and development. They stimulate him to be a self-starter. Relevant to the employee's higher-level needs, they include such things as earned recognition, achievement, contribution, increased authority and responsibility, growth, advancement, and especially the job itself. Where the hygiene factors are largely extrinsic to the man doing the work and the job itself, the satisfiers concentrate on these two key variables.

Both sets of factors are necessary, but they serve different purposes. The causes of demotivation and job dissatisfaction must be removed by the prudent use of the hygiene factors. However, a person may seek and accept as much of this set as possible without being motivated to do a better job. It is primarily the satisfiers that give him incentive in his work. In fact, motivaters can often compensate for a lack of maintainers, but the reverse is rarely true. Finally, there are people who, for one reason or another, seek hygiene factors with little concern for the satisfiers. Most want a balanced diet of the two, with emphasis on the latter.

Chris Argyris

The thesis Chris Argyris[4] proposes is loud and clear—traditional organizational principles, structures, and procedures are incompatible with the mental health of employees. Such classical ideas as task specialization, chain of command, unity of direction, and tight budgets and controls, at least as they have been implemented in the past, are calculated to make subordinates passive and submissive, allowing them little direction of their work world. As a result, employees become apathetic, engage in self-protective defense mechanisms, or fight the system. Since organizations are willing to pay high wages to get adults to act in a less than mature manner, "It is not difficult to see why some students of organizations suggest that immature and even mentally retarded individuals would probably make excellent employees. . . ."

Warren G. Bennis

Seeking to avoid such polarizations as human relations versus scientific management and employee satisfactions versus organizational requirements, Bennis [5] sees the firm as an adaptive, problem-solving, innovative system operating in and coping with rapidly changing environments. Bureaucracy and the organization man are doomed. The day of democracy and the professional is at hand. Democracy entails full and free communication, regardless of position; reliance on consensus rather than coercion or compromise; influence based on competence rather than power; a climate that allows for the expression of emotions as well as task-oriented actions; and an acceptance of conflict, coupled with a willingness to deal with it on rational grounds.

Bennis sees the organization of the future as populated with knowledge workers who have a high level of education and expertise. Status, rank, and permanent roles will yield to temporary task forces and changing project groups. The manager will function as a coordinator or link pin. The major problem of the company will be to keep ahead or abreast of an ever-changing and turbulent pattern of environments. Its major challenges will be

Integration: synthesizing employee needs and management objectives.
Social influence: distributing authority and power effectively.
Collaboration: managing and resolving conflicts.
Adaptation: responding appropriately to changes induced by the environment.
Revitalization: dealing with problems of growth and decay.

Guiding Principles for the Manager-Leader

The executive who would engender in his people a will to work might give some thought to the implications of the following ideas.

1. Motivation does not mean doing things to or for people. The manager's task is to channel already existing drives toward an integration of organizational and individual satisfactions.

2. Motivation, like beauty, is in the eye of the beholder. Thus, one man's motivating meat may well be another's demotivating poison. The research findings may be generally true but individually ineffective, depending on many variables.

3. Each worker is very like all other employees in some ways,

like some others in some ways, and like no other in some ways. The manager looks for constants in the workforce but realizes that human differences are the rule, not the exception.

4. People are not elevators or Pavlovian dogs. They have no hot button that can be pressed to secure the desired results. A grocery list of satisfiers cannot be matched to a laundry list of needs.

5. The most realistic and effective motivater is the job itself. If the employee is convinced that his work not only makes a valued organizational contribution but also meets at least some of his important aspirations, then there will be less reliance on extrinsic carrots.

6. Workers want to satisfy a range of needs rather than satiate one or two. The executive should offer his people opportunities to experience a balanced diet of satisfactions rather than relying on those that would motivate him.

7. For real motivation of subordinates, changes in corporate structures and managerial attitudes are necessary. If the firm does not allow people to achieve and grow and if the manager's attitudes are negative, the best motivational efforts and techniques may be negated.

8. Motivation by imposition is as futile as management by imposition. Analysis must precede understanding, which must come before a choice of techniques. There is no need to dissect employees. It is necessary, however, to have some inkling of why they are working and what returns they expect from their jobs. No manager has the right to psychoanalyze his people. Not only is this an invasion of privacy, but amateur psychiatry is like amateur brain surgery—there are no survivors.

9. An experimental approach is a must. The executive should prudently test various techniques to discover which are most effective with each employee. If he adapts the authorities' dicta to his people rather than slavishly following them like a robot, he will soon discover which are the most practical within the ever present environmental constraints.

10. No manager-leader can sustain the motivation of his subordinates if he does not allow them to motivate him. The best way to influence their thinking and behavior is to be open to their influence.

11. All motivational efforts must be congruent with the execu-

tive's overall pattern of management. If he is ineffective as a manager, his motivational procedures will fail.

12. Finally, it is the *man* in the manager who exerts the greatest impact in motivating or demotivating. To motivate is to move people through influence. What the leader says or does is far less important than the kind of human being he is.

Implementing Motivational Principles

The manager-leader must have motivational strategies for dealing with each individual and group, superior, subordinate, or peer, even as he has planning strategies. A given approach may secure quite diverse reactions from different people; praise may stimulate one to put forth more effort but lull another into complacence. And different approaches may obtain the same results from different people; this man responds well to praise and that one to constructive criticism.

It would help greatly, as pointed out several times before, if executives would accept the fact that employees join and remain with a firm principally to satisfy their own needs, wants, and ambitions, even as the corporation thought of its own needs when it hired them. The real challenge of the manager-leader is to change a relationship that began on a basis of self-interest into one that produces mutual need satisfaction for both parties.

With this basic purpose in mind, the manager can begin to utilize the almost endless motivational methods that have been proposed. When possible, he can appeal to higher-level needs through delegation, participative management, and job enrichment. He can offer special assignments and projects. He can grant greater autonomy to those who prove that they can handle it intelligently and allow them freedom to use their own ideas. He can call on pride. He can give his people some say in how the work is done and some part in decision making. As the employee is expected to adjust to the requirements of the company, so the organization is well advised to accommodate itself to him, within the limits imposed by the demands for efficient operation. This is not soft or human relations management. It is prudent management, since it recognizes the fact that employees can offer increased productivity or withhold it any time they wish to.

In seeking to motivate, the manager-leader needs to come down to the linoleum level of practicality. There are a few people, as Leonard Sayles and George Strauss [6] contend, who find their work so engrossing that they satisfy most of their needs in, on, and through the job; with them, appeals to the higher-level needs are most effective. There are others who find much of their need satisfaction around the job; for them, an adequate salary, good fringe benefits, a considerate supervisor, a congenial work group, excellent working conditions, and humane company policies sum up what they seem to desire—a nice place to work, with a good boss and friendly people. Still others look upon their work as merely a necessary means for meeting their needs off the job. They want the money and other prerogatives from their employment so as to satisfy their wants outside the organization. It is as naive to think that every worker or even the majority in some situations will respond well to higher-level need motivation as it is to assume that people labor only for money.

Another piece of linoleum-level thinking concerns the use of substitute motivations. In many departments, it would be economically prohibitive to rearrange things so that greater emphasis is placed on ego needs. Often, too, the technology of production looms so large that there is little room for such incentives as job enrichment. More than a few jobs, though absolutely necessary, are dull. As long as these realities exist, the manager will have to make abundant use of incentives, even though he realizes that they will produce only transient improvement. The reverse of this coin concerns the people doing the work. Not everyone has a yearning to be creative or innovative; some are not eager for challenging jobs. Others might well find a greater degree of autonomy and participation in decision making rather unsettling; their dependent personalities need not freedom but structure and reassurance. The practicing manager must tailor his motivational techniques to each subordinate's needs.

Before he can learn what those needs are, however, he must earn the *right* to learn about them. They will not be revealed to him unless he first gains the respect and confidence of the employee. Moreover, needs are rarely revealed openly. Accord-

ingly, familiarity with theories of motivation is hardly sole sufficient. The manager must be sensitive to the signals and cues
that employees send forth in their daily behavior. Without this
awareness, he will be maladroit in fitting his motivational approaches to them. He must also develop his own style. Because
a technique is validated in the research or has worked well for
someone else, it does not follow that he will be either comfortable with it or adept in using it. Finally, the manager needs patience with himself as he works out his solutions to motivational
problems. The task requires people-thinking, not thing-thinking.
And people-thinking never provides quick, neat answers.

Problems of Job Satisfaction and Morale

Motivation, job satisfaction, and morale have this in common:
they are all more emotional than intellectual in nature. The only
logic that applies to them is the logic of the individual or group
affected. This is the major reason they are so difficult to understand or cope with. They are personal and subjective. In this
context, the psychological real takes precedence over the onto-
logical real.

Job Satisfaction

A person may be satisfied with his work even though the uninvolved observer sees little evidence of this; the converse, of
course, is equally true. Job satisfaction is the subordinate's *feeling* that he is securing from his whole work environment—the
job, superiors, the work group, the organization, and perhaps
even life in general—what he seeks from it and has a right
to obtain. The subjective element explains why different studies
yield somewhat different results and even studies of the same
groups at different times yield less than identical findings. The
saving grace is that people in a given company or type of work
who have similar class backgrounds, education, cultural values,
attitudes, interests, customs, and mores tend to seek from their
jobs many of the same benefits, though their order of priorities
may vary.

In one of the most thorough reviews ever made of the literature, Vroom concluded that the following determinants have some bearing on the job satisfaction of most employees: [7]

Determinant	Factors Involved
Supervision.	Satisfaction with the leadership.
	Consideration from superiors.
	Interaction with leaders.
	Employee-centered supervision.
	Participation in decision making.
	Ability to influence job conditions.
	Degree of autonomy.
	Amount of recognition.
Work group.	Attractiveness of the group.
	Ability to satisfy worker needs.
	Small and cohesive rather than large groups.
	Positive interaction among members.
	Acceptance and liking by the group.
	Interdependence of group and individual goals.
Job content.	Job level and status.
	Job enlargement, job enrichment, and job rotation.
	Control over work methods.
	Control over work pace.
	Use of skills and abilities.
	Success in work performance.
	Responsibility.
Wages.	Relative standing rather than the absolute wage level.
Promotion opportunities.	Fair competition for advancement; may have a negative effect on the fearful or unambitious.
Hours of work.	Shift work; may have negative consequences depending on use of leisure time, family reactions, and so forth.

It is not possible to spell out precisely how the manager can capitalize on these factors for three reasons. First, each worker develops his own subjective blueprint of the satisfaction mix that will meet his expectations. Second, organizational resources and requirements will dictate to a considerable extent the perimeters within which the leader must function. Finally, his own personality and views will bear strongly on just how much of each factor he can and should provide for his workforce. In the end analysis, job satisfaction is like happiness—both are personal quests. All the executive can do is help each subordinate attain a reasonable degree of satisfaction. Contrary to popular opinion, fewer than one in five workers are genuinely dissatisfied with their work, although all have their pet peeves. Be that as it may, job satisfaction will generally involve the following variables, modified by more general contingencies like the worker's age, sex, marital status, intelligence, personality, and career objectives:

Amount of skill necessary for success.
Variety of the work.
Degree of independence.
Ability to control either how the work is done or the work pace.
Degree of commitment to the work.
Prestige of the job—status.
Opportunities to achieve.
Amount of challenge.
Degree of responsibility.
Opportunities to use talents and judgment.
Rewards for success.
Amount of authority.

Morale

Morale, like motivation and job satisfaction, is an emotional rather than a rational phenomenon. Unlike them, it refers to a group reaction rather than an individual one. It is inappropriate to speak of an individual worker's morale, even though some authorities do so.

Long ago Daniel Katz concluded, on the basis of the early studies conducted by the Survey Research Center of the University of Michigan, that there are at least four crucial dimensions of morale: satisfaction with the job done, pride in the work group, satisfaction with wages received and promotional opportunities available in the company, and identification with the firm and its objectives. The permutations and combinations that are possible among these four factors should forewarn the manager-leader that high morale is not easily come by.[8] Rather it is the result of persistent effort to help subordinates develop a "we" spirit, to help them attain their personal objectives by achieving organizational goals, to engender among the workforce a sense of responsibility for the group's aims, to provide opportunities for each worker to contribute significantly to company objectives, and to enable them to see for themselves that the organization is improving and prospering.

There is a persistent myth that good morale is correlated with high productivity. This is not necessarily true. Almost any combination is possible: high morale and low production, high morale and high production, low morale and temporary high production, low morale and low production. The manager builds a work team which is convinced that the best way to attain group and individual goals is by contributing to the overall success of the organization. As has been emphasized, the group exerts tremendous influence on its members. If they are at odds with each other or collectively dislike the company or despise the work, then the manager has his task cut out for him. On the other hand, if they accept him and each other and find that the organization is fair, then he has a great human resource for building both high productivity *and* high morale. Far too little time and energy have been devoted to energizing the work group as a cohesive entity, which consists of much more than merely the sum of the individuals it comprises. Managers are only now beginning to learn how to function effectively with and through work groups.

cooperating
through communicating

An unbeatable combination in boxing is a deft left hook coupled with a stunning right cross. In managerial leadership, the winning combination is motivation that energizes subordinates and communication that influences them to put out the little bit extra that spells the difference between the ordinary and the superordinary. Coordination is an executive responsibility; it must be insured even though at times this may require firmness or even force from the manager. Cooperation, however, is a people proposition. There is some truth to the idea that a commanding general only makes a motion to advance in a battle; the motion is not really carried until each soldier and group cast an affirmative vote. The leader who is not getting through to his people with the impact he seeks soon discovers that they neither heed his communications nor try to keep him aware of the things he should and must know.

The technology of communication, from xerography to the picture phone, has improved dramatically. Techniques have been explained over and over. There are hundreds of books and thousands of articles and lectures on the subject. On the human side, the educational level of both managers and employees has been rising continuously. These facts, taken in isolation, might suggest that communication problems were near a reasonable solution. Only the naive would imagine that such is the case. Executives complain that managers do not level with them.

Managers, caught in the middle between the upper echelons and subordinates, feel at times not merely a communications gap but a vacuum. Employees, of course, gripe that they do not know what is going on, how the boss feels about them, or what their future is in the company, not to mention the universal cry that nobody listens to them. For all the advances in technology, technique, and education, few companies are happy with their communications network.

Communication: The Mechanical Process

The mechanics of the communication process are easily outlined.

— Two or more people or a person and a machine bear a relationship to each other that necessitates interaction.

— There is a *need, problem, or situation* requiring communication, and the interchange is mutually beneficial.

— The initiator of the communication has certain objectives that he seeks to attain through the process.

— A *message* is formulated that presumably embodies the intentions of the sender.

— A *channel* or combination of channels is selected for the transmission of the message.

— The message is *encoded* in appropriate language.

— It is *transmitted* and *received*.

— It is *decoded* by the recipient.

— It is *understood* with the same meaning that it originally had for the sender.

— The sender secures *feedback* to confirm receipt and understanding.

— The recipient *behaves* in line with the objectives of the sender.

If this is all there is to the communication process, one wonders why it has been estimated that we tend to retain 10 percent of what we read, 20 percent of what we hear, 30 percent of what we see, and 50 percent of what we see and hear. These discouraging estimates are supported by research findings. In one of his studies, Argyris found that 62 percent of the technicians and 61 percent of the engineers investigated knew how their superiors felt about their work "only indirectly"; another 35 and 22 percent respectively did not know.[1]

Communication: The Human Process

Managers are speaking, reading, writing, listening beings who spend 70 to 80 percent of their time in some form of communication. Mastery of techniques is essential. Yet overconcern for this aspect of the process can actually interfere with the human experience; public-speaking teachers, for example, are rarely well-known orators. What the manager-leader needs, therefore, is not a review of the mechanics of communication—these are already available—but an understanding of what takes place when a person attempts to communicate.

A Human Transaction

Communication is a form of influence. It is a human experience. It involves not a unilateral bludgeoning, with one person active and the other passive, but rather a relationship in which both parties play distinct but complementary roles. Certain principles follow from this.

Sender and receiver hear and see subjectively and selectively. Communication is really a sorting process on the part of both originator and recipient. The essential, important, and incidental are determined not by logic alone but rather by a curious mix of cognitive and emotional factors. It is common knowledge that people tend to magnify what is pleasing and to block out what is unpleasant. The communicator must try to determine in advance just what is likely to be magnified beyond the limits of his intentions and what will be glossed over or ignored.

A way of seeing and hearing is at the same time a way of NOT seeing and hearing. This applies with equal weight to sender and receiver. The two tendencies in combination inevitably produce tunnel vision for both parties. The leader focuses on what is significant to him but realizes that his job is to communicate it in such a way that it will have the same valence for the recipient.

Premises and assumptions underlie all communication. Failure to check the premises and assumptions that a communication rests on is a fruitful source of misunderstanding. The hidden presuppositions can involve the goodwill of the recipient, his vocabulary level, and a host of other factors. It is at times necessary to make certain assumptions, but they should be reasonable and rational.

All communication reflects attitudes. Attitudes are treacherous for several reasons. They are often unconscious. They govern our perceptions of reality. They serve to enhance or protect our self-concepts. If the communicator fails to take into account the attitudes and sentiments he and the receiver have toward each other, then it is predictable that any attempt to communicate will result in more heat than light, more static than clarity.

Communication is an experience-based phenomenon. An ethnic or religious joke may be considered humorous when told by a dear friend but intolerably offensive if related by an enemy or stranger. Accordingly, the prudent communicator reviews his relationship and past experience with the other party.

Communication is a function of the receiver's expectations. The toastmaster and speakers at a Friars Club "roasting" belittle the honored guest. Since insults are part of the tribal ritual, he accepts them in good spirit. The climate is expected to be comically abusive, even though the occasion is a form of earned recognition and affection. In like manner, every individual has certain preconceptions concerning what should be communicated to him and how. One is not offhand with the company president. As far as possible, the manager must be mindful of the expectations of the other person.

An Intellectual Transaction

One of the major purposes of communication is the transmission of information. This may involve the dissemination of ideas or data. It may take the form of face-to-face conversations, reports, memos, or directives. In any event, the goal is understanding. William Haney has offered some excellent comments on communication and suggestions for increasing the clarity of comprehension.[2]

Observation and judgment are related but distinct processes. Because an engineer is sitting with his eyes closed and his feet on the desk, it does not necessarily follow that he is goofing off. He may very well be deep in thought. It is a natural tendency to leap from what we perceive to a judgment of the phenomenon. The manager observes carefully. He then extracts meaning from the observed data, drawing his conclusions from this meaning.

He who discriminates well communicates well. One characteristic of intelligent people is that they perceive differences where duller folk see only similarities, and they are aware of similarities when their opposite numbers see only differences. The golden rule, as we saw, is a classic example of oversimplification. The fact is that, because of individual differences, treating others as we would like to be treated may be the very worst way to communicate. Consideration may be interpreted as weakness if the manager is a gentleman who must relate to thick-skinned employees. On the other hand, the rough-and-ready leader who is naturally aggressive may sandpaper the sensibilities of subordinates if they have a concern for politeness.

Either-or thinking can muddy communication. Communication is simplified if we treat objective data or people as black or white. Unfortunately, this often introduces needless noise into the relationship. Haney advises that the communicator be on guard against confusing contradictories with contraries. A contradictory allows for no middle position; one either is a college graduate or is not. A contrary, on the other hand, allows for a middle ground; one may be of medium height, being neither tall nor short. Failure to consider many alternatives, a win-lose attitude when disagreements arise, and an itch to force people and ideas into mutually exclusive categories all play hob with clear communication.

Words are uncertain vehicles for the transmission of ideas. Words take their meaning from a variety of sources other than their dictionary definition. If this were not true, then *democracy* would have the same denotation for the Russian as for the Englishman. The unwary manager assumes that a superior, peer, or subordinate will attach to a given word the same meaning it has for him. It is far wiser, as Haney suggests, to think of words as empty cups. What is important is not the content the communicator puts into the cups but the meaning the receiver is likely to take out of them. Over and beyond this, words are not only signs pointing to intellectual meaning; they can at times serve as symbols heavy with emotional undertones. The use of nerve-pinching terms stimulates a person to tune out the communicator.

Messages should be organized according to the logic of the recipient. Abstractions have an attraction for scientists and philosophers; they can leave the ordinary person cold. When the manager-leader is overly intent on his objectives, when he organizes the message according to his mental set or habit rather than with forethought, when he uses a logic that is merely self-convincing, he risks failing abysmally in his efforts to transmit ideas to others. After all, the receivers are interested primarily not in his objectives but in their own. The only communications they will react well to are those that they find natural and comfortable. If the communicator does not form what he has to say or write along the wavelengths of the recipients, then they will either block out the message or distort it.

The executive should be on guard against allness. Allness exists when the sender assumes that his communication contains all that can be said or written on the topic at hand, or takes it for granted that what he communicates is important and what he omits is unimportant. This error is quite common. Too often management communicates material that it considers significant without giving much thought to the needs and wants of employees.

Agreement must be genuine, not merely apparent. Perhaps the most useless question a manager can ask a subordinate is, "Do you understand?" Obviously, the latter understands whatever is in his head; he may not comprehend the message in the manner that the sender intended. This problem can easily occur in matters of delegation of authority, discipline, coaching, counseling, and performance reviews. Unless the degree of understanding is tested, hard feelings can arise when the subordinate acts in goodwill on the basis of *his* understanding only to have the superior rebuke him on the basis of *his*. Whether the agreement is partial or complete can be readily checked if the leader will ask, "Would you please express in any way you wish just what you think I want you to do?"

A Psychological Transaction

Communication is any form of interaction—words, written materials, facial expressions, body language, silence, and so on

—that conveys meaning, feelings, and attitudes between the parties involved. Organizing a message logically is not overly difficult; organizing it so as to get the impact one desires is never easy.

If possible, the communication should contain something of value to the other party. All people are self-centered; few are selfish. The self-centered person places himself high in the order of his priorities, whereas the selfish individual has no priorities —he pins his attention on himself. Whether the communicator likes it or not, the receiver has two questions: what's in the communication for himself and how it will affect him. It is absurd to expect subordinates to be interested in what higher management has to say simply because the latter wishes to communicate. No relationship can long endure if it satisfies the needs of but one party. An employee more readily accepts changes in procedures if their real or potential advantages are pointed out to him. He executes orders more effectively if the reasons for them are explained. He finds discipline less distasteful if he not only knows why he is being chewed out but also is aware of the benefits that can accrue to him if he alters his behavior.

Whatever is received is received according to the mode of being of the receiver. This seemingly abstract formulation from Saint Thomas Aquinas contains many practical hints for the manager. It implies that he must know not only his objectives but what the receiver is likely to do with them after the message disappears behind his eyes or ears, when it will no longer be controllable by the originator. The hearer or reader must re-create the message that he receives. Unless the communicator takes pains to make sure that the recomposed message is the same as the original, the recipient will take the easy way out and re-create it in his own image and likeness. This tendency is a bountiful source of misunderstandings and affronts. Many people are annoyed at Marshall McLuhan because he seems to go out of his way to raise the level of his fog index; he does little to facilitate understanding. Abstruse terms, technical jargon, far-out analogies, foreign phrases, and pretentious language all violate this principle. So, too, do so-called buzz words, particularly the negative kind that arouse hostile feelings instead of contributing to clear comprehension.

In communication, manner is usually more important than meaning. When a communication results in alienation rather than understanding and cooperation, it often is because of the tone of the message rather than its content. The intentions of the communicator are secondary. What the receiver hears or reads and how he reacts to it are primary. To the originator, an order may seem reasonable, but his tone of voice may prompt subordinates to react as though it were an imperious command. It is particularly necessary for the executive to be wary of his manner whenever he is required to communicate something that he knows his people will find disagreeable.

An Environmental Transaction

Technological advances have caused many problems in communication precisely because the transmission machinery is so widespread. The ease with which material can be duplicated results in mountains of messages. Often a manager simply ignores much of the written matter that flows into his office. Needless paperwork, reports on which no action is taken, memos that do not inform, and directives that are not obeyed produce a peculiar form of organizational hardening of the arteries. It is as valuable for the leader to know when *not* to communicate as when to do so and how.

Selecting the right channel is important. Some managers suffer from meetingitis. Trivial matters may be discussed, or meetings may be held ritualistically even though they do not yield an adequate return on invested time and energy. It is wise to use a meeting as a last resort, when the message can be disseminated with equal effectiveness in no other way. A conference of eight people that lasts for two hours consumes at least two man-days of time. Although meetings obviously have their place, they tend to be like executive luncheons; far too much time is wasted for the results accomplished. Be this as it may, for one situation, an eyeball-to-eyeball conversation may be best; at other times, an all-hands memo; in a third case, a short and well-planned meeting. Whatever channel is utilized, it should be selected with a view to producing the results that the manager desires.

It is dangerous to overload a given channel. When one medium of communication is used to the neglect of others available, people have a way of resolving their own difficulties. They filter out the messages that they consider unimportant, assign their own priorities of attention, and resort to formalistic responses that are organizationally acceptable but do not attain the objectives of the communicator. At best, channel overload delays action, piles up messages, and dulls subordinates' attention.

The structure of the group must be conducive to the free flow of communication. Experiments have shown that the way a group is structured can have telling effects on the communication process. In a star arrangement, people can talk only to the leader, who can communicate with all the group members. In a circular structure, a person can communicate only with the two people on his right and left. In a free-flowing structure, any individual can communicate with any other. The results are interesting. The star arrangement is most orderly, efficient, and rapid as far as problem-solving activities are concerned. The circular is the slowest and least effective. The free-flowing setup is not so efficient as the star, but the members are more enthusiastic and enjoy the experience more. In addition, they are more innovative and resolve complex problems involving value judgments more quickly. Thus, regimentation may give good short-term results but prevent subordinates from deriving satisfaction from the communication process. On the other hand, too permissive an arrangement may be satisfying but very short on practical results.

The picture is not the reality. Rudolf Flesch has observed that writing is like an iceberg; one-ninth you see, eight-ninths you do not. The part that gets on paper is very small compared with the part that goes on in your head. The same, of course, is true of the receiver of the message. Over and beyond this, when the sender formulates the communication, he makes a selective word map of some idea or feeling that he has. This he sends forth in the form of a message. The receiver must now build his picture of the same reality, using the denotations and connotations of the message as his instruments. Both parties, as Alfred Korzybski warns, are dealing not with the reality itself but with two maps of it. Einstein once compared an attempt to understand reality with a man trying to understand the mechanism of a closed watch that he cannot open. He can see its face and hands, hear its ticking, and so on. From all this he can form a picture of the mechanism, but he will never be certain that his picture is an exact replica of the article itself. Communication is thus the exchange of different pictures of the same reality. The communicator must see to it that the recipient's picture is as congruent as possible with his own.

Communication is organizationally determined. The sources of environmental interference in the communication process are manifold. The authority and power structures can greatly hamper the flow of interchanges; following the chain of command may be sound in principle, but it can produce bothersome delays. There are accepted ways of communicating within a given firm or department. Customs and mores already exist. Precedents have been set. There are established ways of communicating with which superiors, peers, and subordinates feel at ease. Naturally, to violate these givens is to risk damaging the impact of one's message.

Organizational pressures can wreak havoc with communication. As organizations become integrated systems in which a given unit may affect any or all other units, as management must concentrate increasingly on building cohesive work groups and coordinating their efforts, the amount of interaction grows geometrically. Knowledge is doubling about every decade. Communication is difficult because of the sheer volume of what comes to the executive's attention daily. As one company president commented, "Every once in a while, I get so frustrated I throw all the damn papers behind me so I can get some work done." The tempo in most firms has also increased. Pressures not only mount but tend to come from a wider spectrum of sources. Increased specialization adds its own exotic confusion. Marketing, engineering, production, industrial relations, accounting, and finance all have their technical jargon. Unless the communication patterns and procedures are well planned, many managers will slowly slip further and further behind. It is said that Napoleon, as an experiment, once did not read a single communication for two weeks. When he did read them, he found that he had missed little or nothing at all. Many executives, in desperation, are tempted to imitate his example. Overcommunication can be just as deadening as overmanagement can.

What Can the Manager-Leader Do About All This?

It has been said that the typical manager does not need a plethora of techniques and procedures; there are probably more already at hand than he can use at any given time. What he requires are basic principles, for two simple reasons: (1) principles govern the implementation of techniques; (2) techniques make for rigidity, whereas principles make for flexibility. The following ideas may help the leader grasp what happens when one person communicates with another.

Communication is a relationship in which the sender controls only half of the transaction; the receiver probably controls the more important half. It is a form of interaction to which the recipient possibly brings as much as or more than the communicator.

Four images are crucial to the communication process. The first is the *self-image* of the sender, and the second is the *other-image* that he has of the receiver. These two images must be as accurate as possible. If the communicator is truly an expert, his messages will reflect this; if not, he must adjust to this reality. If he erroneously perceives the receiver as an unimportant person, it is predictable that his communication will take on a condescending tone. The second two images are accepted as psychological givens. A superior who fancies himself a financial expert must be dealt with on the basis of this *self-concept*, at least initially, even though his expertise may be quite limited. To affront this self-concept is to make communication impossible. Finally, the sender must be aware of the *image that the receiver has of him*. If the latter thinks well of him, then he can communicate rather openly. If, correctly or incorrectly, the other person has little respect for him or his ability, then the communication must be tailored to these reactions. Far too many managers communicate from the base of their title, position, and status rather than from the quality of the relationship that exists between them and their employees.

If the sender will note, before he tries to transmit a message, how close in sound the word *communication* is to the words *common, community,* and *communion,* he will prevent much misunderstanding. What he and the receiver have in common automatically both defines the areas of possible communication and sets up the limits within which it must take place. Where they have little in common, there can be little communication. Community refers to shared objectives, values, interests, and attitudes. Where there is no sense of community, attempts to interact are futile. This is as true of relationships between manager and subordinates as it is between management and labor, or mainland China and the United States. This is why it is sad to see some puerile supervisors seeking to increase the psychological and sociological distance between themselves and their key subordinates when they should be endeavoring to do just the opposite. Communion means to commune. When one communes he seeks to be as candid and authentic as the situation requires. He shows the other individual the courtesy of listening to what he has to say, even though he may disagree or find it somewhat distasteful.

It is well for the communicator to recall that the receiver exists as the center of his own world of psychological experience. The *real* for him is the reality he experiences, not what he is told. Hence the best way to get through to anyone is first to adopt his frame of reference and to be mindful of his viewpoint. This implies far more than merely putting one's self in the other fellow's shoes. It is more like getting into his skin, thinking his thoughts, feeling his feelings. Thinking and feeling *for* and *about* the receiver is one thing. Thinking and feeling *with* him is a far more difficult task.

Before trying to communicate with anyone, the manager would be well advised to "get behind him" imaginatively and try to see the world as it appears in the eyes of the receiver, to hear the world as it sounds in his ears. One may disagree with what he sees and hears through this process. But this is irrelevant—the purpose of getting out of one's self is understanding, not necessarily agreement. In fact, where disagreement exists, the manager may be able to master the all-too-absent art of disagreeing agreeably! With some insight into how the recipient of the message views reality and their relationship, the communicator can now fashion his communication to get the impact he seeks.

It is important for the communicator to realize that the very organs that he is limited to—tongue, gestures, fingers, and so on—are precisely the organs that are useless to the receiver, who can use only his eyes and ears. If the sender does not, in a sense, *reverse the organ language,* he will never be very effective. An analogy that makes sense to him may be lost on the receiver; a vocabulary level with which he feels comfortable may be above or below that of the recipient; evidence or statistics that are particularly clear to him may be a mystery to the other person. He must constantly ask himself, "How will it appear in the eyes and ears of the receiver?"

Before any communication takes place, the sender might review six key questions. Three apply to him: (1) What do I *intend* to say or write? (2) What will I *actually* say or write, sometimes in spite of my good intentions? (3) What will I really *mean,* what will be the *emotional impact* of what I say or write? The other three questions apply to the receiver: (1) What does he *expect* to hear or read? (2) What will he *actually* read or hear, at times despite what is said or written? (3) How will he *feel* about what he reads or hears?

The manager-leader must bear in mind that his purpose is not to impress but to communicate, not to carry on a semantic handball game but to get through to the other person or group. Accordingly, his task is threefold: (1) to translate what is significant to him so that it will be *acceptable* to the receiver; if it is not acceptable, the message will be rejected; (2) to translate what is important to him so that it is *meaningful* to the receiver, on his terms rather than those of the sender; (3) to translate what is significant to the sender into terms that will have the *impact* he seeks on the receiver. If these three conditions are not met, then the communication will at best be limited, at worst nil.

Regardless of the authority or status of the communicator, it is essential that he take for granted that, in the process of communicating, he is more the *servant* than the *master* of his people. He may dictate the goals, but the receiver dictates the manner of communication to which he will respond positively. This is a very difficult truth for most executives to accept emotionally.

The Art of Listening

The communications coin has two sides—sending and receiving. There is an old saying that any leader might well take to heart: if God wanted men to talk twice as much as they listen, he would have given them two mouths and one ear. Listening is difficult because it allows the speaker to take the lead in a joint relationship. Small wonder that most people engage in *marginal* listening, which involves little more than sporadically attentive hearing.[3] Another pitfall is *evaluative* listening—listening with the fists cocked, listening in order to disagree with, rebut, or shoot down the communicator. If the leader wishes to listen in a *projective* manner and put himself in the frame of reference of the speaker, the following suggestions may be of some assistance.

Pay complete attention. The average hearing speed is four to six times speaking speed. Distraction and woolgathering are ever present dangers. If the listener allows himself to be sidetracked by selected buzz words or does not give his whole attention to the speaker, then he will lose a great deal of the message. But there is more to listening than mental attentiveness. One listens with his whole being. Facial expressions, gestures, and postures all play a part in the process. No one is going to talk for long to an unresponsive stony face. A smile, an uh-huh, or even an mmh reassures the other party that the manager is still with him.

Listen for the real message. The listening process is like the X-ray process. As the latter cuts through muscle, tissue, and so on to get to the site it is aimed at, so the listener X-rays through the words and the silences to come to grips with the true message. Is the communication basically intellectual or emotional? Do I listen for meaning, or am I attracted and distracted by the words that convey the meaning? Do I search for the connotation of the gestures and other elements of the transmission, or am I content to deal with the denotation of the words only? These are excellent questions for the manager to ask himself.

Listen for what is not said. At times, the message is contained in the pauses, the silences, the omissions. Although the manager is not expected to search for arcane meanings, reading between the lines is an essential skill.

Listen encouragingly. It is difficult at times to hold one's tongue. It takes self-discipline to let a person have his say without undue interruption. One aspect of this practice involves the charity of silence. The manager should let some statements go by, rejecting the temptation to pour vinegar into an open wound, prove that the person is wrong, or make him feel inferior or inadequate.

Listen prudently. It is not necessary for the manager to listen to everything that a person may want to say. In fact, at times he may have to prevent someone from baring his chest unduly. A person under pressure naturally tends to unburden himself when he feels that he has a sympathetic shoulder and an empathic ear available to him. The manager can protect both himself and the speaker by asking himself the following questions: (1) Is the matter job-related? (2) Is it within my authority and responsibility? (3) Is it within my competence to handle effectively? If not, then a supportive referral should be made to other sources in or outside the firm that can cope with the difficulty.

Listen to learn. The interchange should be a learning experience for both parties. The skillful listener can learn a great deal about the speaker; after all, every time a person opens his mouth, he reveals himself to the shrewd observer. The listener can also learn something about himself by catching himself in his behavior, as Horney recommended—noting his own reactions to attack, criticism, praise, flattery, and so on. Finally, he can learn a great deal about the relationship between himself and the speaker from how frank they are with one another, whether and to what extent either party feels a need to be defensive, and what the sensitive areas are that one or the other tends to avoid and why.

The Art of Asking Questions

Helping the Speaker Continue

Any speaker needs two sorts of reaction: stimuli to keep him talking and cues that assure him he is getting across to the listener.

The first sort of intervention might consist of *nondirective questions*, ones that cannot be answered with a simple yes or no but rather require reasonably complete statements. These questions can take any of the following forms, depending on the circumstances: "Do you care to go into the matter further?" "Would you like to talk about it a bit?" "What happened then?" "How did you feel when this took place?" "What did you think of the course of action that was adopted?" "How did you react to this?" Questions of this type prime the speaker's vocal cords.

As for cues that the speaker is being understood, the manager can *rephrase the content* of what has been said in some way: "It appears that you considered the change inappropriate because it would create confusion for your work group and hinder their efficiency. Is that it?" or "You were sure of your position, but you couldn't convince the boss. Is that what you're saying?" At other times, it is important to *recognize the feelings* that have been ventilated. This, too, can be done by asking questions, often in statement form, that recap the sentiments expressed or implied: "You must have felt that you had been treated rather shabbily," or "You feel that you work very hard but your efforts are not appreciated—am I right?" Finally, the manager can also *confirm agreement with guiding questions*. For instance, when he and his vis-à-vis seem to concur on a given point, he might ask, "Then do we both feel that this is the right thing to do?" The hope here is to consolidate the progress made while laying the groundwork for further agreement.

Fitting the Question to the Quest

Apart from the types of question already considered, the manager-leader needs to use a variety of other approaches. Many executives use the same pattern of inquiry over and over, regardless of the situation; many habitually limit the scope of their queries. To counteract these practices, the manager-leader might consider how adroitly he questions groups and individuals for the following purposes.

To check understanding: *"Your contention is that we are overmanned in certain departments but undermanned in others, with a resulting imbalance in the workloads. Is that it?"*

To establish reasons: *"I realize that it's been customary to handle problems of this sort in the way you've described. But I wonder, why have we dealt with them like this?"*

To obtain reactions: *"This is how we tentatively plan to go about making the transition. What do you think of it?"*

To obtain suggestions: *"I think that this plan is basically sound, but I also realize it probably has flaws in it that I'm not aware of. Have you any suggestions for making it more foolproof?"*

To act as a devil's advocate: *"This looks fine on paper. But what unanticipated difficulties are we likely to get into if we establish a zero defects program in one department but not in the others?"*

To draw on past experience: *"This is a new one for us. On the other hand, we've been in this business for a long time. Have we ever run into something similar in the past? What can we draw on from our past experience to help us attack this situation?"*

To discover the source: *"We all know that it's company policy to promote on the basis of merit. How did this rumor get started that minority-group people couldn't make supervisor?"*

To focus attention: *"We've been talking about several problems. In fact, at times we've bounced back and forth from one to the other. Now, which do you feel is the core problem we should start with?"*

To obtain feedback: *"We've been following this procedure for some time. What exactly have been the benefits and disadvantages from your viewpoint as a department head?"*

To stimulate reflective thinking: *"We've considered a great number of things. But is there a danger that we may have been examining symptoms rather than causes? What do you feel are the root reasons for the things we've been discussing?"*

To emphasize ethical considerations: *"I realize that what has been proposed would be efficient. But in the long run, would it be fair to everybody concerned?"*

To secure opinions: *"As you know, it has been proposed to merge department X with department Y. What is your view of this proposal?"*

To arouse provocative discussion: *"Do you think that a job enrichment program would do anything for the kind of people who work with us?"*

To ascertain intensity of feeling: *"I realize that you're in favor of this change. But how important is it to you?"*

To determine reluctance or eagerness to move ahead: *"There seems to be general agreement on the merits of the proposal. Should we start as soon as possible or think it over for a while before committing ourselves to action?"*

To test for consensus: *"We've looked at this from many angles. Does everybody feel that this is the way we should go, or are there some who have doubts about it?"*

To prevent too quick agreement: *"We've all agreed about what should be done. But we seem to have agreed so quickly that I wonder whether we've thought this thing through. Would it be wise for all of us to mull it over for another week and then take it up again?"*

To obtain evaluations: *"Where do you feel that you've done a superior job? Where might you have fallen down on the job?"*

To follow up: *"Last time we agreed that you would spend at least 15 percent of your time training your salesmen. How has it worked out?"*

To explore resources: *"Now we know what we want to do. But what personnel resources do we have to do it effectively?"*

Making the Meeting Productive

In group meetings, there are four specific types of questions that can be used to keep the group moving toward the intended objectives, to control it, and to draw out its best thinking.

The overhead question. The overhead question is used to get the discussion started. It is thrown out to the participants in the hope that some of the more talkative will catch the ball and run with it. It can also be a means of getting someone to summarize what has been accomplished up to a given point. Examples of this sort of question are "I've explained the problem that confronts us, gentlemen. Does anyone have any suggestions for how we should go about coping with it?" and "We seem to have covered quite a bit of ground. Would anyone care to summarize what we've agreed upon?"

The rhetorical question. A rhetorical question requires no answer. It is used to arouse interest, to focus attention, or to impel the group to think more deeply. Here are some examples: "The company has been enjoying prosperity up to now. I wonder, though—what adjustments might we have to make if we lost two-thirds of our government contracts?" "Consultative management seems to be a sound idea. But where would we draw the line on employees' participating in decision making? Is there such a thing as partial democracy? Or will they want to intrude in areas that management considers its prerogative?"

The returned question. The manager-leader may return a

question for one asked when he wishes to help the questioner find the answer himself rather than provide him with a neatly wrapped solution. It might go somewhat like this: "Tom, you've brought up an interesting problem. On the other hand, you are nearer than anybody else to it and have lived with it longer than anyone here. On the basis of your experience, what do you think might be the best way of handling it?"

The redirected question. When it is clear that the questioner is not capable of providing his own answer, the manager can relay it to the group as a whole in some such manner as the following: "Jack has brought up a vital question. Can anyone help him out?" Another method is to redirect the question to a group member who is competent to reply, for example: "Jack has brought up a vital question. Tom, didn't you run into this when you were general foreman? How did you handle it then?"

The variety of questions that the manager-leader has in his armory is not of primary importance. The essential thing is that he master the art of asking the right question of the right person at the right time and in the right way. His real purpose is not merely to secure the desired information but additionally to help others learn and to build a more cooperative relationship with them.

chapter eleven

developing subordinates

No amount of leadership strength can replace the need for the manager to develop his key people. As has been said, great leaders at times leave weak organizations; great managers never do. The aim of subordinate development is to give people a sense of purpose in working with, rather than merely for, the manager. Although any interested superior can do many things to help his people grow, four areas are critical. He must work out with them the objectives for which they will be held responsible; this requires the setting of achievement targets. He must provide them with reasonable assistance in attaining these goals through coaching and counseling, and he must insure them sufficient freedom to achieve, which involves delegation. And he must hold them accountable for the results of their efforts, which is the function of performance and development reviews.

Setting Achievement Targets

More time, thought, and effort has been devoted to the refinement of concepts and techniques of setting standards of performance or achievement targets by The Presidents Association (an affiliate of the American Management Association) than by any other organization in the world. The writer happily acknowledges his gratitude to the members of this organization.[1]

As President Woodrow Wilson said of a different subject, achievement targets should be "open covenants, openly arrived at." They are a part of work planning that establishes the ground rules by which the efforts of the supervisor or manager and his immediate superior are coordinated. Setting performance standards can benefit all concerned. It fosters the attainment of relevant organizational objectives. At the same time, it assures the subordinate that the firm can be a suitable vehicle for his career plans since it intends to reward achievement.

There is considerable confusion regarding the term *performance standards*. Defining it briefly may provide a small ray of light. The typical manager or supervisor has two related responsibilities. One concerns the work of the unit for which he is accountable. The organization requires certain group outputs, and he has the task of seeing that they are forthcoming. While he is accountable for the results produced by his people, he is not expected to achieve them personally. They are a function of his skill in working with and through his subordinates, and they constitute *group achievement targets*. Thus, a manager might be responsible for increasing sales in his district by 8 percent in a six-month period. Performance standards are *personal achievement targets*. They are set in the work-planning process that goes on between a manager and his boss. The aim is to obtain certain outputs from the manager. Group outputs are derived from the role that a given department or section plays in the total organization. Performance standards build on a man's position description. They are an achievement contract spelling out the conditions that will prevail when the subordinate does his job well. The present discussion is limited to standards so defined.

Effective achievement targets embody the following characteristics:

— They are the result of negotiation between superior and subordinate as to what constitutes a job well done.
— Whenever possible, they are quantified and measurable. Qualitative terms should be used only as a last resort.
— Vague terms such as "normally," "sometimes," and "few" are avoided since they are readily misinterpreted.
— They are fair to the subordinate in that they are restricted to factors over which he has control and fair to the organization in that they are directed to acceptable rather than mediocre performance.
— They are either positive ("Devote 20 percent of meeting time to

the development of the sales force") or negative ("Turnover is to be less than 5 percent").
— They are attainable and yet stimulate the subordinate's best efforts.
— They are geared to the job to be done, not the personality of the doer.
— They reflect a rational order of priorities.
— They cover a definite time period, after which they will be reviewed and revised.

Benefits for the Subordinate

Every sport has a twofold definition: the kind of game and its perimeters are signaled by nets, goal posts, bases, and so on, and the criteria of acceptable output are known to those responsible for it. Both the pitcher with a 20 and 3 record and the one whose record is 4 and 10 know just where they stand. Thus, standards not only give a supervisor a sense of direction but also enable him to invest his energy purposefully. They assure him that he will be evaluated on the basis of his performance rather than such irrelevancies as politics, favoritism, seniority, and so on. Even the president's son must meet preestablished norms. More importantly, standards make it possible for the supervisor to experience these eight selfs:

Self-commitment. Since the manager or supervisor has participated in setting the standards, he is likely to accept them and strive to measure up to them.

Self-planning. Knowing the specific results for which he will be held accountable, he can now plan how best to attain them.

Self-motivation. If the standards are realistic, he is challenged to achieve them.

Self-supervision. Since the goals are clear, the burden of supervision is shifted from his superior to himself.

Self-discipline. Like a conscientious athlete, he will tend to discipline himself rather than wait until his boss checks up on him.

Self-management. Standards, in a sense, are a vote of confidence on the part of the superior. The supervisor thus has the freedom to manage his own resources so as to attain his goals.

Self-development. Since standards represent acceptable rather than mediocre performance he is challenged to stretch to achieve them.

Self-reward. Fulfilling his part of the achievement contract enables him to enjoy the satisfaction that comes from increased competence.

The eight selfs do not imply that the superior abdicates his responsibility for the performance of his subordinate. The question here is one of priorities. The superior intrudes only when the subordinate fails or is incapable of surmounting an obstacle. One aspect of joint standard setting that has at times been overlooked is that it allows the superior to cope with the differences in his key people while safeguarding the legitimate concerns of the organization.

Benefits for the Organization

Consensus on the results to be produced lessens the need to fly by the seat of one's pants and reduces the amount of fire fighting. If each person achieves, then corporate goals will be attained. Standards prevent a situation best described by an executive when he said, "We are paying full salaries to too many people who have already left us but who are still on board." Moreover, promotables can be identified early and manpower planning can be simplified. Failure to reach the targets set provides a basis for coaching and counseling. Analysis of the reasons for the failure may help the person improve or lead to his transfer to another area in the firm where success is possible. At times, it may be to his advantage as well as the organization's to terminate him. Most managers are understandably reluctant to let a key subordinate go. When the evidence is clear that a worker cannot or will not cut the mustard, to do anything else is unfair to the firm and to him. The employer has no plans for the incompetent; the employee becomes more frustrated the longer he lives with failure.

Establishing Achievement Targets

Two presidents attended an executive development program. Each became a true believer in performance standards. One, upon his return home, sequestered himself in his office for several days and wrote up achievement targets for his vice-presidents. When he completed this chore, he broke the news to them. After six months had passed and nothing had happened, he was surprised and annoyed. The other president wrote up his own standards and then discussed them with his top management team, securing their reactions and suggestions. Then, one by one, each vice-president went through the same process.

This account illustrates how and how *not* to go about formulating achievement targets. The best way, as stated earlier, is for the subordinate to draw up the conditions that will prevail when each aspect of his overall job is well done, using his position description as a starting point. Most jobs can be broken down into three to five major components. Perhaps three or four aims for each component will be more than sufficient, especially if the subordinate focuses on make-or-break elements. It is often advisable for him to give each component a weight indicating its relative importance. When he has done his homework, he can get together with his superior. They then work out realistic and fair criteria of success.

It is not possible in a brief space to describe fully the mechanics of establishing standards of performance according to a management by objectives philosophy. Anyone who is interested can attend the Management Course at AMA or one of the programs offered by The Presidents Association. The key ideas are these: (1) a make-or-break aspect of the job is selected; (2) an activity—action verb—is described; (3) the objective to be attained by this activity is specified; and (4) the criterion of success is defined as precisely as possible. For instance, one element of a salesman's job may be new business development. Thus his *activity* will be to make at least five calls each week on potential customers. The *purpose* of this activity is to generate new business and increase sales. The *criterion* is that his work will be up to standard when at least one of these "cold" calls results in a sale.

Cautions

Three major dangers must be averted when achievement targets are being set. There is a temptation for the superior subtly to impose his views on the subordinate; any form of imposition triggers the subordinate's rejection mechanisms. The subordinate may be inclined to bite off too much the first time around; agreement on a few productive standards is better than energy-wasting attempts to produce comprehensive lists. Or he may be carried away by idealism; setting the standards defeatingly high brings on frustration. In addition, the superior and subordinate must be willing to invest the thought, time, and effort required for the review and revision of standards over a period of time. If they cannot do this, it might be wiser not to start the process at all.

Coaching

The aim of coaching is to help the employee become a more proficient worker. Since it is a form of teaching, it must follow known principles of learning. Some of these are illustrated in the following brief adaptation of an actual interview.

MANAGER: Tom, you said you wanted to see me. What's up?

TOM: Dick, I need an assistant.

MANAGER: You need an assistant?

TOM: Yes. The workload is too much. I just don't have enough time to get through it, even if I come in early, stay late, and take work home some weekends.

MANAGER: Tom, if you really need an assistant, we'll get you one. But I wonder if this is the basic problem.

TOM: What do you mean?

MANAGER: Well, there are four of you fellows who report to me, right? Each has about the same workload, though it varies from time to time. Yet you are the only one who's asking for an assistant. Could you help me understand this?

TOM: I can't speak for the other fellows. All I know is that I need an assistant. I don't have enough time, that's the trouble.

MANAGER: I realize that you work hard. But do you work *smart?* Is it a question of not having enough time or of not making the best use of the time that you do have?

TOM: You've lost me.

MANAGER: Well, maybe it's a question of organizing your work and time so as to get the best possible results.

Tom: I *am* organized.

Manager: Are you getting the results you'd like to get?

Tom: I'd like to get better results. That's why I need an assistant.

Manager: As I said, you'll get one if you need one. But if this isn't the real problem, getting an assistant won't solve things, will it? Could it be that you're trying to do too much personally? That you haven't thought through your priorities?

Tom: What do you mean?

Manager: How did you describe what a supervisor does in the supervisor improvement program you attended?

Tom: The supervisor is someone who gets desired results with and through his subordinates.

Manager: And how do you determine which jobs are *yours* and which are your *people's*?

Tom: Well, I handle the important things myself and distribute the rest to my people.

Manager: And how do you decide what the important things are?

Tom: I know from experience. I handle the things I'm best at and let my people do the rest. This way, things get done best.

Manager: Have you ever thought of classifying everything that comes your way into two broad categories—those you alone can do or should do and those someone else can do or should do?

Tom: No. I've never looked at it that way. How would I do it?

Manager: Well, instead of just talking about it, why don't we try a little experiment? Recently, I was at a management development program, and we had to do an in-basket exercise. It consisted of a group of problems, requests, decisions that had to be made, and so on. We were given one hour to decide whether we would handle each item ourselves, delegate it to a subordinate, take action promptly, postpone action, or what. Each man worked individually. Later we discussed the decisions each of us made.

Tom: That sounds interesting. Why didn't we have one of those exercises during our supervisor improvement program?

Manager: I have a copy of the exercise in my file. Why don't I get it and you can run through some of the items, O.K.?

Tom: Yes. I'd like to see how I make out.

Manager: Here it is. Now, just do the first five items.

[*Tom studies the various items and makes notes on the course of action he would take. After about 20 minutes, he has finished the first five items.*]

Tom: That *was* interesting. How did I do?

Manager: Well, it's not a school test. Why don't I do the same items you did? Then we can compare notes.

[*The manager runs through the same items. He shows his notes to Tom.*]

Tom: Well, what do you know? Of the five things, I would have handled three myself, but you would handle only one. I must be doing something wrong.

Manager: Tom, it's not a matter of doing right or doing wrong. We're discussing how you might possibly get the work done without having to come in early, stay late, or take work home, right?

Tom: Yes.

Manager: For about the next two weeks, why don't you try classifying everything you're now doing into the two groups I mentioned—what you alone can or should do and what should be delegated to one or other of your subordinates? Would that save you time?

Tom: Well, I don't expect miracles. But I can give it a try and see what happens.

Manager: Good. Then we can get together again and discuss how things are going. All right?

Tom: I sure hope it works. Thanks for your help.

What learning principles and suggestions are contained in this abbreviated interview?

— Coaching must grapple with the subordinate's real problems, not merely with their symptoms.

— Coaching must satisfy a felt need on the part of the subordinate. Imposed learning is short-lived. Coaching is most effective when a psychological readiness to learn exists.

— The subordinate must be motivated to respond well to the coaching. He must see some reward for himself in it.

— The subordinate is responsible for his own learning. He must participate and be active in the coaching process, which is a cooperative effort to diagnose his difficulties, explore alternative solutions, and formulate practical ways of dealing with them.

— No real learning has taken place unless it results in new ideas, improved skills, and especially changed behavior on the part of the subordinate.

— Follow-through is necessary if the learning is to be evaluated and reinforced.

— Feedback to the subordinate on his performance should be as quick and supportive as possible. Successes must be underscored and must outnumber failures. The experience of progress toward increased competence is essential.

The manager-leader need not be an expert on learning theories. But he must realize that coaching connotes more than merely telling, showing, selling, or demonstrating something to a subordinate. Further, though he coaches his people perhaps more from self-interested motives (such as saving himself time) than from altruism, his efforts nonetheless make them better able to operate on their own and to harvest the satisfaction of competence.

Counseling

The purpose of coaching is to help the employee be more efficient. The purpose of counseling is to help the employee become a better-adjusted human being within his work environment. Every executive must deal with the petulant complainer, the organizational conniver, the isolated loner, the self-important know-it-all, the abrasive troublemaker—the list is well nigh endless. The manager should avoid two extremes of response. One is to maintain that the personal difficulties of subordinates are none of his business. Employees are paid to perform. As long as they do so, they can take their private problems to experts in or outside the organization. The other extreme is the missionary reaction, seen in the manager who is tempted to run a clinic on company time, prying indelicately into matters beyond his capabilities and legitimate concern. It is a fact that human dilemmas enervate a worker and reduce his efficiency. To ignore them is folly; to probe into them unprofessionally is self-defeating and potentially dangerous. A middle ground is defined by such questions as these: What principles should guide the superior's efforts to counsel his people? What approaches should he take to appropriate job-related counseling? What kinds of counseling are relevant to the manager-leader's job?

Some Counseling Principles

Any subordinate with a disruptive personal problem is bound to feel uncertain, anxious, ashamed, or angry at himself. If the manager cannot be supportive in his attitude, then he should not even try to counsel him. Additionally, he must be nonmoralistic and shockproof. What the employee needs is not so much sympathy and reassurance as empathy and understanding. He looks for someone who will help him work his own way through his difficulty. Thus, the aim of the leader is to establish a climate in which authentic communication can flow freely. His role is to help the subordinate gain insight and learn. As Horney once said, when a therapist and a client deal jointly with a problem, it is much like climbing a mountain that neither has ever climbed before. The advantage that the therapist has is that he is much more familiar with mountain climbing in general. This is a good model for the executive, although he is not expected to be a therapist or psychoanalyst.

The purpose of counseling is not merely to deal with the immediate problem but to help the employee learn methods for coping with his future difficulties. Thus, the manager *thinks and feels with* him as the subordinate *thinks and feels through* his conflict or frustration. Although the subordinate is the overt leader, dominating the talk, the manager subtly guides him to analyze his difficulty, discover and evaluate possible courses of action, and reach a solution that the subordinate finds acceptable and that is realistic.

All problems can be classified into three general categories. There are those that are surely within the competence and responsibility of the manager. A bright, aggressive young man who seeks to move ahead faster than the organization can possibly permit has a problem the manager can legitimately take up. So, too, has a good man who has been passed over for a promotion and is turning sour. The second class of problem is clearly beyond the manager's ability to handle, such as alcoholism and deep, prolonged depressions. In such cases, what is needed is the most expert assistance available in the company or community. Here there is a danger that the subordinate may feel the manager is giving him the brushoff. The person must be shown that the leader will continue to be concerned about his problem, and that he is being referred to another resource only to insure him the best available help.

The third classification is the most nettlesome to handle— cases where the executive is not sure whether he is getting over his head. How far should he become involved? A sound rule of thumb is, don't open a coffin unless you are pretty sure you can put all the bones back together again. The manager can listen until—and only until—he gets the drift of the difficulty. If he then thinks that he cannot or should not deal with the problem, he can refer the person to a competent department, such as personnel or medical. In gray areas, it is better to err on the side of caution than to blunder into a counseling relationship that may prove hurtful to both parties.

Possible Counseling Approaches

Conceptually, counseling may be thought of as ranging along a continuum.

Threatening.	Threats promote fear rather than learning.
Exhortation.	Appeals to the use of common sense, willpower, self-respect, and the like pressure the person to shape up and fly right without helping him discover how.
Lecturing.	Monologues make the manager feel good but ordinarily are useless to the subordinate. More often than not, the latter has already tried most of the gems presented but to no avail.

These three approaches are not counseling at all. They are merely forms of coercion and pressure.

Reassurance.	Soothing words tend to prop up the subordinate. While reassurance has a part to play in counseling, comforting phrases are hardly a substitute for rational programs for improvement.
Advice giving.	Suggestions also have a place in counseling. The manager must be wary of the fact, however, that they may be only *his* suggestions. The employee may find them rather impractical. Too many suggestions render the subordinate deaf to the counseling.
Social reinforcement.	Relying on the social nature of man, the manager capitalizes on the behavior of reference groups which the subordinate esteems, pointing out how others succeed, the social rewards that will be forthcoming, and so on. The employee's positive comments and actions are reinforced with praise and approval.

These three techniques have a function to play in counseling, but they do not constitute counseling interaction as such. At best, they are likely to give only short-term results. Overdone, they get in the way of the subordinate's efforts to cope with his difficulty.

Directive guidance.	The manager is quite active when he provides directive guidance. He makes suggestions, proposes alternatives, asks directive questions, and sees to it that the employee considers practical solutions. He places at his disposal his greater knowledge and experience to attain mutually acceptable solutions.
Problem solving.	Again, the manager may be rather active in suggesting ways out of the problem. Yet he works with the employee in reaching a rational solution. He does not overdirect the subordinate's thinking but helps him weave his way through his dilemma.

Nondirective guidance. The manager asks open-end questions, provides nondirective leads, reflects the feelings that the subordinate has expressed, and restates the content of his remarks. He is far from passive when he supplies such nondirective guidance. He strives to serve in an active but subtle encouraging role as the employee arrives at a subjectively meaningful resolution of his difficulty that will also be socially and organizationally acceptable.

These three approaches can be called counseling in the strict sense. The executive uses one or another, singly or in combination, according to the needs of a given employee and his problem. It should be emphasized that merely listening, offering a person opportunities to get a difficulty off his chest, is not counseling. It is a form of uninvolved politeness or patience with catharsis, even though at one time or another it may be necessary to listen quietly as a person unburdens himself.

Legitimate Counseling Problems for the Manager-Leader

Performance counseling. Overachievers and underachievers are not unknown in most organizations. When a subordinate is lacking in motivation or when his attitudes are such as to militate against his progress, counseling is obviously called for. Aimless and goalless employees who have superior talents are fit subjects for counseling. On the other hand, the man who is racing his motor so hard to achieve that he is likely to burn himself out before his time probably requires some guidance. A third appropriate candidate for performance counseling is the employee whose views of and reactions to the firm's normal regimen or its authority figures are such as to be self-damaging in the long run. Any counseling effort expended in changing these attitudes may be energy well invested.

Career counseling. Some of the most perplexed subordinates are those who have so many talents that they cannot decide which way they should go. Helping such a person formulate a practical career plan is more than charity; it well may be the best way to keep him with the firm. If he sees where it is possible for him to go in the organization and how to get there, he may not only be more satisfied in his job but also strive to grow and learn. At the opposite extreme is the employee who is nearing retirement. More and more, retirement is becoming a problem that should be handled by the personnel department. With the far longer span of active years often promised by greater life expectancy, counseling with regard to a second career is becoming increasingly necessary.

Job adjustment counseling. Every firm has built-in organizational frustrations in the form of requirements, policies, rules, procedures, customs, mores, taboos, and folkways. Pressures, some of them unfair, exist in every department. If the employee is to derive an element of psychic income from his daily work, he must learn to adjust to such realities within the limits of his convictions. Help in this area is needed by everyone at some time or other.

Social adjustment counseling. Organizations are composed of groups of people with whom one must interact. Some are easy to live with; others tend to annoy or disturb a given employee. A great deal of the executive's time will be spent helping people relate to one another if he is shrewd. His task is to build a cohesive, cooperating work team. It would be a miracle if his group developed such a character without his counseling some of its members on how best to deal with their peers and subordinates.

Personal adjustment counseling. The extent to which the manager-leader can or should become involved in the strictly personal frustrations and conflicts of his people is a decision that he must make in terms of the caveats already presented.

Delegating

Andrew Carnegie once remarked that when a man realizes he can call others in to help him do a better job than he can do alone, he has taken a big step in life. In like manner, Teddy Roosevelt observed that the best executive is the one who has sense enough to pick good men to do what he wants done and self-restraint enough to keep from meddling with them while they do it. These comments speak to the core of delegation, whose key concepts are meaningful work, authority, autonomy, and accountability. Few managers need to be convinced of the advantages of delegation in this day and age. Yet managers and subordinates alike at times reject it, for a variety of reasons. As the following rundown shows, these reasons are often mirror images.

Managers	Subordinates
Unwillingness to let go some authority.	Unwillingness to take on additional responsibility.
Failure to see delegation as a means of building team effort.	Failure to see delegation as a means of growing and learning.
Ignorance of what to delegate.	Feeling that only distasteful chores or trivia are delegated.
Ignorance of how to delegate.	Confusion as to the manager's expectations.
Restricting delegation to one or two subordinates.	Group pressures not to volunteer.
Failure to support subordinates executing delegated authority.	An attitude of once burned, twice shy.
Insistence that delegated duties be done as they would do them.	Resentment at not being given credit for common sense.
Jealousy of their better people.	Fear of incurring the boss's wrath.
Preference for handling things personally.	Eagerness to delegate upward in order to keep the boss busy.
Lack of trust in their people.	Lack of respect for the manager.
Fear of taking prudent risks.	Fear of being chewed out for even minor mistakes.
Failure to develop their people.	Lack of skill in handling delegated authority.
Failure to reward achievement.	Feeling of not being appreciated.
Delegation by abdication.	Feeling of being used and abused.

Managers	Subordinates
Indian-giver delegation.	Not knowing where one stands.
Delegation of responsibility but little authority.	Ignorance of the authority and its limits granted by delegation.

It is clear from this comparison that delegation is far more than a mechanical process. Every act of delegation is rooted in the relationship that exists between the subordinate and his boss, the mutual confidence and respect they have for one another, the ideas and attitudes that each brings to the transaction, and the potential rewards and satisfactions that each perceives as coming from it. Accordingly, two problems are of significance: what should be delegated and how to delegate in a motivating manner.

What Should Be Delegated?

Delegation is a process of job enrichment. Unless what is delegated represents a challenge for growth and achievement over and above the perimeters outlined in the position description, nothing much will happen. Moreover, the manager must resist a temptation to delegate things that he dislikes handling. Subordinates are not stupid; they readily perceive that such spinoffs are no more than rank-has-its-privileges in action.

No manager can delegate away his ultimate responsibility for what his subordinates do. Even so, it is inane to impose additional responsibilities upon them without simultaneously sharing with them the necessary authority to produce the results expected. It is naive to assert that the authority should equal the responsibility. Every organization will give every person more responsibility than authority if for no other reason than that it is so easy to add to the former and so difficult to part with the latter.

An act of delegation is at once a vote of confidence in and a test of the subordinate. Both authority and autonomy must be granted in due measure. The employee need not be a master of the organization's fate, but he surely should be the captain of his destiny. As long as the limits of authority and autonomy are mutually understood, he should be free to work out his salvation as he sees fit. The obverse of the need for autonomy is the need for strict accountability for results.

Thus, delegation can be thought of as a box surrounding a significant unit of work. On the four sides, defining the limits of the work, are the walls of contribution, authority, autonomy, and accountability.

How to Delegate

Understand the strengths and limitations of each key subordinate. One subordinate's delegation meat is another's delegation poison. What one perceives as an attempt to help him develop another may perceive as an unsubtle attempt to maneuver him into doing the boss's job when he does not receive the boss' pay. Knowing one's subordinates involves far more than generally appreciating their assets and deficiencies. It entails a specific awareness of their attitudes toward delegation and their ambition to grow and advance.

Delegate as part of a development plan. Delegation should not consist of a haphazard or discrete series of incidents. It should be a process of planned growth. According to one legend, Hercules became the strongest man in the world by lifting the same calf every day until it became a full-grown bull. The purpose of delegation is to strengthen the subordinate's managerial muscles, not to give him an occupational hernia. Initially, the manager-leader fits the back to the burden and the burden to the back. As subordinates grow in competence, he makes the challenges and tests more exacting. This planning process requires patience on the manager's part. It is hardly likely that subordinates will perform with the polish or perfection that he may possess. A certain number of errors are to be anticipated since the goal is improvement. Learning from blunders helps people avoid repeating them.

Spell out the ground rules. Three people can perceive a delegated authority in three different ways: one will magnify it, another will minimize it, and the third will interpret it rather accurately. This is only human. The manager can prevent heartburn at a later date for himself and his subordinate if they agree on the areas where the latter is

— Free to decide and act on his own initiative.

— Free to decide and act on his own but required to keep his superior or another department informed of his behavior.

— Free to decide and act only after consulting with his superior or the manager of another department whose work or relations with his own group may be seriously affected by the action taken.

— Free to decide and act only after receiving specific permission from his superior or the manager of the other department.

— Not free to decide and act since the superior reserves such matters to himself.

Go from monitoring to self-management. At the outset, the executive would be wise to keep his finger on the pulse of his subordinate's actions, though without intruding, for the reason that even well-intentioned disasters are no less distasteful. As the subordinate proves himself, the superior can tactfully ease himself out of the picture, allowing the subordinate to supervise himself. It is prudent, however, to set up in advance checkpoints and check times when the two will get together to discuss progress and problems.

Reward performance. Any substantial improvement on the part of the subordinate must be rewarded, even if only verbally. Since one learns what he lives and produces what is rewarded, delegation may prove to be more demotivating than motivating if the manager seems unaware or unappreciative of the subordinate's efforts.

Performance Reviews

Both the organization and the employee have certain rights. It is rightful that the firm know just how well the individual has performed. The employee has the right to know just what the firm thinks of his performance and what its plans are for him. Since both parties have such reasonable expectations, it is surprising that both tend to dislike appraisals and reviews. Contrary to so-called common sense, a study by General Electric indicated that praise has little lasting effect on performance. Criticism has a negative effect; the defensiveness it produces results in inferior performance.

There are many aspects of organizational life that can limit the effectiveness of performance reviews; these are beyond the control of the individual manager. He can, however, control certain debilitating factors to some extent.

He can make sure that he and the subordinate set mutually acceptable achievement targets at the outset of the review period. If this is not done, the manager is usually forced to act on the basis of mere personal impressions or what the subordinate has done recently.

A negative climate, mental set, or pattern of attitudes can preclude a productive review. Often the good intentions brought to the review are undercut by such things as the discomfort of the manager, the defensiveness of the subordinate, a tendency to concentrate on personality rather than performance, or a habit of giving the subordinate a once-over lightly—a few pats on the head and raps on the knuckles rather than a balanced consideration of hits and misses.

A good review represents a fine blending of earned recognition for work well done, constructive criticism, coaching, joint problem solving, and planning for future improvement. Such benefits cannot be obtained if the manager fails to plan for the interview, neglects to allow sufficient time for it, dominates the talking, or merely goes through the motions.

The manager should not mix a review of subordinate performance with a consideration of a salary increase. When this occurs, the employee is so distracted by the prospect of his raise that he gives little attention to efforts to help him improve.

Formal appraisals take place once or twice a year. If the manager neglects to appraise the subordinate informally from day to day, the latter correctly has a sense of being put upon since the review deals with history, which at this date he cannot alter.

Performance Reviews versus Development Reviews

Two different reviews should be held and at different times. The reason for this is that the purposes are radically different.

The *development review* is geared primarily to the improvement of the employee. It is noncompetitive in that he is not compared with any of his equals. It is an outward sign of the firm's desire to help him become more effective, even if he leaves the organization. It endeavors to help him capitalize more fully on strong points and remedy weak ones. Coaching and perhaps even counseling play a key role in the interaction.

The *performance review* is by nature competitive. The employee is measured not only against his own job standards but also against the performance of his peers. The organization has a money pie that is only so large. The size of the wedge that a given subordinate receives depends on his overall contribution to the company or department. He is obviously competing with others at his level who also are struggling for as large a wedge as possible. This does not imply that the purpose of the performance review is solely or even principally to distribute rewards. The manager and his subordinate together evaluate past performance in order to plan future improvement. Thus, a well-conducted review should aim to accomplish at least some of the following.

— To discover jointly how practical were the objectives and standards originally agreed upon and to modify them if need be.
— To recognize, reward, and thank the subordinate for superior productivity so as to motivate him for the future.
— To analyze together the reasons for past failures with a view to evolving a plan for preventing their repetition.
— To discover how the subordinate feels about his job, his coworkers, the superior, and the organization.
— To let him know frankly what the organization thinks of his past performance.
— To improve the working relationship that exists between the man and his boss, including aspects of the latter's management style that may be preventing the subordinate from performing according to his capabilities.
— To answer job-related questions that the subordinate may have on his mind.

Conducting the Performance Review

The performance review takes place after the manager has evaluated the work of his subordinate and discussed his appraisal with his superior in order both to keep him informed and perhaps to receive suggestions and advice from him. How the manager conducts the interview is a matter of planning, attitude, and technique. KISS is a good motto in this regard—keep it simple and supportive. One method is to adopt a Socratic and nondirective approach, asking such questions as the following:

— Would you care to discuss the areas where you feel that you have performed better than acceptably? Why do you think that you did so well? Could you give me a few instances?
— Where do you feel that you did an acceptable job? Could you offer some examples? Why do you think that your work was only average?
— In what areas do you really feel that you did less than an acceptable job? Could you pick out a few details? Why was your work less than acceptable?
— What is your program for improvement?
— What do you have going for you, and how do you intend to capitalize on it to improve?
— What obstacles do you foresee in carrying out your own self-improvement program, and how do you plan to overcome them?
— How can I help you implement your plan?

These questions are not to be asked in a mechanical or routine fashion, of course. It may take the greater part of an hour to cover them. At appropriate times, the manager will tactfully interject his views as the representative of the firm. But his real task is to help the subordinate become more sensitive to his own performance and the need for self-improvement, to encourage him to conceive a new view of his job and a new determination to do it well. The subordinate must be very active in, if not in charge of, the interview. If the manager finds it necessary to demur from the employee's evaluation of his own past performance, he should disagree agreeably. When this spirit prevails, even distasteful subjects can be discussed openly, because the superior is functioning not as a judge or a needling critic but rather as a partner in the subordinate's pursuit of competence.

chapter twelve

coping with tensions

Behind the executive mask lies a very fallible, imperfect human being. Behind the facade of strength and poise is a person who is all too subject to the strains of a demanding and complex life style. Every leader must wrestle with his anxieties, even when he radiates an impressive air of self-confidence. He must contend with his frustrations. He must deal competently with his conflicts. He must introduce order into the turbulent ingredients of his personality.

Since the executive is as human as his subordinates and yet must cope with far more fragmenting and irritating stresses, it behooves him to gain some understanding of his inner dynamics. Managers are eager to learn what makes others tick. They are generally far less eager to learn what makes them tick. This does not imply that the leader is to become a do-it-yourself psychologist and then busy himself plastering mental-health Band-Aids on the results of self-punishing introspections. It does mean that, before he seeks to influence others, he should have a frank encounter with himself as a unique person. Often, if he has troubles, the trouble is not with superiors, peers, or subordinates but with himself. Until he learns to cope successfully with his own problems and tensions, he will tend to project his difficulties on others in one way or another, pay an inordinate price for whatever career success comes his way, and get little or no satisfaction from this success.

Problems of Stress

The common denominator of all stress or tension is a feeling of discomfort. This may range from mild disquiet to acute anxiety. Hence, it is well to make certain distinctions.

Stresses are experienced feelings; they are not the obstacles that give rise to them. Every human being has two basic drives: to maintain psychological equilibrium and harmony and to actualize his potential. Whenever one perceives any threat to these drives, he experiences a certain amount of stress.

When tension is realistic and mild, it can be highly useful. The job of the leader is not to tranquilize all tension in his people, as is the practice under paternalistic management. It is to create constructive tension, which can then be channeled into productive effort. As for himself, the executive should look upon tension as his lever for achievement. All challenges to oneself are based on stress situations in which the ultimate outcome is not sure. Stress forces us to organize our behavior to meet these situations. Mountain climbers, athletes, scientists, all people who really excel seek out stress-producing situations to test their mettle and make them stretch so as to achieve far more than they have in the past.

Overwhelming tension, however, can be destructive. It interferes with a person's perception, preventing him from seeing reality objectively; it confuses his cognitive processes, preventing him from reasoning logically about reality; it disorganizes his behavior, so that he acts maladaptively; it gives rise to emotions that are at best unproductive and at worst harmful to him.

Frustration and Conflict

The manager-leader may be blocked by three types of stress producers. He can be stymied by material objects, as every salesman whose car will not start when he is in a hurry knows very well. He may be thwarted in his interpersonal and social relations. Or he may find that the source of his problem is not external but in himself. When the obstruction is environmental, it is called *frustration*. The person finds that his ongoing behavior or efforts to satisfy his needs are foiled by things or people outside himself. *Conflict* exists when he seeks to satisfy two antagonistic drives or need patterns simultaneously, despite the fact that this is impossible in a given set of circumstances.

Frustration

Although many situations involve both frustration and conflict, it is better to keep the two experiences conceptually discrete. For one thing, frustration externally caused is often considerably easier to handle. The manager beset by a nettlesome corporate problem can often utilize problem analysis techniques to resolve it. The man who is shut off from a desired promotion can acquire the skills that are prerequisite to it. The executive who is faced with a job that is too big for him can ask for a transfer. He may even restructure the job to meet his talents. As a last resort, he can flee the field and seek employment elsewhere.

It is not to be inferred from this that frustration and conflict are passing inconveniences. At times, they can be very disorganizing. The following incident is an eye-opener in this regard.

George had gone to the very best schools, graduating from an Ivy League university with honors. During World War II, he had been landing officer on an attack carrier, one of the most demanding jobs on the ship. After the war, he entered a finance company that his father had helped establish. He was given a title but little responsibility. After his father's death, George was slowly relegated to obscurity despite his obvious talents. His routine was to come to work, read the newspapers until midday, lunch for perhaps two hours, putter aimlessly around the office, and go home. No one paid much attention to George, preferring to work around him. When he came for counseling, he was dejected and filled with resentment. Over a period of time, he learned to assert himself, to inject his voice into company decisions, to pull weight with his peers at the top. He not only resolved many of his problems but gradually made increasingly important contributions to the firm's success.

Conflict

One can generally learn to live with externally provoked frustrations, however bothersome they may be. The people behind the Iron Curtain live with their oppressors, and primitives live with their harsh environments. But when the frustration is internally generated, the situation can be very difficult. A man becomes his own judge and jury, perhaps even his own tormentor. Three basic kinds of conflict have been identified.

Approach-approach. A manager wishes to be liked by the Indians. Yet he wants to have an outstanding performance record, be thought well of by the chiefs, and get promoted. In certain conditions, he may feel that it is impossible to attain both objectives at the same time. Hence, he can be pulled in opposite directions.

Avoidance-avoidance. A man finds himself between the devil and the deep blue sea when he wishes to avoid two unpleasant courses of action or situations but must choose one or the other. For instance, a manager discovers that his boss, an old friend, has been systematically cheating the company in a serious way. If he fails to bring the matter to the attention of higher management, he may be accused of neglect of duty and may even end up as the fall guy for his boss's chicanery. On the other hand, he does not want to violate his own ethical code by letting the superior's cheating pass; nor does he wish to be the instrument of his friend's downfall. He is literally the man in the middle: no matter what he does, it will hurt someone.

Approach-avoidance. When Lee A. Iacocca, president of the Ford Motor Company, was a fledgling salesman at the outset of his career, he was told by his boss, Charlie Beacham, to change his name from Lido to Lee. No one knows what Iacocca's reactions were to this demand. It is known that he was and is very proud of his Italian heritage, as is true of so many successful sons of immigrant parents. It can be imagined that Iacocca was drawn to the possibility of pleasing his boss and getting ahead while at the same time he was undoubtedly repelled by the idea of changing his name. To be attracted to and repelled by the same object, person, or situation is most painful.

A man may find the status and power of a promotion highly desirable and yet resent many of the things that must be done to get or keep the new position. The following incident illustrates what can happen when a manager is confronted with such a conflict.

A manager is offered a much-desired promotion. He is eager to accept it because it means a giant step up the organization ladder. Unfortunately, it requires that he move from a large metropolis with many cultural and other advantages to a small town where they are notable by their absence. His wife, a college graduate who is liberal in her politics, active in a little-theater group, and attuned to big-city life, is adamant that they should not move to a small town, even if this means passing up the promotion. Their two children, of high school age, are also less than enthusiastic about the move. After a week of talking the matter over, husband, wife, and children are as far apart as they were at the outset. What can the husband do?

1. He can accept the promotion and simply move his family, regardless of their feelings.
2. He can accept the transfer and leave his family in the city, visiting them on weekends.
3. He can try to bribe his family to move.
4. He can ask his family to experiment with the new town for a year, promising that if everyone is still unhappy at the end of this period, he will request a transfer or get another job.
5. He can refuse the promotion and please his family.
6. He can try to stall his superiors on taking action immediately.
7. He can try to persuade his superiors that he can make a greater contribution by working up the promotion ladder where he is at present.
8. He can ask for a transfer within his present unit of the firm.
9. He can get another job.

The Adjustment Process

When a person's ongoing or customary behavior is thwarted by a frustration or conflict, he will be motivated to resolve the difficulty. From this standpoint, stress, needs, drives, activity, behavior, and adjustment are all intertwined. What the typical executive needs is not a clinical analysis of the adjustment process but some understanding of the dynamics involved that he can apply to the realities of his own corporate situation.

The process of adjustment is best illustrated as a sequence of events.

A manager,

with all his past experiences, learning, successes, failures, frustration tolerance, habits, interests, attitudes, temperament, and personality,

encounters a thwarting situation
and perceives it as threatening.

His ongoing behavior is blocked. A pattern of needs, desires, or aspirations is blocked either by some external situation or by some internal conflict.

As a result, the manager is stirred up.

He has a drive to overcome the barrier. He is motivated. Tension builds up. According to the perceived threat, feelings and emotions may be strong. He may become more or less confused.

He tries various ways to overcome
the thwarting situation.

He does not give up easily (in this regard, too much frustration tolerance may be as bad as too little). He tries one way after another to cope with the blocking. Different people choose different approaches, ranging from dogged effort based on logical experimentation to random illogical behavior or stereotyped repetition of ineffective actions.

He discovers a tension-reducing response.

Eventually, the manager hits upon a course of action that will enable him to reduce his tension.

It may be adaptive or maladaptive.

Adaptive behavior resolves the difficulty and promotes the manager's growth. Maladaptive behavior gives short-term drive reduction and need satisfaction, but it ultimately hampers his development.

It will then have a tendency to be repeated.

Any behavior, adaptive or maladaptive, that reduces tension and gives even temporary peace tends to be repeated under similar circumstances. This is obvious from the actions of the procrastinator, the liar, the alcoholic, and the compulsive smoker.

How Effective a Solution?

Since any response that reduces a drive will bring some satisfaction, the manager must have criteria for evaluating his efforts to cope with frustration and conflict. Otherwise, he may find to his regret that his behavior gives him short-term relief but long-term trouble. First, he must face up to the barrier or the state of stress. Henry Ford acted like an ostrich when he refused to accept the knowledge, despite a persistent loss of business, that he was doing something wrong. Second, he must base his solution on a realistic appraisal of the problem. People have a talent for manufacturing hobgoblins and then reacting not to the facts but to their imaginings of the facts. Third, his solution should be economical. If it drains him of his resources, the victory is Pyrrhic.

It goes without saying that the manager must reduce his tensions in a manner that is personally, socially, and ethically acceptable. Any measure that violates normal social standards is unacceptable. Since adjustment entails the balanced satisfaction of needs, the manager must treat his difficulties as interrelated. If the solution found does not result in a higher degree of personal integration—and this is always relative—then one need or pattern of needs will be met at the expense of others equally important. The experience of dealing with a thwarting situation should help the manager increase his self-understanding, improve his skill in handling similar problems in the future, and facilitate his efforts to accept and relate to reality as it is, not as he would wish it to be.

There are three major forms of nonintegrating adjustment. The first is recourse to aggression as one moves against people and situations, in Horney's terms. The second is a withdrawal from people or problems to escape the cause of frustration or conflict. The third is self-deception, which enables one to save face and maintain his self-respect.

Aggression as an Adjustment Mechanism

When a human being is blocked, it is normal for him to react aggressively. When there is a possibility of overcoming the obstruction by sheer power, it is natural for him to take a direct approach and roll over it.

Aggression is a two-edged sword. On the one hand, self-assertiveness, determination, and initiative, which are all rooted in aggressive tendencies, are all considered virtues in our society. They enable people to surmount difficulties and meet challenges successfully. Properly directed and governed, therefore, aggression is positive and healthy. But at the other extreme, unbridled aggression can take the form of mindless cruelty.

Negativism. "I came here without a friend, and I expect to leave without a friend. Just as long as I do my job, what difference does it make?" These are the words of a plant manager who had more than average difficulty in his work relationships. Such an attitude is common, for example, in the kind of people who are forever agin' the government. They make waves when none are necessary. They are contentious for no clear reason. They are to a degree rebels without a cause.

Domineering. The American middle-class mother has been accused of being overbearing, of stunting her offspring with oppressive affection; everyone has heard the semihumorous anecdotes about Mama's proclivity for brooding over her young, curing everything from a cold to pneumonia with chicken soup. It is difficult for any manager to find the dividing line between too much dependence and too much independence in his people. If he is domineering, he will lose the good ones, and the rest will become docile and useless. If he holds the reins too lightly, then he may pay the penalty for their misdirected enthusiasm.

Nagging. While nagging is generally attributed to women, especially wives, it is commonplace among men in business. The nit-picking, needling manager is an earthly form of purgatory, if not hell. The real problem here is that usually the nagger means well, but his laudable intentions mask annoying actions. Although subordinates may perceive his good motives, the fact is that they often feel, "You just can't please the S.O.B."

Displacement. Everyone, including managers, must save face. Displacement is one way to do so. The manager who dislikes his superior may hide his hostile feelings from the boss under a mask of agreeableness and impose them instead on his subordinates. This, of course, keeps him out of trouble with the superior but worsens his relationships with employees, who resent being the butt of his displaced aggression. Accordingly, displacement solves one problem only to create or intensify another.

Hostility. Physical assault is rare in modern business. More subtle forms of attack are quite common. Habitual sarcastic remarks, cutting comments, stinging criticism, and demeaning ridicule are favorite weapons of managers who derive pleasure from inflicting pain on defenseless subordinates. Nor are peers and superiors always safe from their shafts. Obviously, bullying, vengefulness, and other forms of hostility are rewarding not so much because they help the perpetrator overcome obstacles but because they give him the feeling of satisfaction that comes from expressing one's superiority over a scapegoat.

Adjustment by Flight

In an article entitled "The Absentee Executive," *Business Week* estimated that the absenteeism among executives is about one out of six in some companies.

It is surprising how ingenious man is in his efforts to escape the demands of the world in which he lives and avoid threats to his sense of personal worth. The easiest way to withdraw from the unpleasant is simple *denial.* Neville Chamberlain, prime minister of Great Britain, signed the Munich Pact sanctioning Hitler's take-over of Czechoslovakia on the argument that this act of appeasement would avert a world war.

Denial is a refusal to consider the evident facts or the objective situation. *Isolation* is another way to evade reality. This it-won't-happen-to-me reaction is a form of intellectual self-deception that can be very tempting. Many groups were inclined to adopt this attitude when Hitler was rising to the summit of his power. Some people do not isolate themselves intellectually but insulate themselves emotionally. Tragedies and injustices that should produce a sense of righteous indignation are ignored. Those who should react and act stay aloof and uninvolved. In the famous play *The Andersonville Trial*, about Union prisoners in a Confederate prison camp, this was brought out with dramatic clarity.

Frustration and conflict do not always produce aggressiveness. There are people who react to them with *apathy*. Rather than attacking what blocks them, they show indifference. *Daydreaming* and *absent-mindedness* are still other forms of withdrawal from a disturbing situation. These are among the favorite resorts of workers who feel that higher management is not interested in them. Since they are compelled to submit to the directives of management and cannot lash back, they take refuge in a protective apathy. Monotonous jobs also prompt people to be present physically but mentally and emotionally absent.

There are four additional ways in which people in industry frequently avoid the demands of reality: *overindulgence, hypochondria, regression,* and *drug abuse.*

Although overindulgence in eating, sleeping, and other escapes is common, it is drinking that is a major industrial problem. Some 6½ million alcoholics use the cup that cheers to pull the curtain of oblivion over the pressures of life. Alcoholism accounts for about 3 percent of all industrial absenteeism. Drinking problems cost private enterprise $2 billion or more each year. Alcoholism is the fourth most serious health problem in the United States. The dreary litany of the dreadful results of the grape and the grain is almost endless, and yet the number of problem drinkers and alcoholics grows annually.

Hypochondria is an insidious method of escaping reality. Every human being is naturally sympathetic toward someone who is ill. Yet the hypochondriac is rarely sick from physical causes. If he is, the disorder is likely to be an effect of his state of mind. He is obsessively preoccupied with his bodily functions, health, and imagined ills. Unlike the malingerer, who is well aware that he is feigning sickness to avoid unpleasant tasks, the hypochondriac is convinced that he is in poor health, even after the most thorough physical examination has indicated that nothing is organically wrong with him. No amount of objective evidence will shake his belief. Flight into illness is a self-protective device. It enables the person to have his cake and eat it in that he runs away from the normal demands of his job while securing the fringe benefit of human sympathy, at least for a time.

Regression to the familiar is a retreat from current tensions to the security of a type of behavior that was appropriate to an earlier age or position but is useless in dealing with the present. Related to regression is *fixation*. Where the regressor retreats under strain, the fixated person freezes his behavior at a point where it is comfortable. The first turns back from challenges, growth, and maturity; the second fails to grow up in the first place.

A newcomer on the escape scene is drug abuse. Most middle-age executives shudder at the very idea, whereas younger people are more tolerant in their attitudes. Some drugs are obviously addictive and degenerative, but claims are made that others are more benign. Be that as it may, a number of things are evident. First, drug abuse is on the rise. Every company has some sort of narcotics problem among its people. In fact, one corporation estimates that up to 6 percent of its 30,000 employees may be in trouble with drugs. Second, the problem is likely to get worse before it gets better. Despite the arguments pro and con certain drugs, the fact is that they are crutches. As such, they prevent the user from learning how to cope with stress in a way that is conducive to balanced adjustment. Some people might be surprised to learn that in at least one Japanese camp in World War II, American prisoners were given marijuana to keep them quiet and docile. Finally, the habitual use of anything to evade reality, regardless of its other effects, does not contribute ultimately to mental health.

Adjustment by Self-Deception

Many people clearly recognize that attacking reality and withdrawing from it are ineffective ways of handling stress. Yet human nature dictates that they defend their self-concept as worthwhile beings at all costs. Thus, when threatened with a sense of failure, guilt, or inferiority, they will at times resort to the self-deceptions called *defense mechanisms*. A more accurate phrase would be *protective mechanisms,* since their purpose is to safeguard the ego. Rather than present a detailed description of each of these devices, it will better serve our purposes to give a series of examples of self-deceivers, following each illustration with a brief explanation.

> "Mr. X, the assistant manager, will be a pest. He will interrupt you with questions that have nothing to do with the topic under discussion. He will disagree with you on some minor point that is not worth two cents. If you form buzz groups, he will leave his group and buttonhole you. After the session is ended, he will hang around to impress you with his experience in other companies."

Attention getting is the most elemental defense mechanism. It can be positive or negative, direct or subtle. In any form, its purpose is to draw notice and approval. Attention seekers are a nuisance to the manager-leader because they force him to focus on them and give him little hope of getting a return on his invested time and effort. They also irritate their peers since they try to hog the stage.

> "Tom has gone about as far as his boot-strap operation will take him in this company. But he doesn't seem to mind very much. He is the Boy Scout leader, he is very active in local politics, and he is head of several church and social groups."

> "Peter is an odd one. He's so small that a good wind would blow him away. But he's a physical fitness nut. He jogs five miles a day. He will challenge anyone to an Indian hand wrestle. Get him to tell you how, pound for pound, jockeys are the strongest people in the world."

Compensation is the practice of substituting satisfaction from one kind of achievement for the lack of it in another area. Its purpose is to reduce the sense of uselessness that might result from outright failure. The real question is not the form that the compensatory behavior takes but rather how genuine the substituted attainment is. Tom is getting real achievement outside the firm even though he is blocked in it. Peter is compensating by overreacting to his small physique. But so did Helen Keller overreact to her blindness and deafness.

"Joe never got out of high school. But his kid is getting his Ph.D. in physics at M.I.T. Joe has two M.I.T. emblems on the rear window of his car. All he ever talks about is that boy of his."

Identification is a less well adjusted form of compensation. Instead of obtaining satisfaction from his own accomplishments, the person basks in the reflected glory of someone with whom he is associated. The so-called company man and the "My son, the doctor" parent are familiar examples of identification.

"I know that they passed me over for the job of department head. But I'd really hate to have that job. The in-fighting, the pressures from the vice-president, the worry about meeting deadlines and performance objectives—no, thanks. That's not for me."

"Sure, Peter will be promoted after his overseas assignment. I know that few people get that kind of transfer. But he has to uproot his family, he'll be living with foreigners, and he's got to learn a new language and get used to new customs. I'd rather stay in my present job. Even though it doesn't mean a promotion, it's perfect for me. I prefer it."

Rationalization is a form of self-protection that provides socially acceptable reasons or excuses for behavior rather than the true reasons. The purpose of the false explanations is to make the behavior appear rational and logical. In the first case, we have an example of sour grapes. Like the fox in the fable who could not reach the grapes, the man claims that what he cannot have is not worth having. "She's beautiful but dumb" and "He's got lots of theory but no common sense" are examples of rationalization. The second quote illustrates a sweet lemon approach. In this instance, the rationalizer contends not only that the unattainable is not worth having but that what he now has is preferable to what is beyond his reach.

"What can I do with the lousy people personnel sends me? God couldn't get the job done with these clods. I know how to manage, but these people are unmanageable. Besides, you can't trust higher management. They speak with a forked tongue. They're trying to get blood from a stone. Then when you need their support, they act sneaky and leave you out on a limb."

A harmful type of rationalization is *buck passing*, or pushing blame onto something or someone else; this is what the carpenter does who always blames his tools. Blaming others relieves the manager of feelings of inadequacy. The example also illustrates another form of rationalization: *projection*, or attributing to another faults that really reside in oneself. Ineffective managers invariably see their superiors as lacking in competence.

"You never get a break around here. The higher-ups don't understand how hard I work and what I have to deal with. All they want are results. They don't give a hang for my feelings. You'd think that they would have a heart for people at my level."

Sympathism is a childish plea for a shoulder to cry on. It expresses the attitude that one is in an afflicted position for which nobody has any understanding or feeling. The emotional tone is one of "You should feel sorry for my unfortunate plight and let me lean on you."

"I'm really much too good for this job. With my education and experience, you'd think that they would give me a real managerial position. But we have idiots who set the criteria for promotion while dunces kill themselves to meet them. If they would only recognize real talent, I wouldn't be stuck in this dead end. I'm not going to degrade myself by trying to please a bunch of incompetents."

Egocentrism protects the ego by enabling the manager to excuse lack of success on the ground of his superiority. Instead of paying the price of achievement, he adopts an attitude of self-importance combined with condescension toward others.

Some Observations on Inadequate Adjustment Mechanisms

Every manager *now and then* attacks reality, withdraws from it, and resorts to protective mechanisms. The difference between the average executive and the one who hurts his development and social relations is one of degree, not kind. It is the habitual use of maladaptive ways of dealing with reality that gets people into difficulties. Moreover, self-defeating behavior patterns cannot be neatly compartmentalized. The various types overlap and are interrelated. Nor is the behavior conscious and deliberate; if it were, it would be easier to eradicate. The person has experimented with it and found that it removes threat, reduces tension, and preserves his self-esteem for a short time. Since nothing succeeds like success, he repeats the pattern, despite the fact that in the long run it makes him hard to live with and interferes with his effectiveness.

It does little good for the executive to attempt a depth analysis of maladjustment, whether his own or a subordinate's. It is obvious that one adopts self-hurtful behavior because he feels inadequate, insecure, or inferior; it is clear that he is overreacting out of fear, worry, or anxiety. But if the manager-leader has some understanding of what lies behind the conduct, he is less likely to be disturbed by it. More importantly, he will be in a better position to help himself or the employee substitute acceptable and efficient attitudes and responses. The manner in which a person acts, however irrational it seems to the uninvolved observer, serves the purpose of preserving his self-concept. What he needs is not moralistic judgments but assistance in replacing stunting reactions with behavior that is more rewarding for him and more productive for the firm.

Behind the Facade of Success

Men of intelligence who carry the burdens of authority and responsibility must from time to time contend with conflicting elements in their personalities. Many of these distressing difficulties are created by our culture. In our society, with its residue of the Puritan ethos, the executive must channel his drives and expectations according to societal norms. He must compete vigorously, *but* he must cooperate with peers. He must keep No. 1 front and center, *but* he must have a certain compassion for his fellow man. He must retain his own identity, *but* he must conform to the will of the majority. He must cling to his own independence, *but* he must learn how to identify with and accept legitimate authority. He must cling to his personal code of ethics, *but* he must abide the unethical behavior of others. He must move forward in the rat race since to stand still is to lose ground, *but* he must live a balanced life as a spouse, parent, and citizen—as a human being.

The list of antitheses with which the manager must wrestle is almost endless. In an earlier era, he might have shrugged them off on the basis that the business of America is business. Today, he must be attuned to the demands of society. A schizophrenic existence is no more workable for the executive than it is for the village moron. His life must have integration and a wholesome harmony. Personal adequacy is not to be confused with mere technical competence. Maturity must not be confused with the ability to make money, important as this is. Personal fulfillment must not be confused with material acquisitions. Self-understanding, self-acceptance, and self-esteem are not to be confused with status, power, or the trappings of high position.

Equating these inner traits with outer signs of strength further complicates the executive's struggle to balance conflicting cultural demands. And were these burdens not enough, he must grapple with three major enemies within the gates—fear, worry, and anxiety.

Fear and Worry

Fear is an emotion produced by a specific threat that prompts a person, wisely or unwisely, to flee if flight is possible. Worry is the fear of some *future* event about which one has incomplete knowledge and over which he has little or no direct control. Fear can be either rational or irrational. So can its absence. In a period of labor cutbacks, the person who has been deliberately doing less than acceptable work and is not fearful of losing his job simply does not understand the predicament he is in. On the other hand, the man who has been doing excellent work for years is foolish to worry about losing his job during a time of company growth. When the fear is proportionate to the cause, it is adaptive; when it is disproportionate, it is maladaptive.

Worry is more difficult to handle. Since it generally concerns the future, it is almost a perfect obstacle to functioning. The man who is worried about a possible demotion or a heart attack necessarily feels strong tension. This, of course, lessens the clarity of his thought processes, which makes it even more difficult for him to deal with his situation. Some people are chronic worriers. They keep the emotional pot simmering. Their prolonged fretting can indeed produce physical symptoms, which the worrywart interprets as confirmation of his forebodings. It is common knowledge that beginning medical students at times feel that they have the diseases they are studying; they become hypersensitive to the symptoms, and their perceptions are distorted.

Coping with Fear and Worry

Fear and worry are emotional reactions. Emotions make good servants but tyrannical masters, as we saw earlier. Therefore, these feelings should be looked on as problems to be solved. The following comments may prove of some use in controlling them.

1. It helps to admit frankly that the fear or worry exists. It is useless to shut one's eyes to it or to fancy that it will go away. Owning up to it is quite different, however, from exaggerating it so that it grows out of all proportion.

2. Fear or worry cannot be crushed by willpower. It is as futile to try to overcome it by direct attack as it is to try to blow out an electric light.

3. The cause of the feeling should be evaluated. Understanding the relationship between the cause and the emotion may indicate that there is no real reason for the reaction. A man who has just had a thorough physical examination has no need to worry about arteriosclerosis.

4. The executive should do what must be done, despite the feeling. Pushing the panic button only worsens it. There is a story about a British officer who was told by one of his men just before an assault, "Sir, your knees are shaking." The officer replied, "Son, if they knew where they had to carry me in a few minutes, they would fall off."

5. A woman who is fearful of mice can often control her feelings by acting on the basis of knowledge rather than emotion. Acting-as-if does not involve self-deception. It is a determination to do what is logical and rational in spite of one's state.

6. The executive should not put off an attempt to resolve the

fear or worry. It will rarely disappear by itself, as said above. If his efforts are unsuccessful, then he should seek out competent help promptly.

7. Relief activities can clear the head. Again, this is not an example of kidding oneself. Taking time out from fretting helps prevent it from building up unnecessarily. The person is well aware that he intends to return to the fear or worry, but he wishes to do so refreshed.

8. If possible, something positive and pleasant should be associated with the cause of the fear or worry. An important trip with the boss or a make-or-break presentation at a top-level meeting can cause fear. But it can also be used to motivate one to do his best. It can also be seen as an opportunity to succeed and make a positive impression on higher management.

9. Concentrate on the emotion, not the source. Focusing on the cause will increase the intensity of *any* feeling, positive or negative. If a man is afraid of his superior, constantly thinking about him will only aggravate the fear. It is like throwing gasoline on a fire. On the other hand, an emotion is like a fog: it often disappears under the sunlight of reason. The subordinate who is afraid of his superior should ask himself such questions as "What good is the fear doing me?" and "Why am I wasting my time and energy in unproductive ways?" Answers to questions of this sort weaken the power of the fear or worry.

Anxiety

Anxiety, like fear and worry, can be either rational or irrational. When it is rational, it represents a mature concern about an issue that is in doubt. When it is irrational, it makes the person resort to ineffectual methods of dealing with it. Everyone experiences this feeling at times. As Fulton J. Sheen has said, "Everyone has anxiety; fortunately, everyone does not have an anxiety complex." In fact, moderate anxiety, like moderate fear, can be a positive motivation to do a better job. The anxiety resulting from poor performance that is incompatible with a young salesman's self-concept and self-esteem may impel him to master his craft.

It is intense and prolonged anxiety that is disabling. It drains a person because it stems from a persistent conflict that has never been resolved. Most authorities agree that anxiety is the common core from which all neurotic behavior arises. The real problem is that anxiety is vague, pervasive, and painful but difficult to pinpoint and analyze. To make matters worse, the sufferer has habitually used inefficient methods for allaying his anxiety that do not even get close to its source. Eventually, feelings of helplessness, guilt, anger against himself, and isolation set in. He feels inadequate and immature. His sense of worth is greatly impaired.

The manager whose feelings about his superiors are hypersensitive or ambivalent because he has never worked through his attitudes toward authority may twist and turn as he will. He may try this and that technique for relating to them, but sooner or later, latent resentment will break through his carefully cultivated protective devices. The same applies to the manager who basically desires to be dependent but is forced by his position to act with relative independence. The best course of action for these men is to seek professional help and work through the conflicts that are causing their damaging behavior. The worst thing for them to do is to continue treating the behavioral symptoms rather than the roots of the difficulty in a defensive process of self-deception. This only guarantees the perpetuation of the anxiety cycle: from pain to ineffectual tension-relieving activities to short-term peace of mind to greater guilt and self-resentment, and so on without any lasting solution.

The Well-Adjusted Manager-Leader

Listing the characteristics of the well-balanced, mature manager-leader is of little use. Lists are static, and human personality is always dynamic; the lists say nothing of the interaction of attributes. On the other hand, most reasonably well adjusted people have certain traits in common. They are objective; they do not engage in self-deception to any significant extent. An executive showed objectivity when he remarked, "My quick temper is a great hindrance. I have to watch it or it gets me into hot water." They also have a fair measure of self-understanding in that they are aware of their strong and weak points without allowing the former to blind them to the latter. Self-acceptance—the ability to live with oneself contentedly but without complacence—is also an indication of maturity. To like oneself while trying to grow and improve gives inner peace.

Aristotle said that man is the only animal with a sense of humor. The ability to smile at oneself now and then is a healthy sign. The maladjusted person always takes himself far too seriously; for him, everything is grim. Most adults have learned to give and receive affection and friendship easily and without embarrassment. While everyone has certain eccentricities, the well-integrated personality is relatively free from quirks that hamper social relations. Adjusted people have developed problem-solving skills and techniques for controlling their emotions that keep their reactions in proportion. Their frustration threshold is reasonably high, and they are flexible and adaptable in coping with tension-producing situations.

At a deeper level, the mature manager knows who he is, what he stands for, and where he is going. This indicates that he has formulated a system of values that gives meaning to his life and developed a positive sense of direction in his career. Over and beyond these, he secures a reasonable amount of satisfaction from his work; he may not have a job that makes his heart sing, but he has one that enables him to meet at least some of his higher needs.

business ethics

There is probably no more bothersome item on the management agenda than business ethics. High-sounding platitudes abound. Clear ideas are notable by their absence. Absolutists insist that everything is either good or bad. Relativists contend that it all depends. Skeptics despair of finding a code of ethics that a majority of executives will accept. Cynics snicker at the lofty propositions espoused by megacorporations that dominate their markets. Pragmatists snort that ethics is a luxury for the small entrepreneur. Realists of goodwill query, "In a pluralistic society with disparate philosophies and religions, whose ethical system are we talking about?"

The situation is worsened by the fact that even institutions to which executives look for guidance have had little influence on their business behavior.

When 103 managers were asked to rate six factors according to their influence on their moral behavior, education was placed last. Both executives who had taken a formal college course in ethics and those who had not responded to nine selected ethical situations similarly. Religiously affiliated managers gave answers to ethical problems that were not notably different from those given by participants who were not identified with a formal religion. Businessmen as a general rule do not look with any great confidence to their clergymen for practical guidance on ethical problems, even though they would appreciate realistic instruction in this area.[1]

The subject of ethics is all rather confusing to the executive. Perhaps, after all, business is nothing more than a boxing match in which bluffing, in-fighting, and cheating are permissible as long as they remain within the rather generous perimeters of legality.

Considering the Options

"People of the same trade seldom meet together but the conversation ends in a conspiracy against the public, or in some diversion to raise prices." This statement of Adam Smith's in 1776 would strike a responsive chord in the hearts of many two centuries later. A system of ethics is like oxygen. We take it for granted until an egregious violation of minimal moral standards sends a shock wave through the business community. God's in his heaven and all's well with the world until a disaster like the electric company case breaks. Let seven high-level officials go to jail, let the companies involved be fined almost $2 million, let some 1,700 law suits be filed with the potential costs ranging from $1½ to 2 billion, then some soul searching will take place —at least until the crisis passes.

Granted that the entire field of ethics is something of a maze, it behooves the manager-leader to give some thought to available options. If little or no effort is expended to solidify the moral foundations of executive action, what is the glue that will keep society together? If discussions of corporate ethics are met with a sly smile, what will block a gradual return to a jungle and jugular concept of human relationships? If ethical guidelines are eroded to the point of impotence, what will prevent the pyramid climbers from dominating economic society?

Ethics is like democracy, of which Winston Churchill said, it is the worst possible form of government until one considers the alternatives. Arthur Hull Hayes, former president of CBS Radio, claimed that he was called upon to make a moral decision almost every day. And Thomas J. Watson, Jr. once wrote, "Beliefs always come before policies, practices and goals. The latter must always be altered if they are seen to violate fundamental beliefs. The only sacred cow in an organization should be its basic philosophy of doing business." However perplexing the task, the manager-leader must have a candid encounter with his values.

Ethics or Legislation?

Few executives would deny the need for a common denominator of moral principles. Many would contend, however, that a special variety of business ethics is needless. The purpose of an organization is to supply goods and services in the quantities and qualities desired by the public at prices it is willing to pay. Profits are a reward for providing the community with these goods and services more efficiently than competitors. By doing so, a firm makes its proper contribution to the community and the common good. Ethics has reference to a human being; the corporation is not a human being. It has been established by law, and its sole responsibility is to respect legal boundaries as it prospers and grows. Thus, legislation and the manager's conscience are all that are needed; talk of ethics is superfluous. Morality equals legality.

The contrary viewpoint maintains that such an approach is incredibly naive. The law is largely negative and minimal. It is generally behind the times in that it usually constitutes a reaction, not action. It represents neither the ideal nor even the desirable; it is the best compromise that conflicting interests allow. Moreover, the law is static, whereas business and industry are dynamic and ever changing; relying solely on legislation would force executives to deal with current problems on the basis of a past orientation. Finally, if the law were to be the only foundation, then managers would be overwhelmed, since no number of enactments can take into account all the varieties of human experience or the vicissitudes of human nature.

It is equally simple-minded, according to this viewpoint, to depend only on the manager's conscience and goodwill. To leave crucial matters of morality to one man's personal judgment is dangerous. The range of individual differences and the disparities in executives' backgrounds and training foredoom such a practice. For better or worse, some managers have refined and sensitive consciences, whereas others are far more callous. One will have a mature and well-informed conscience; another's will be barely an eyelid above the pigsty. To expect such people to coordinate their practices or even compete without spelling out the game rules is ridiculous. Many authorities maintain that every disruptive psychological problem is ultimately a moral (not to be confused with a religious) problem. It arises from a conflict between a person's behavior and his convictions. Finally, man must live in an ethical cosmos, not an ethical chaos. The good is superior to the expedient; ends are more important than means. Chesterton once remarked that if he owned a boardinghouse, he would be more concerned about his roomers' philosophy of life than their income. Only if they had ethical standards would he be sure of getting his rent.

Ethics as a Science

Ethics is a practical, normative, philosophical science that studies and evaluates the rightness or wrongness of voluntary human acts. Per se, it has nothing to do with formal religion. Ethics relies on the proper use of reason, religion on revelation. Religion requires faith; ethics demands intellectual honesty and rationality. The truths of religion, in a sense, are final and complete; those of ethics are always incomplete. Using different sources and methodologies, both provide principles and directives for human conduct.

Calling ethics a science will shock those who restrict the term to the investigation of physical phenomena. Basically, science is an attitude of mind and an approach to the study of reality. Any science has certain characteristics: it is an organized body of knowledge, and this knowledge is demonstrable and valid in the light of available evidence; it allows certain phenomena to be described, explained, and predicted, within limits; it is universal in that its basic concepts do not vary widely according to contingencies of time and place; it provides guiding laws and principles; and it applies a defined methodology and perspective to pertinent subject matter.

If one will not constrain the term *science* to the restrictive perimeters of the physical disciplines, and if one will grant that there are many scientific methods, then ethics meets the definition. Moral laws can be as valid as the law of gravity. One cannot, however, expect to approach material and moral realities in the same manner. The precise study of organic symptoms, for instance, will tell us nothing of mental disorders. Since ethics is a human science like psychology and medicine, it cannot provide answers with the same degree of precision as, let us say, chemistry does. Even today, it is more accurate to speak of the *practice* of medicine than of the *science* of medicine. Thus, ethics is an incomplete science. What the manager-leader needs is a moral road map to indicate the way he should go. This is all that the science of ethics seeks to provide.

Theories of Ethics

It is interesting that man has not always had a need for economic theory. He has always felt the need for an ethical system. In fact, economics grew out of what was called moral philosophy. Hence, it is not surprising that man has experimented with various ethical orientations.

Hedonism, especially in materialistic cultures, has always had a strong appeal. If a thing or act gives pleasure, it is good; if it is painful, it is bad. Plucking the day and living it up for the present have been tried and have always failed to satisfy reflective men. At times, Kant's concept of doing one's duty has been attractive. If every man but did his duty, the world would be in great shape. Unfortunately, as Stalin proved so well, much depends on who defines the duty. Stoicism appeals to the higher aspects of man. One must live according to reason, disciplining emotions and sensual desires. When he overcomes the irrational elements in his makeup, he can live not only a self-sufficient but a good life.

Utilitarianism has a persuasive appeal. After all, what could be more beneficial than the greatest good for the greatest number? When this principle violates the natural rights of even one human being, however, it degenerates into despotism. Theoretically, at least, it might constitute the greatest good for the greatest number to eliminate all the insane or aged or those with IQs below 70. Pragmatism has a peculiar attraction for Americans. If it works, it must be good. An experimental, instrumental cast of mind can readily subvert such an approach and turn it to the service of self-interest. The fact is that what may be "good" pragmatically may be unjust.

The social contracts of Hobbes and Rousseau, based respectively on fear of one's fellow man and confidence in the innate goodness of humankind, are built on a societywide agreement to respect the rights of others; this agreement is administered by the state or insured by men's benevolence for each other. Situation ethics, a recent arrival on the scene, contends that nothing is absolute; everything depends on the context in which it occurs. What may be wrong in one set of circumstances may be perfectly licit in a different set.

The difficulty with all these theories is not that they are wrong but that they are limited and incomplete. They have no provisos that protect the weak against the strong or the minority against the tyranny of the majority.

What about custom, tradition, and religion? Custom and tradition, to be sure, are often distillations of tested experience. On the other hand, both are geared to the past rather than to the present or future. Both are likely to preserve the bad as well as the good. Slavery was sanctioned by custom and tradition in Athens and America even though it violated the most basic of all human rights. As for religion, in a melting-pot culture characterized by many sects, religion has much to contribute. But it fails to provide a common denominator that all Christians, Jews, and other theists, not to mention agnostics and atheists, will accept.

Possible Sources of Ethics

The most obvious source of ethics is the state, that is, the whole of the body politic. Whatever the state decrees to be ethical automatically becomes so. Unhappily, the state is a man-made institution and subject to all the foibles of its creators. Moreover, every human being has certain rights that even the state may not abrogate.

At the opposite extreme is individual judgment. Whatever a person judges to be ethical or unethical is so. This, of course, is the position of those who refuse to submit to the draft. They decide that a given war or all warring is immoral; therefore, it is immoral. Yet if all matters are left to the discretion of the individual citizen, if each person is free to decide which laws he will or will not accept, the entire fabric of society is rent. What agency, then, will be vested with the authority to require the individual to accept the consequences of his actions, an obligation corresponding to his right and duty to follow his inner convictions?

Law is the last resort of those who seek an ethical system. According to the historical record, however, man-made laws have a way sometimes of being unjust. Moreover, what man has made, man can unmake. This represents a rather shaky base for consistent ethical behavior.

A Way out of the Ethical Woods

Man, no matter where he is found on this earth, has at least four common characteristics. He is *rational* in that he can use his intellect to understand, to reason, and to judge. He is *social* in that he is constituted to live in community with his fellow men. In certain conditions, he is *self-determining;* certain acts and responsibility for them are imputable to him. Granted that man does not always think rationally, and granted that he may at times act on the basis of emotion rather than objective facts, he still remains fundamentally endowed with reason and freedom. Lastly, man is "the only animal who knows." Since he knows the moral quality of his behavior, he can feel both guilt and self-approval.

It follows from man's essential sameness wherever he is found that a study of his nature can reveal certain basic principles of how he should act and how others should treat him. The first finding of such an analysis is that every man possesses certain human rights. A right is merely a title to what is consistent with a person's nature and necessary for his well-balanced development. These so-called natural rights cannot be enumerated to the last detail. A man's ability to exercise them, of course, will vary according to the cultural matrix and the resources of the community in which he lives. Be that as it may, he has at least the following innate rights: to justice; to privacy; to his reputation and good name; to freedom of movement; to an education that will equip him to marry and raise a family decently; to a job, and to enough income to provide not only the necessities of life but also at least some of the better things of life; to adequate housing; to proper medical care, whether he can pay for it or not; to association with his fellows to promote common interests, as occurs in unions and management associations; to a certain amount of leisure; to reasonable protection against the problems of old age.

The trouble with ethics is that, whereas everyone is conscious of his due, most are somewhat reluctant to acknowledge their duties. Rights are not a one-way street. For every right, there exists a corresponding obligation. If the worker has a claim to a fair day's pay, he has a moral responsibility to provide a fair day's work in return. One of the most blatant derelictions in modern society is the failure to carry out responsibilities conscientiously. Needless to say, there is no proportionate renunciation of rights. In ethics as in all things else, nothing returns nothing. Everything has a price that must be paid.

Ethics and Human Conduct

Every science is, by definition, incomplete and evolving. To expect of ethical science either pat formulas that can be mechanically applied to every situation or final answers to every possible problem is jejune. A study of man living in community and responsible to a degree for the welfare of his fellow men reveals the following precepts.

The primary principle. The basic principle of ethics is that man is made to do good and to avoid evil. This principle is as universal as Newton's laws. Thus, in Kant's terms, the manager must never use anyone as a mere means to his personal ends nor allow anyone to use him so. Again in Kant's terms, the manager should decide what he is going to do or not do according to whether he would be willing to have his decision applied to and used by all men as a universal law.

The outstanding anthropologist Clyde Kluckhohn has maintained that his studies do not support the notion of ethical relativism. The obligation to do good and avoid evil is recognized and accepted in every culture. Differences in interpretation reflect differences in the cultures themselves and arise from the fact that the culture is in the personality and the personality in the culture. One can no more violate this basic ethical law over the long term than he can physical laws. As persistent and heavy drinking, excessive smoking, or dope addiction eventually catches up with a person, so too do habitual violations of this fundamental principle. Education will, of course, help a man clarify what is good or evil. But education is not enough; he needs to commit himself to doing what is right, with due allowances made for human frailties. Theodore Roosevelt once remarked that a tramp will steal a ride on a railroad car, but if he is sent to college and educated, he will steal the railroad.

The secondary principles. The categorical imperative to do good and avoid evil is evident to anyone with a modicum of intelligence and experience. Grasping and practicing the secondary principles, however, require considerable gray matter and education, for the distinctions and discriminations to be made can be subtle. For instance, it is not immediately evident whether euthanasia is good or bad. Some of the questions executives must answer are nettlesome and require extensive examination before a definitive conclusion can be reached. When does a company's right to know about its new employees become a violation of their right to privacy? What are the limits beyond which psychological testing cannot be carried, even though probing into a man's personality may yield useful information for the firm? Has an organization the right to interview the wife of a prospective manager? What ethical problems are involved in maintaining so-called data banks or dossiers of information that the subjects may not know about and can never see? In what conditions may a polygraph be used? What ethical considerations enter into demotions and dismissals? Nettlesome as these problems are, men of goodwill who persistently search for what is right can reach firm conclusions and draw up practical guidelines for appropriate behavior. Were this not true, then professions such as accounting, law, and medicine would have no codes of conduct.

Most informed men of goodwill can come to some agreement on the secondary principles, even though unanimity is of course not to be expected. A good example of this is found in *Ethical Standards of Psychologists:*

> [*The committee*] *had to decide whether to concern itself with only issues that were clearly a matter of ethics, in the sense of bearing moral implications, or whether to extend its concern to include matters of professional practice and*

of courtesy. The decision was made to define ethics broadly . . . and although the dividing lines between ethics and good practice and courtesy are often hard to draw, the committee has made an attempt at such differentiation, lest all issues be reduced to the least common denominator of courtesy.[2]

The tertiary principles. Given the same information and about the same education and goodwill, men can draw different conclusions in areas that are not clearly black or white. It is the gray that is confusing. Only the most callous of conscience would seriously contend that securing call girls for a customer in order to facilitate a sale is a matter of ethical indifference. By any name, procuring or pimping violates moral concepts, not to mention human dignity and self-respect. But the matter is different when it comes to questions like these:

Is it ethical for a small firm staffed with otherwise unemployable people to pay them less than a living wage if the alternative is that it go out of business and throw them out on the street?

Is it ethical for a businessman to engage in certain unethical practices to counteract the strategies of a competitor who has little or no regard for ethical behavior?

Is it ethical for a tobacco company to manufacture marijuana cigarettes if it is legal?

Is it ethical for a doctor to recommend that his patients go to a hospital built by a corporation that he has stock in?

Is it ethical for a company that is making a reasonable profit to move from one locality to another, leaving the employees in the lurch even though certain financial measures are taken to make the separation as painless as possible, if the reasons for the move are to increase profits, escape a union, and obtain certain tax benefits?

Is it ethical for a firm to give preferential treatment in employment and promotions to competent members of minority and disadvantaged groups, although there are other, better-qualified contenders?

It is quite possible for executives to disagree over the ethics of such questions as these, despite the fact that they may be equally educated and equally dedicated to sound principles.

Moral Knowledge or Moral Courage?

To know what is the right thing to do is usually far easier than to do it. The manager-leader is not expected to be any more perfect than the general run of mankind. On the other hand, expectations and mandates rise as authority, power, and influence accrue to a person. What might be frowned upon in a private citizen can become intolerable in that same citizen as a candidate for a seat on the Supreme Court. Rank has not only its privileges but its increased responsibility to give an example of impeccable conduct. Human frailties in high places are understandable. They cannot be considered mere peccadilloes as they might be in people of lower station. To paraphrase President Truman, if the executive cannot bear the ethical heat, let him stay out of the organizational kitchen.

What can the conscientious manager-leader do who desires to combine, as best he can within his all too human limitations, ethical behavior and practical actions that produce growth and profits?

He can develop an informed conscience. In the final analysis, everyone must follow his conscience. Conscience, contrary to popular belief, is not a matter of feelings or emotions. It is an intellectual process whereby an executive judges whether an act or course of action is good and therefore should be done, or bad and therefore should be avoided. It is also the function of conscience to compel a man to experience guilt *consequent* to an act that is contrary to his convictions. In the first role, feelings and emotions have little to do with conscience; in the second, they play an important part. But the executive's conscience must be informed; he must seriously undertake to discover what makes for ethical and unethical behavior. Additionally, it must be mature, realistic, and sensitive. The manager must avoid a primitive absolutism that makes him rigid and a rubber-band relativism that makes him a moral zero. Like mathematics, ethics has constants and variables. The intellectual constants give a man a sense of direction and purpose; the variables must be taken into account for a specific decision. But the constants cannot be sacrificed to the variables.

He can do his best to seek justice. Justice obtains when each person is rendered his due. *Exchange* or *contract* justice exists between people who are equal with respect to the matter at hand. Its purpose is to protect the rights of individuals. It is evident whenever one endeavors to be fair in his dealings with others. This is a minimum requisite in the manager-leader's conduct. *Distributive* justice is involved in the relationship between a society and its members. It requires the fair distribution of both the benefits and the burdens of a given community among its members. *Corrective* justice endeavors to rectify wrongs that have been done and to redress legitimate grievances. *Social* justice requires that every man contribute to the common good of society. The executive must be alert to his responsibilities in these areas if he is to act in a generally ethical manner.

He can develop a realistic personal code of conduct. The typical manager does not need intellectual enlightenment nearly so much as he needs the intestinal fortitude to live by a personal code that is reasonably valid and operationally effective. He is not meant to be holier than thou. On the other hand, he is less than a man if he habitually takes refuge behind the specious defense that "Everyone else is doing it"; in fact, this is exactly what he often complains about in his children. Circumstances, it is true, may at times impel or compel him to act contrary to his code. Ultimately, however, he will have to decide which is better: to live with success at any price or to live with himself.

In developing his code of conduct, the manager-leader can begin with a fixed intention to do good and avoid evil whenever this is possible. He can continue by taking Kant's injunctions to heart: never to use another person as a mere means to his own ends, and never to allow another to use him for his ends. He can then ask himself whether he would want his actions to become universal law for all men. In addition, he might give ear to some questions similar to ones proposed by Edmond Cahn, professor of law at New York University: [3]

— How would the action look to the public if all the facts, interests, motives, and profits were known?

— How would it look if the consequences were entirely different from those the executive expects?

— If he finds himself arguing that it is a nigh-on universal practice, then he might test his position by assuming that his is the unique example of this act. How does it appear in this light?

— If a tempting unethical act will keep or advance him in his job and thus enable him to do much future good, is the act not wrong nonetheless and the excuse a self-deception?

— How would he see the act if it were done by his most detested adversary?

— Does he believe that the act will cast honor or shame on the community?

He can give an example. The manager-leader influence for good or the opposite, in the final analysis, stems not so much from what he knows or thinks but rather from what he does and is. The executive can test almost all conduct, at least intellectually, by asking the following questions: Would he want what he does to appear on the first page of *The New York Times,* with a complete explanation of his true reasons for his action? And would he want his own children to work for a manager who implements in his day-to-day activities the ethical principles and practices that he himself follows? Would he be willing to defend publicly, before a panel of his peers, every major decision or course of action that has serious ethical implications?

Perfection is not meant for this life. Improvement is not only possible but necessary, especially in the realm of ethical behavior. This is all that can be expected of the conscientious manager.

Problems of Social Responsibility

If ethical considerations are calculated to stimulate the nerve endings of businessmen, discussions of the social responsibilities of corporations and executives have a way of provoking volatile opinions and emotions. Why is this so?

In a conversation with a member of a foreign embassy, the writer found himself listening to the following train of thought. Americans are just beginning to learn to live within the limits of a bounded environment. Up to now, they have lived a life of lotus eaters. A virgin country with undeveloped resources was just yearning to be exploited.

"Now," he continued, "you Americans are reaching a stage of development that we Europeans had to face up to many years ago. Your natural resources are not limitless. You must wrestle with the side effects and aftermath of your industrial revolution. The land is no longer free for the taking; nor is it endlessly fertile. It must be husbanded and managed. Problems of population, pollution, housing, recreation, employment, health, education, and old age are not to be solved by appealing to private enterprise or rugged individualism or by great outpourings of government money. You Americans are now being forced to act like adults. From now on, you will have to think through your values, order your national priorities, and realize that you cannot have everything at once. Even America's resources are exhaustible."

There is, of course, much truth in the statements of this European. Too often, business and industry have acted as though God gave them national resources to use as they saw fit, unmindful of the repugnant offshoots of their operations. Someone has said that by the year 2000, we shall be firing missiles from the tops of mountains of garbage produced by an affluent society. Yet industrial progress has a price tag. One-fifth of our people live in poverty while another fifth live a borderline existence. The ill-housed, the ill-fed, and the ill-clothed remind us that the golden side of democratic capitalism is not the whole story. Ecological convulsions loom large on the horizon, and, perhaps more often than is genuinely fair, their causes are traced to industry. Be that as it may, organizations can no longer expect to tap national resources without regard for the consequences.

In the words of a noted business leader, the day when industry was allowed to enjoy obscure prosperity is as dead as a dodo. The American people seem determined to compel large corporations to recognize that, if making money is a legitimate objective, making a good society will be one of their most insistent demands in the next few decades.

Models for Corporate Conduct

In an excellent monograph, *Corporate Social Responsibilities,* Clarence C. Walton has examined the entire problem clearly and succinctly.[4] He derives from his research six major models that are open to corporations: (1) the austere model, (2) the household model, (3) the vendor model, (4) the investment model, (5) the civic model, (6) the artistic model.

The austere model. The austere view of the business firm maintains that it is an economic entity first, last, and always. Its perennial goal is to maximize profits. It consists of two groups: (1) the shareholders and the prime movers who generate profits and (2) everyone and everything else that represents a resource to be utilized for this end. Although executives may do much to improve society and further the condition of mankind, all such efforts must have a profit orientation. Individuals and groups may contribute to the common good but on their own time and with their own money. Organizational resources are not to be diverted from profit seeking. In a literal sense, the business of business is business; all else is extraneous to the major purpose of a company.

It would be an injustice to impute motives of selfishness to executives who uphold this theory, which is defended by such worthies as Andrew Hacker, Theodore Levitt, Milton Friedman, and others. Its proponents contend that, should the corporation abandon or water down its principal purpose by attending to societal problems, more harm than good would result. No other arm of the community can adequately make up for its failure to perform its proper task. Private enterprise contributes to society by making money, paying taxes, providing employment, raising the economic level of the nation, and giving people opportunities to improve themselves. Competition should be keen and intensive but fair and in accord with the law. These functions will benefit society in the long run. Furthermore, executives lack the time and know-how to deal competently with social ills. Their efforts to do so would be futile and would turn a productive corporation with an efficient corps of managers into an amateur social service with inept workers who, instead of tending to their profit-producing knitting, would blunder into the maze of social problems filled with high purposes but doomed to fail.

The household model. According to the household concept, a firm's employees have important and definite rights. The corporation is a kind of extended family in which top management plays something of a *padrone* role. The company does not simply pursue profits single-mindedly and formulate cold, impersonal strategies to this end. Its human assets, the employees, have a claim on it that is at least equal if not actually superior to that of the investors. Although profit is a sine qua non for survival and growth, it must not be obtained at the expense of the personal or collective rights of employees. Hence, the maximization of profits is at most a secondary aim. The purpose of profit is to provide not only a fair return on investment to owners but also steady work at good wages with good working conditions for people who, given these satisfactions, will produce even higher earnings. Human rights, then, take precedence over property rights.

It is clear that such an approach may bring about organizational paternalism, although it need not. The fact is that most large corporations endeavor to protect their employees from the specter of economic uncertainty. It is perhaps one of the greatest merits of American industry that the average employee has *not* turned to the government to insure his present and future economic security. Rather, he has relied on the conscience of the company; to the credit of private enterprise, he has rarely been disappointed.

The vendor model. Where the austere model spotlights the shareholders and the household model the corporate team, of which the employees are a major part, the vendor model puts the consumer front and center. Instead of being an *internal* game among shareholders, executives, and unions and employees, this approach focuses attention on the *external* responsibilities of the firm. People like Ralph Nader have the vendor model in mind when they argue forcefully for the rights of the customer, that often forgotten man. The vendor kind of firm emphasizes its intention to provide high-quality goods and services to those who pay for them, replacing "Let the buyer beware" with "Let the seller be honest." The benefit to the public is no less real if the motive is self-serving: the realization that the consumer may rise up in his collective wrath and see to it that binding government strictures are placed on private enterprise. The truth-in-lending and truth-in-packaging laws are tokens of what may ultimately come to companies that fail in their social responsibility to consumers.

The investment model. At one time, it would have been unheard-of for a corporation to devote part of the shareholders' profits to endowing an educational institution, building a park, or otherwise improving the community. In fact, top management's right to donate funds to such projects has been challenged—unsuccessfully—in the courts: it is accepted that the prudent use of some of a firm's income for social purposes is well within the prerogatives of those who are responsible for the good health of the organization.

The firm following the investment model fully expects to secure a generous return on its investment in the social good over the long haul. Its fundamental principle is not altruism but a pragmatic self-interest. The corporation intends to continue, if possible, *in perpetuum*. It is dependent on the sufferance of the government and the benevolence of the public. Often it feels that it can perform an extracorporate job more effectively than government agencies or other groups in the community. To generate goodwill, to protect its future, to defend against government incursions, *and* to contribute to the general welfare, it takes on certain activities that may temporarily reduce its return on assets in the hope of increasing it ultimately. One can hire the disadvantaged not out of love for one's fellow man but because just one segment of it, the black population, represents at least a $30 billion market that must grow as Negroes move up the economic ladder.

The civic model. Activities like the following would be legitimate under a civic model of corporate social responsibility. A company spends millions of dollars installing devices that will lower or eliminate air and water pollution in a city. A corporation recruits disadvantaged people of all races and creeds, trains them on its premises and with its own resources, and places them on its payroll. A firm allows a manager to serve for a year with pay as a special adviser to a mayor or governor. A group of insurance companies provide funds for the renewal of a ghetto neighborhood, the planning and execution of the project being done by the residents. A corporation opens up a plant in a high-risk area of a community to help it in its bootstrap program.

Although the reasons for taking them on are varied, projects such as these are not geared to immediate or even perhaps long-term profits. The company lives in the community and feels a need to be a good citizen. The civic model implies a commitment to making democracy work. The key principle is that the general welfare is superior to mere profits. Hence, the executive is convinced that beyond making a profit, which is an obvious necessity, he has an obligation to improve and refine the democratic system and actualize its potential more fully. He is conscious of the general applicability of Alfred Sloan's statement that the automobile industry has "a tremendously valuable franchise from the United States and should respect it."

The artistic model. In a postindustrial culture, in which a social ethic and leisure time are becoming more prominent, it well may be that the artistic model of corporate social responsibility may receive greater emphasis. The first industrial revolution replaced human muscle, thus providing far greater leisure for the worker than he had ever dreamed possible. The second industrial revolution is substituting machine brains for human. The knowledge explosion, advances in technical methods, automation, and similar developments give promise of unprecedented amounts of free time. The artistic model, which is now receiving minimal attention, maintains that the social responsibility of corporations does not stop at contributing to the common good but includes beautifying the communities in which they exist. Accordingly, there is no reason a firm should not help fund libraries and museums and sponsor plays, concerts, and other cultural endeavors.

It may well be a proper concern of the company to improve the esthetic quality of life enjoyed by the citizens of a community. A humane, responsible, creative society that enables a man not only to make a living but also to appreciate and enjoy the finer aspects of life is the aim of the artistic model. In fact, "muse products" currently receive 5 percent of all corporate giving. What is more, studies show that a cultured environment stimulates employees: they work better when "officially" exposed to art or music. Even so, it is granted, such a concept of the role of the corporation seems a bit farfetched at present. Yet it may be a promising model for the future.

Where Does This Leave the Manager-Leader?

The executive must fashion for himself a personal code of ethical behavior under the guidance of valid principles and standards. This is the foundation for building his role in society. His most demanding task as architect of that role is not to be merely an economic success but to become as complete a human being as possible; economic success at the expense of more important values has a way of leaving a taste of ashes in one's mouth. This implies that he must evolve his own order of priorities, distinguishing what is essential and important from what is only incidental for living as a well-balanced, integrated, and mature person.

The dominant constituent of our culture is the corporate society, which sets in large measure the tone and ethos of society as a whole. It is taken for granted that the manager-leader will strive to perfect himself in his craft and attain whatever success is possible. We are far from an age that admires those who turn their backs on the economic system. On the other hand, the economic man is but one facet of God's creation. The manager-leader must give as well as take, must contribute as well as receive. So must the corporation. The austere model may be theoretically possible, but in present conditions it is practically unrealistic. The artistic model, however, is a bit far out, even though events seem to be moving slowly in this direction. The household model harks back to an outdated era in which paternalism held sway. Hence, perhaps some combination of the vendor, investment, and civic models would be most appropriate.

the manager-leader: catalyst for change

Three things are certain about the future. It will be radically different from the past; it will be somewhat different from the present; it will be rather different from what we expect it to be. As Benjamin Disraeli once remarked, the expected often does not occur, whereas the unexpected does. Who, for instance, in the 1950s, predicted the restiveness of disadvantaged groups, the rebelliousness of students, and the *cause célèbre* that the Vietnam conflict became in the 1960s—the three most important developments in that decade?

The manager-leader must nonetheless have an eye to the future, even if simply to avoid becoming its victim. Knowledge multiplies and techniques proliferate. Not since the Reformation have basic values been so challenged. Not since the Renaissance has there been such concern for the quality of life on this planet. With so many movements afoot and so much of existence in a state of flux, it is risky to predict what is to come. Yet, undeniably, the future will one day be the present. When this happens, doors will be open to the prepared and shut in the faces of the unprepared.

Rather than launch into a lexicon of the changes that loom on the horizons, it might be more realistic to limit the discussion to two factors that are already upon us: the need for innovation and managerial leadership in the introduction of change.

Performance, Creativity, and Innovation

The three terms *performance, creativity,* and *innovation* are subject to much confusion. *Performance* means productivity based on past and present concepts, procedures, and processes. *Creativity* is the ability to fabricate the brilliant idea, the striking breakthrough. The product of creativity is invention. *Innovation* is an act that strives to produce small, incremental improvements on what is accepted today. It looks for newer and better solutions to old and current problems, solutions tied to some practical objective and geared to some measurable operational result. Companies have found to their regret that it is self-defeating to seek only creativity. As one authority has observed, "Even when new developments emerged from the R&D process, the odds were often estimated as high as eight or nine out of ten that they would fail commercially." Moreover, there is some question regarding just how many truly creative people the average organization can sustain. In fact, a firm populated by inventive types would find it difficult to operate in a well-coordinated manner and with reasonably consistent administrative procedures.

If the aim of creativity is invention, that of innovation is improvement. Managers are not paid to create; they are paid to become more effective and to operate increasingly effective organizations. Although the manager-leader should encourage creativity in every realistic way, he should not hold his breath for it, since lightning has a frustrating way of striking as it will. And even when a truly creative idea has been proposed, years may pass before conditions are right for its implementation. Innovation, however, can be readily translated into operations strategies. Moreover, unlike creativity, which requires intellectual acumen of a high order, innovation demands no great intelligence. Its principal characteristics are a dissatisfaction with the good enough and a focused concern for improvement. It is difficult to create or invent something that is entirely new. It is relatively easy to improve what already exists. Creativity may be more thrilling, but innovation is more realistic in the average firm or department.

Why Aren't People More Innovative?

The innovator must have an attitude that constructively challenges accepted ways of seeing or doing things, a conviction that anything made by man can be improved by man if he but thinks about it in a new way, an ability to blend familiar concepts and processes into novel combinations, skill in translating and transferring perceptions from one situation to another that at first blush seems to be entirely different, a refusal now and then to be constrained by the seemingly rational and logical, and a willingness to maintain flexibility in the face of failure.

How many years did it take before manufacturers of refrigerators put them on wheels and why did it take so long to think of setting windows in oven doors, although both articles had been with us for generations? Why is it that when the simplest innovation is introduced, a common reaction is, "Why didn't I think of that?" The reasons people are not more innovative, despite the fact that under the right conditions most of us enjoy the experience, stem from at least three sources: the organization's philosophy and tone, the personality of the worker, and pressures from peers.

The Organization's Philosophy

ABC Company is a very large manufacturing organization. It fared well for years, but then it began to see its share of the market drop as more determined and innovative competitors entered the field. Almost unconsciously, the top echelons had remained content with the status quo. Lower-level managers had been extremely likable, conforming, pliant, and modest producers. Rarely had anyone said or done anything extraordinary that might have gotten him tossed out of the organizational ark. Under the pressure of keener competition and a falling profit picture, top management set about changing the corporate course. The firm diversified into previously unthought-of fields. It encouraged professional management. It gave the "golden handshake" to key officials who could not or would not get cracking. It brought carefully selected young tigers on board. It demanded performance of a high order and rewarded it reasonably well. In return, actions, suggestions, ideas, and questions reached the top that would never have been proposed before. Requests and even demands came from the lower levels that made some old-timers shake their heads in a mixture of grudging admiration and wonderment. In the meantime, the growth and profit pictures improved slowly but measurably.

DEF Corporation is the largest firm in its industry. For decades, it was content to be first among its peers. Then, under new leadership, it ventured into new but related fields. It built a research facility and a very profitable international operation. As part of a self-development program, each person in a management or supervisory position was asked to scrutinize his job with a view to suggesting one or more practical improvements. Although relatively only a few people took on self-imposed chores of cost reduction, in less than one year a total of some $2 million was saved. Comparable improvements were forthcoming in other operational areas. The idea of improvement has caught on and is being pursued vigorously.

These two examples illustrate certain facts about the impact of an organization's climate on innovation.

Despite the accepted stereotype, it is not true that the large organization is a constricting force. Actually, the evidence shows that it is the locus of most innovation, though innovation is found wherever the corporate philosophy and atmosphere are supportive. Second, improvement is encouraged when competence rather than merely position rules. Third, innovation flourishes when the company or department demands and rewards it. In this regard, the manager-leader is both intellectually cruel and humanely encouraging—cruel in that he tolerates no nonsense and insists that each subordinate improve his work, encouraging in that he is open to new ideas as long as they are based on evidence or experience. Without this supportive spirit, the smog of premature criticism will kill off even the best of suggestions.

The innovative executive takes it for granted that some original proposals will force him to restructure his role and relationships to some extent. Moreover, he is aware of his preferences and aversions and resolves to prevent them from blinding him to the new. For better or worse, innovation is where one finds it, regardless of status or title. More imaginative ideas have been done in by the negative attitudes of authorities than by lack of evidence. Finally, the manager seeks to build a climate that welcomes innovation by rewarding growth in and through one's job. It is shameful that subordinates expend so much of their innovative energies *after* the workday has ended.

The Personality of the Worker

At times, the employees are hostile to innovation. Although people are not born that way, some become that way for a variety of reasons. They are their own worst enemies as far as venturing into the arena of the novel is concerned, and their personality structures are not going to change overnight if at all.

Some people have so little confidence in themselves as human beings that it is useless to expect innovation from them. They are secure only when life is organized and predictable. The unknown frightens and disturbs them. Among these are compulsive conformers, who find it painful to be out of step with either authorities or the group. This can breed habits of dependence and an excessive desire for approval, which can thwart the innovative potential of the brightest head.

Fear of failure or even criticism overwhelms some people; they find that the risk involved in sticking their necks out is too much to bear. Fear of loss of status, too, makes certain people perceive improvement as a threat. They are failure avoiders rather than success seekers.

Overspecialization and preoccupation with a narrow field of endeavor or expertise can blind one to new vistas. Everybody is familiar with the accountant who never sees meaning in his data and with the controller who has no feel for finance. Similarly, emotional overinvolvement with an idea or procedure can prompt one either to resist a different view or to listen with his claws. In addition, idolizing rationality at times prevents a person from mentally manipulating seemingly illogical combinations and the apparently absurd just to see what happens. All these forms of extreme behavior exemplify a rigidity that destroys the openness, flexibility, and sensitivity essential to innovation. A refusal to experiment is lethal to imagination, as is the attitude that there is nothing new under the sun.

Since everyone suffers more or less from each of these fears at one time or another, what separates the truly innovative man from the mere pretender? Because the culture now tends to deify the new, the manager must be able to tell the mere poseur from the genuine article. The following characteristics, habitually revealed day in and day out, tend to distinguish the two.

The Innovator	The Pseudo-Innovator
Is intellectually inquisitive.	Is cynically curious.
Is constructively critical.	Is corrosively critical.
Seeks to improve the operation.	Seeks to impress others.
Has firm convictions but listens to the ideas of others.	Resents honest and constructive criticism.
Tends to be a loner at times.	Tends to rob the ideas of others.
Is relatively unconcerned with the more superficial aspects of organizational protocol.	Is likely to emphasize organizational protocol if it magnifies his ego or status.
Is persistent; carries on well in spite of opposition.	Attacks opposition, is easily discouraged, and pouts readily.
Pushes ideas through to completion.	Flits from idea to idea, making many starts but few completions.
Usually has a sense of humor.	Shows little humor, and that tends to be caustic.
Is able to take disagreement in stride.	Takes disagreement as a personal affront.
Does not relate easily to authority but accepts it as a fact of life.	Generally resents authority and wastes energy fighting or undermining it.

The Innovator	The Pseudo-Innovator
Is zealous for his ideas and programs.	Is zealous for his prerogatives and status.
Prefers complexity.	Prefers the attention-getting or shocking.
Deviates only when needful.	Deviates for the sake of being different.
Usually not adept in human relations.	Often quite adroit in human relations of the manipulative kind.
Is nonconformist in a natural and unconcerned manner.	Is noncomformist for purposes of display.
Is solid and thorough, willing to persevere for lasting results.	Is shallow, settling for superficial results.
In his own way, is genuinely interested in the success of the operation.	Has a personal ax to grind.

Pressures from Peers

Many if not most of the pressures against innovation arise not from the higher levels of management but rather from immediate superiors and coworkers. A subordinate does not have to live with the top executives; he must work out harmonious relationships with his boss and fellows. If the former throws cold water on new ideas, all innovative efforts will be aborted. If the latter punish the man who makes innovative waves, he must have considerable intestinal fortitude in order to continue in his course.

The innovator is much like a saint: we admire him in theory, but in real life he is a pain in the neck to his peers because he makes them feel guilty. They realize that they should be doing what he is doing. The easiest way to deal with such a nuisance is to shoot him down. The rewards and punishments doled out by the peer group are not only more immediate than those management has in its control but are often far more compelling. The manager must therefore take special steps to engender in his work team a spirit that welcomes innovation.

Actualizing the Potential for Innovation

Although the organizational climate and peer groups can make it harder or easier for the manager to stimulate his own and his subordinates' innovative powers, ultimately he must bestir himself in his own behalf. A simple strategy will enable him and his key people to become more imaginative than they have been in the past: each can question his skill in utilizing the four crucial resources that every executive brings to his work—time, thought, talent, and behavior.

How am I investing my time, thought, talent, and behavior?

Why do I invest them in this way?

What am I doing personally?

Why am I doing it?

What am I doing that I should be delegating?

How can this be delegated to others?

What is my order of priorities in my tasks?

Does this classification reflect their relative importance?

What are my work routines?

Are they the result of habit or careful planning?

Am I managing work or results?

How can I manage results more effectively?

What am I not doing that I should be doing?

How can I squeeze out time to do it?

How many improvements have I engineered in the last six months?

How have they worked out, and what have I learned from them?

How open am I to new ways of getting results?

How can I convince my people that I am interested in their innovative suggestions?

What have I done about the practical suggestions of subordinates in the past?

How can I make certain that action is taken on the good suggestions?

Am I rewarding compliance and docility?

How can I reward improvement?

Does my management style stimulate people to improve?

How can I adjust my habitual style to encourage improvement?

No one is born an innovator. The ability to come up with small improvements that work in the direction of greater effectiveness and profitability has little to do with either deep intelligence or broad experience, though the more one has of these precious commodities, the better. Innovation, like science, is a matter more of attitude than of techniques. For this reason, the manager-leader does not need so-called brainstorming sessions nearly so much as he needs to be authentic in his insistence that he really wants improvements and intends to reward them. He will find gimmicks far less useful than a climate that stimulates his people to think in a new way about old procedures and practices. Encouragement alone, however, is not sufficient; most people need training in actualizing their potential for innovation. What can the manager, who is already under a great deal of pressure, do to tap this potential in his subordinates?

He can give his people an example by thinking about his own job and the way he carries it out and by reorienting his activities as needed toward achieving objectives rather than merely doing work. Ships are not the only things that collect barnacles; everyone unwittingly wastes some energy on unproductive pursuits.

He can periodically review the requirements that he imposes on his people with the purpose of determining to what extent they are necessary and germane to the objectives sought and to what extent they merely represent his personal preferences.

He can look at his work team with a new eye, asking himself who still has the horsepower and desire to contribute and who is resting content with past achievements.

He can act as a consultant to his people in their efforts to innovate. At times, he may serve as a devil's advocate, forcing a subordinate to think through the operational consequences of what appears to be a bright idea; at other times, he may help an employee modify a good suggestion in order to make it more efficient and more relevant to the organization.

He can set aside time now and then during his periodic meetings for a group analysis of suggestions or problems submitted by members of his work group. In this way, all team members help each person improve.

He can designate one member of his key group to lead a discussion about a specific aspect of the operation at a meeting. The person knows in advance that he will be called upon to chair this part of the meeting. It is made clear that the purpose is to elicit suggestions for improving the operation, not merely to hold a gripe session, and all are expected to contribute according to their expertise.

While remaining within the constraints of the organization's policies and practices, he can allow each subordinate to listen to his own drummer, protecting him from pressures to conform in matters where conformity leads to mediocrity rather than progress.

The definite steps that the manager takes to promote improvement are not nearly so important as his underlying supporting attitude. Whatever the avenue to innovation, most employees get satisfaction from the challenge to contribute.

Organizational Renewal

Academically, the rule is, publish or perish. Organizationally, the principle is, change or perish. Organizational charts, which often still represent little more than maps of position authority, are increasingly reflecting the authority of competence and expertise. Companies are being forced to deal less with *locals,* people whose primary loyalty rests in their firm and who plan to remain with it for the rest of their lives, and more with *cosmopolitans,* who have a primary allegiance to their career so that they will change employers to advance their plans. With a workforce that is getting more and more education, the day when the average supervisor or manager is content to stretch himself on the rack of organizational demands is passing. In fact, the next decade will see far more consideration given to changing the organization so that people can achieve than to changing the man so that he fits organizational requirements.

With the accelerating pace of social and cultural changes, it would be remarkable if the typical company could afford the luxury of advancing at a snail's speed. There is a movement away from a static structure and toward task and venture forces geared to specific accomplishments and goals. The situation is already such that almost every executive has some subordinate managers who are brighter and better prepared than he is. Management Development, according to Lawrence A. Appley, is now an outmoded idea. This concept, spelled with a capital *M* and *D,* has been interpreted as a specialized, separate activity that could operate apart from normal, day-to-day business operations and could be abandoned whenever the economic picture tightened ever so little. Today, what is needed is a professional management program carried on by precept and example within a professionally managed organization, since approximately four-fifths of the manager's development comes from the climate and the situation he functions in and the practices he adopts.

This means that the board of directors, the chairman, the president, the executive vice-president, every other officer, top-middle management, middle management, foremen, and supervisors all know professional management, have been trained in their part in it, and are trying their level best to practice it effectively under constant guidance, review, and drive.[1]

This does not imply that programs off company premises are not helpful or even necessary. It does mean that it is a waste of time and money to send people even to excellent courses if the organization does not allow them to practice what they have been taught. In the firm of the near future, the emphasis will be placed on self-development and on development by one's superiors, enriched by cross-fertilization with programs on the outside by those especially equipped to provide them.

An Illustrative Case of Organizational Renewal

In 1961, the Harwood Company bought out its major competitor, the Weldon Company. Both firms were quite similar in many key respects, ranging from family ownership to history and growth in the same industry. They were dissimilar in that Harwood deliberately adhered to a participative management philosophy, whereas Weldon clung to the traditional methods normally used in the garment industry. And despite the fact that the two firms had had similar performance records in the past, Weldon was in dire straits by the early 1960s, while Harwood was enjoying prosperity.

Harwood set about building a renewal program for Weldon. Several types of change were instituted simultaneously: the work environment and procedures were modernized; training, development, and communications programs were improved; participative approaches were introduced to heighten performance; and the work system was linked to the organizational social system.

Within two years, Weldon moved from a loss to a profit position. Employee performance, motivation, and job satisfaction increased. The organization took on the characteristics of an adaptive, self-controlling, integrated, participative system. A reevaluation in 1969, four and a half years after Harwood ceased to pay special attention to Weldon from headquarters, indicated the following: (1) the firm was still profitable; (2) managers had moved from a harsh-benevolent authoritarian approach to one that was more participative; (3) employees' earnings were at a relatively high level; (4) between 1964 and 1969, there was increased concern for production *without* any lessened concern for employee satisfactions; (5) there was no evidence that the organization was tending to regress to former ways of doing things.[2]

The interesting aspect of this organizational metamorphosis is that it involved looking at the firm as an integrated system. It was not sufficient to initiate one or a few changes alone—develop managers, improve human relations, establish money incentives, reorganize the company structure, introduce new machinery and production methods, or give employees more say in how things were done. A force-field concept called for the application of technical, cognitive, motivational, organizational, and behavioral influences more or less simultaneously. This may not be feasible in many organizations—the power figure at Harwood was a highly respected and sophisticated psychologist as well as an expert executive. It well may be that a given company will prefer to make haste slowly by introducing modifications gradually. Even so, those in command must be aware that change in a given sector of the organization will require adjustments in others, since basic changes have a way of affecting related operations.

Some Other·Studies of Less Drastic Changes

Rarely is it necessary to remodel an entire organization; in fact, few executives possess the fortitude to make the attempt. More often than not, change is limited to improvements of ongoing processes.

Robert N. Ford has reported the results of 19 studies carried on in the Bell System.[3] Although they varied as to the jobs affected and the people involved, the main thrust of the experiments was to make the jobs themselves the principal source of employee motivation by loading them vertically so as to make them more challenging. This job enrichment program gave the worker more authority, independence, and responsibility, a far more vital change than mere job enlargement, which only rearranges a job's components. The following list gives some idea of how the jobs were enriched.

Method of Loading	Motivater Invoked
Removing some controls without removing accountability.	Responsibility and personal achievement.
Increasing employees' accountability for their own work.	Responsibility and recognition.
Providing a whole, natural unit of work.	Responsibility, achievement, and recognition.
Expanding job freedom, that is, giving additional authority to do and decide.	Responsibility, achievement, and recognition.
Making periodic reports directly available to the worker himself rather than to the supervisor.	Internal recognition.
Introducing new and more difficult tasks not previously handled.	Growth and learning.
Assigning specific or specialized tasks to people and thus helping them become experts.	Responsibility, growth, and advancement.

On the 19 studies, 9 were evaluated as being "outstandingly successful," one was rated a "complete flop," and the remaining 9 were "moderately successful." Overwhelmingly, the subjects of the experiments were favorably disposed toward their job enrichment program, even though it meant that they would have to measure up to greater demands for performance. Productivity, quality of performance, customer reaction, and other criteria either improved or held their own. Turnover was reduced generally and in one instance remarkably, representing a great saving in dollars. Apparently, most people prefer to do a whole job of their own, even though the demands increase, than to be responsible for a fragment of a job with a limited purview.

Lester Coch and John R. P. French, Jr. have reported the outcomes of three different approaches to the introduction of production changes to more or less matched groups of sewing-machine operators.[4] With the *no-participation* group, the workers were told in advance about the proposed change, the reasons were explained, and questions were answered by management. With the *participation through representation* group, the need for the change in production methods was dramatically explained to all concerned in a group meeting. The workers then selected certain operators to receive special training in the new methods. They, in turn, made suggestions to management and served as trainers for the other workers. With the *total participation* group, all the operators took part in designing the new jobs and made many suggestions.

What were the results? The no-participation group's productivity dropped more than 20 percent. In fact, things reached such a pass that the work group had to be disbanded. The represented group's production dropped temporarily but then recovered within 14 days. The attitudes and cooperation of the workers were good; there were no quits for 40 days. The total participation group fared best of all. It recovered its former productivity within a few days and at the end of a month was 15 percent above its former standard; again, no quits occurred in the first 40 days.

Robert Blake and his associates have proposed an approach through their Managerial Grid® to effect organizational renewal.[5] The program, which may take from three to five years to be lastingly effective, consists of six stages: (1) a *laboratory sem-*

inar, a one-week conference devoted to analyzing team performance and individual managerial styles; (2) *team development*
back on the job, with the manager and his people exploring
their own management patterns and practices as a team and
working out their own guides for team management; (3) *inter-group development,* concentrating on relations between work
groups and departments, in which cooperative problem solving
replaces a win-lose attitude; (4) *organizational goal setting,*
which addresses problems that require commitments at all levels
of the firm, such as cost control, profit improvement, and union-management relationships; (5) *goal attainment,* the use of task
forces to come up with corrective measures for the problems de-
fined in stage 4; and (6) *stabilization,* continuing efforts to prevent regression to old ways of doing things and organizational
slippage.

Does it all work out in practice? An independent evaluation,
not conducted by Blake and his associates, reached positive conclusions regarding the implementation of the program in a company employing some 4,000 people. After 800 managers, technical people, and supervisors had been put through the first stage,
the program was run within the organization. The following
specific results were obtained. The program was at least partly
responsible for at least several millions of dollars of cost savings
and profit increases. It seemed to account for a sizable increase
in employee productivity. Relationships between the firm and its
corporate parent, the union, and the community were better
than they had ever been in the past. There was some evidence
of major shifts in the attitudes, values, and behavior patterns of
the managers, who reported improvement in boss-subordinate,
group, and intergroup relations. Subordinate managers felt that
colleague support was more important than the support of superiors as a factor contributing to improvement.

Suggestions for the Manager-Leader

The worst possible thing the manager could do would be to
rush heedlessly into change. Contrary to the results reported
above, there are instances in which attempts to use democratic
or participative methods have failed miserably. The changes

summarized were proposed by highly skilled behavioral scientists and were introduced with the strong support of top management. The average line manager often lacks both these desiderata. However, in general, subordinate participation has helped produce one or more of the benefits of higher productivity, increased satisfaction, better quality of work, greater teamwork, less resistance to change, reduced turnover and absenteeism, and a deeper sense of responsibility in groups and individuals.[6]

Even so, there are those who have no compelling desire to participate, regardless of what experts and academicians think *should* be the case. These people, whom Herzberg calls "hygiene seekers," are apparently content to put in a day's work and then look for their need satisfaction in off-the-job activities. Moreover, some employees simply do not have the competence to participate constructively. In fact, the manager may be caused considerable trouble by people who feel that they have a right to contribute but who lack the necessary knowledge or experience to do so effectively. Again, subordinates may judge that a given matter means little or nothing to them. Participation in policy formulation may be attractive to managers but seem useless and a waste of time to the rank and file. Then too, advanced technology may make participation regarding certain changes meaningless; it is the technology that dominates, not the wishes of the worker. Finally, if involving subordinates means wasting time on needless discussion or requires those who know to bow before the will of the majority, it will do more harm than good.

Any firm or department is an arena in which environmental, cognitive, behavioral, technological, and social forces are always interacting. If the manager thinks of it this way, he will realize that his real task is not to adopt a change but rather to adapt it to an ongoing system with a configuration all its own. Two extremes are to be avoided: imposing change, which is as useless as trying to force-feed a baby; and overindulging in consultative or shared management, which is an invitation to failure and shattered morale.

The following guidelines may be useful to the executive who desires to move his organization toward increased effectiveness.

As much as possible, he should build on the already existing strengths of the company or department and work within the ongoing system. Change for the sake of change is hardly a virtue. Euphoric optimism is no substitute for careful planning. The only justification of a major alteration is the improvement of individual, group, and organizational productivity. Many people feel comfortable with things as they are; they may identify with authority figures who have established the present system and may perceive the innovation as an unjust criticism of accepted ways of doing things. Hence, their emotional reactions may make them impervious to the reasons for and advantages of the proposed change.

He should determine precisely how far he must go in order to achieve the intended results and then make only the necessary changes. What people fear are uncertainty and the unknown, not change as such. A compulsive itch to remake the world tells one more about the manager than it does about his people. Any substantial change requires far more restructuring of ideas, habits, attitudes, relationships, and interactions than the naive suspect. If major surgery is necessary, it must be done, but it is foolish to risk incurring needless opposition because of overkill.

Unless the change is of an emergency nature, he ought not try to rush or push people into acceptance. Novelty has a certain shock effect. People need time to mull over a proposed change, to live with it, to convince themselves of its merits. They require a certain amount of lead time to assimilate the prospect into their perceptions, attitudes, and habits. Reasonable opportunities must be given them to ask questions, to make suggestions if they are competent to do so, and to ventilate their feelings. For this reason, an ounce of preventative exposure to the change is better than a pound of cure for negative reactions after it has been introduced.

He should get as solid a front of support for the change as possible. Since organizations are sociopolitical complexes, it is obviously necessary either to win over or to neutralize power figures who are in a position to facilitate or hamper the introduction and acceptance of a proposed change. Such figures may include one's superiors, union representatives, key subordinates, and nonformal group leaders. The crucial terms are *involvement, acceptance,* and *commitment.* Conviction cannot be coerced. It is impossible to manipulate key people to abide by a change to which they are hostile.

He must plan the phasing of the implementation with utmost care. Every detail of the proposed change must be scrutinized for its beneficial or disruptive potential. A point of entry that promises the least resistance and the greatest success must be determined. Timing is critical. Preliminary communication and feedback are essential. The stages by which the change will be put into effect must be decided. Should a pilot experiment be made? Should the change be introduced simultaneously in different departments? In what sequence will the change be put into practice? In short, every effort must be made to prevent the occurrence of unanticipated adverse consequences.

Strategies and tactics should be chosen in advance for coping with rational and irrational resistance. No change has ever worked out exactly as intended by the originator. As noted before, Murphy's laws seem to have universal application: if anything can go wrong, it will; it always takes longer than we thought it would. The manager-leader must be armed with methods for dealing with a variety of resisters—the intellectually unconvinced, who may nonetheless have goodwill; the strident critics of the change who have no foundation of evidence for their opposition; the foot shufflers, who go through the motions but have no intention of making the change; the saboteurs, eager to undermine any chance of success; the prophets of doom who fight the change with forebodings; and the self-interested, who find that their status or prerogatives are threatened. Constructive criticism before the change is implemented is to be encouraged. But it should be made clear that once the manager goes into action, he has no intention of allowing oblique resistance to sway him from his course of action. Termites nibbling away post hoc at the change must be dealt with fairly but firmly.

He needs to stay loose. He should have alternative strategies for adapting the change to organizational realities and developments in the light of feedback. Whereas the manager-leader must deal strongly with petulant or malevolent attempts to do in the change, he must also resist the temptation to strive stubbornly to push it through when there is valid evidence that it must be modified if it is to succeed. Bullheadedness is not a laudable executive characteristic. Initial errors and mistakes are inevitable; every change needs debugging. Higher management should be forewarned that at the outset productivity will almost certainly drop off temporarily. Even if the old ways of doing things were less efficient than the new, the employees were able to make them work well because they were totally comfortable with them. They will need time and perhaps training to get used to and get results from new methods. As for the manager, he must be guided by the situation. If the feedback indicates that the change will be more effective after certain modifications, then he would be well advised to make them, even if he finds it a bit embarrassing to do so.

The change should be monitored closely until it proves itself. Far too often, the executive rests content with the mere verbal assent of his subordinates. Votes are taken, plans are made, statements of purpose are prepared, some official communication to the troops is sent forth, the change is authorized by higher management—and the executive sits back certain that all is well with his world. The actual truth is more akin to President Truman's comment, as he was leaving office, that as a general on active duty, Ike gave orders and was sure that they were carried out; but as President, he would give many orders only to find that nothing at all would happen.

If the change is to survive in good health, the manager must monitor it closely from the outset to identify and remedy any fault or resistance. Tight controls may be needed. Reviews of progress must be held periodically. Rewards and punishments may have to be used to convince the reluctant that the manager means business. Reinforcing interest in and support of the innovation is a sine qua non. Then, as the change takes root and proves itself, it will require a diminishing amount of attention. In medical terms, every extensive change begins in the intensive care unit. It advances to normal therapy. This is followed by a recovery and convalescent stage. Finally, it is able to stand on its own feet and make its way unaided.

He should avoid imposing the proposed change and should seek in every way possible to have people internalize it. Intellectual and rational objections to a change can usually be answered by a logical presentation of compelling facts. The problems attendant on any substantial change, however, are more often emotional in character. In an excellent article, Edgar Schein suggests that the leader has four possible courses of action open to him.[7]

— He can impose the change. This may get surface compliance, but it will never secure cooperative acceptance. As soon as the imposed coercive force is lessened, sabotage will surely erupt.

— He can use pressing persuasiveness. It is difficult to resist openly a course of action that the organization and its key authority figures favor. Such an approach may yield short-term results but little more.

— He can lead people to identify with the change. It is human nature to want to be on the winning team and be part of a successful operation. The manager may invoke respect for a superior, a desire to be associated with something better than the old ways of doing things, and a self-concept that prompts one to be well disposed toward the most up-to-date way of running a business to get people to accept the proposed change.

— He can help his people internalize the change. The history of religion is clear proof that imposition is self-defeating. Until the people who are affected by the change and who ultimately will determine its success or failure are convinced that it is beneficial, nothing of lasting worth will take place.

Since resistance and resentment stem chiefly from feelings rather than from reason, the manager must be aware of the three steps that are involved in changing attitudes. The first is to *unfreeze the old views.* Every ethical effort must be made to break up the concrete that binds them and remove their underpinnings. The manager can make it clear that he will not reward old attitudes and ideas. He can throw the weight of organizational power, status, prestige, and influence against former ways of doing things. He can use his own behavior and attitudes as a model for rejecting what was once acceptable. As a plant dies without water, so old emotions and outlooks die when they fail to get reinforcement and rewards. The second step is to *introduce the change.* The key here is to make it as attractive to those affected as possible by highlighting its benefits to them. Conversely, it should be implemented in as unthreatening and undisruptive a way as conditions allow. The final step is to *freeze in the innovation.* To get this process started, the executive has ample organizational resources to reward acceptance. Ultimately, of course, the change must win its own spurs by proving out in practice. If it does not, then the use of rewards to gain continuing compliance is mere manipulation.

Think of the "one thing more." It is not possible to anticipate all the things that may go awry in the future. In human events, the unexpected is the norm. This does not mean that the manager-leader should get himself in a pet fretting about imaginary hobgoblins. Even so, because one brain and two eyes can think and see only so much, the prudent executive steps back when he is convinced that he has touched all the bases and thinks of the "one thing more" to do before committing himself. At this point, participative and consultative management can be of enormous help. McLuhan has said very sagely that fish would be the last ones to discover water. It is always wise and often necessary for the manager to have other people serve as his corrective mirror lest he become the victim of his own views, preferences, and aversions.

References

Chapter 1

1. Victor H. Vroom, *Work and Motivation* (New York: John Wiley & Sons, Inc., 1964), p. 203.
2. Leonard R. Sayles, *Managerial Behavior: Administration in Complex Organizations* (New York: McGraw-Hill Book Company, 1964), pp. 39–50 et passim.
3. Daniel Katz and Robert L. Kahn, *The Social Psychology of Organizations* (New York: John Wiley & Sons, Inc., 1966). See excellent table on p. 312.
4. For a different set of erroneous assumptions regarding leadership, see J. Kelly, *Organizational Behaviour* (Homewood, Ill.: Richard D. Irwin, Inc. and The Dorsey Press, 1969), pp. 130 ff.

Chapter 2

1. Robert N. McMurry, "The Case for Benevolent Autocracy," *Harvard Business Review*, January–February 1958; see also Eugene E. Jennings, "Business Needs Mature Autocrats," *Nation's Business*, September 1958.
2. Anthony Downs, *Inside Bureaucracy* (Boston: Little Brown and Company, 1967), Chapter 9.
3. Erich Fromm, *Man for Himself* (New York: Henry Holt & Company, Inc., 1947); see also Ernest Dale, *Management: Theory and Practice*, 2d ed. (New York: McGraw-Hill Book Company, 1969), pp. 564–565.
4. Peter F. Drucker, *The Age of Discontinuity* (New York: Harper & Row, Publishers, 1968), p. 245.
5. Robert C. Tucker, "The Theory of Charismatic Leadership," *Daedalus*, Summer 1968, pp. 731–756.

Chapter 3

1. See Rensis Likert, *The Human Organization* (New York: McGraw-Hill Book Company, 1967), and *New Patterns of Management* (New York: McGraw-Hill Book Company, 1961).

2. Edwin A. Fleishman and Edwin F. Harris, "Patterns of Leadership Behavior Related to Employee Grievances and Turnover," *Personnel Psychology*, Spring 1962, pp. 43–56.
3. Fred E. Fiedler, *A Theory of Leadership Effectiveness* (New York: McGraw-Hill Book Company, 1967).
4. Abraham Zaleznik, *Human Dilemmas of Leadership* (New York: Harper & Row, Publishers, 1966), p. 1.
5. W. J. Reddin, *Management Styles Diagnostic Test* (Frederickton, N.B., Canada: Managerial Effectiveness, Ltd., 1971); see also idem, *Managerial Effectiveness* (New York: McGraw-Hill Book Company, 1970).
6. Paul Hersey and Kenneth H. Blanchard, *Management of Organizational Behavior: Utilizing Human Resources* (Englewood Cliffs, N.J.: Prentice-Hall, Inc., 1969).
7. Robert R. Blake et al., "Managerial Grid," *Advanced Management*, September 1962, pp. 12–15, 36.

Chapter 4

1. Richard Henry Tawney, *Religion and the Rise of Capitalism* (New York: Harcourt, Brace, 1926); see also Max Weber, *The Protestant Ethic and the Spirit of Capitalism* (New York: Charles Scribner's Sons, 1930).
2. David C. McClelland, *The Achieving Society* (Princeton, N.J.: D. Van Nostrand Company, Inc., 1961), and idem, "Business Drive and National Achievement," *Harvard Business Review*, July–August 1962, pp. 99–112.
3. For a wide-ranging selection of views regarding the nature of man, see Erich Fromm and Ramon Xirau, eds., *The Nature of Man* (New York: The Macmillan Company, 1968).
4. Joan Woodward, *Management and Technology* (London: Her Majesty's Stationery Office, 1958); see also Robert Dubin et al., *Leadership and Productivity: Some Facts of Industrial Life* (San Francisco: Chandler Publishing Company, 1965).
5. Adapted from William F. Whyte, *Organization and Behavior: Theory and Application* (Homewood, Ill.: Richard D. Irwin, Inc. and The Dorsey Press, 1969), pp. 561–562.
6. For an excellent examination of the organization as a social–technical system, coupled with a review of the studies done by the Tavistock Institute, see Robert Cooper and Michael Foster, "Sociotechnical Systems," *American Psychologist*, May 1971, pp. 467–474.
7. Whyte, op. cit., Chapter 14.

8. Glenn A. Bassett, *Management Styles in Transition* (AMA, 1966), Chapter 6.
9. See John M. Pfiffner and Frank P. Sherwood, *Administrative Organization* (Englewood Cliffs, N.J.: Prentice-Hall, Inc., 1960), pp. 18–27.
10. "Winds of Change at Harvard B-School," *The New York Times*, Business and Finance section, October 25, 1970, p. 3.
11. Floyd C. Mann, "Toward an Understanding of the Leadership Role in Formal Organization," in Dubin et al., op. cit., pp. 68–103.

Chapter 5

1. John K. Hemphill, "Job Descriptions for Executives," *Harvard Business Review*, September–October 1959, pp. 55–67.
2. Eugene E. Jennings, *The Executive in Crisis* (East Lansing: Michigan State University, Graduate School of Business Administration, Division of Research, 1965), p. 129.
3. Ibid., pp. 90, 118.
4. David Riesman et al., *The Lonely Crowd: A Study of the Changing American Character* (Garden City, N.Y.: Doubleday and Company, Inc., 1956), p. 42.

Chapter 6

1. Eugene E. Jennings, *The Executive in Crisis* (East Lansing: Michigan State University, Graduate School of Business Administration, Division of Research, 1965). The summaries that follow are adapted from pp. 139–140, 145–147, 147–149.
2. John R. P. French and Bertram Raven, "The Bases of Social Power," in Dorwin Cartwright and A. F. Zander, eds., *Group Dynamics: Research and Theory*, 2d ed. (Evanston, Ill.: Row, Peterson and Company, 1960), pp. 607–623.
3. "The Autobiography of Benjamin Franklin," *Reader's Digest Family Treasury of Great Biographies*, Vol. I (Pleasantville, N.Y.: Reader's Digest Association, 1970), p. 390.
4. Rensis Likert, *The Human Organization* (New York: McGraw-Hill Book Company, 1967); see also Timothy W. Costello and Sheldon S. Zalkind, eds., *Psychology in Administration: A Research Orientation* (Englewood Cliffs, N.J.: Prentice-Hall, Inc., 1963).
5. For a more complete account of this incident, see Ernest Dale, *Management: Theory and Practice*, 2d ed. (New York: McGraw-Hill Book Company, 1969), pp. 132–133.

6. This discussion is based largely on Daniel Katz and Robert L. Kahn, *The Social Psychology of Organizations* (New York: John Wiley & Sons, Inc., 1966), Chapter 7.

Chapter 7

1. David W. Ewing, *The Managerial Mind* (New York: The Free Press, 1964), p. 105.
2. Harry Levinson, *The Exceptional Executive: A Psychological Conception* (Cambridge: Harvard University Press, 1968), pp. 133 ff., especially pp. 139–140.
3. For similar but far less comprehensive tables, see J. Kelly, *Organizational Behaviour* (Homewood, Ill.: Richard D. Irwin, Inc. and The Dorsey Press, 1969), p. 135; also, Charles R. Holloman, "Leadership and Headship: There Is a Difference," *Personnel Administration,* July–August 1968, pp. 38–44.
4. Robert N. Ford, *Motivation Through the Work Itself* (AMA, 1969), p. 83.
5. Robert Tannenbaum and Warren H. Schmidt, "How to Choose a Leadership Pattern," *Harvard Business Review,* March–April 1958, pp. 95–101. The discussion is based on this classic article. The applications and types of behavior are the writer's responsibility.

Chapter 8

1. Based on Samuel A. Culbert and James M. Elden, "An Anatomy of Activism for Executives," *Harvard Business Review,* November–December 1970, p. 136.
2. Reference to this study is found in Douglas McGregor, *The Professional Manager,* Caroline McGregor and Warren G. Bennis, eds. (New York: McGraw-Hill Book Company, 1967), p. 47.
3. David Riesman et al., *The Lonely Crowd: A Study of the Changing American Character* (Garden City, N.Y.: Doubleday and Company, Inc., 1956), p. 349.

Chapter 9

1. Douglas McGregor, *The Human Side of Enterprise* (New York: McGraw-Hill Book Company, Inc., 1960).
2. Abraham H. Maslow, *Motivation and Personality* (New York: Harper & Row, Publishers, 1954).

3. Frederick Herzberg, *Work and the Nature of Man* (Cleveland: The World Publishing Company, 1966).
4. Chris Argyris, *Personality and Organization* (New York: Harper Brothers, Publishers, 1957); see also idem, *Understanding Organizational Behavior* (Homewood, Ill.: The Dorsey Press, Inc., 1960), pp. 8 ff.
5. Warren G. Bennis, *Changing Organizations: Essays on the Development and Evolution of Human Organization* (New York: McGraw-Hill Book Company, 1966).
6. Leonard R. Sayles and George Strauss, *Human Behavior in Organizations* (Englewood Cliffs, N.J.: Prentice-Hall, Inc., 1966), p. 7.
7. See Victor H. Vroom, *Work and Motivation* (New York: John Wiley & Sons, Inc., 1964), pp. 105–159 et seq.
8. B. von Haller Gilmer, *Industrial Psychology* (New York: McGraw-Hill Book Company, 1961), pp. 212–213.

Chapter 10

1. Chris Argyris, *Organization and Innovation* (Homewood, Ill.: Richard D. Irwin, Inc., 1965), p. 36.
2. William V. Haney, *Communication and Organizational Behavior*, rev. ed. (Homewood, Ill.: Richard D. Irwin, Inc., 1967), Chapters 6–15.
3. Edwin B. Flippo, *Management: A Behavioral Approach*, 2d ed. (Boston: Allyn and Bacon, 1970), p. 403.

Chapter 11

1. The discussion in the section on setting achievement targets is based on the views of James L. Hayes, president of the American Management Association, and William V. Oncken, president of William V. Oncken Associates. The discussion is the writer's responsibility.

Chapter 13

1. Based on Raymond Baumhart, S.J., *Ethics in Business* (New York: Holt, Rinehart, and Winston, Inc., 1968), p. 4 et passim.
2. *Ethical Standards of Psychologists* (Washington, D.C.: The American Psychological Association, 1953), p. *ix*.
3. Adapted from similar questions proposed by Edmund Cahn in *The Predicament of Democratic Man* (New York: The Macmil-

lan Company, 1961), pp. 178–180, as quoted in Clarence C. Walton, *Ethos and the Executive: Values in Managerial Decision-Making* (Englewood Cliffs, N.J.: Prentice-Hall, Inc., 1969), p. 91.

4. Based on Clarence C. Walton, *Corporate Social Responsibilities* (Belmont, Calif.: Wadsworth Publishing Company, Inc., 1968), pp. 127–141.

Chapter 14

1. Lawrence A. Appley, "Management Development," address delivered at the meeting of the Associated Merchandising Corporation, White Sulphur Springs, W.Va., April 29, 1964.

2. This summary is adapted from Stanley E. Seashore and David G. Bowers, "Durability of Organizational Change," *American Psychologist*, March 1970, pp. 22–33.

3. Robert N. Ford, *Motivation Through the Work Itself* (AMA, 1969), pp. 29, 188–189.

4. See Lester Coch and John R. P. French, "Overcoming Resistance to Change," *Human Relations*, August 1948, pp. 512–532.

5. Robert R. Blake et al., "Breakthrough in Organization Development," *Harvard Business Review*, November–December 1964, pp. 37–59.

6. Keith Davis, *Human Relations at Work*, 3d ed. (New York: McGraw-Hill Book Company, 1967), Chapter 8.

7. See Edgar H. Schein, "Management Development as a Process of Influence," *Industrial Management Review*, May 1961, pp. 59–77.